Honda MB, MBX, MT & MTX50 Owners Workshop Manual

by Jeremy Churchill

Models covered
MB5. 49cc. US July 1981 to 1982
MB50 S-A. 49cc. UK January 1980 to September 1982
MBX50 S-D. 49cc. UK February 1983 to March 1986
MT50 S-A. 49cc. UK January 1980 to September 1982
MT50 S-E/F. 49cc. UK April 1985 to February 1986
MT50 S-G. 49cc. UK March 1986 to August 1988
MT50 S-J. 49cc. UK August 1988 to September 1990
MT50 S-L. 49cc. UK March 1990 on
MTX50 S-C. 49cc. UK May 1982 to April 1985

ISBN 1 85010 888 9

Printed in England *(731-12R9)*

ABCDE

Haynes Publishing Group
Sparkford Nr Yeovil
Somerset BA22 7JJ England

Haynes Publications, Inc
861 Lawrence Drive
Newbury Park
California 91320 USA

British Library Cataloguing in Publication Data
A catalogue record for this book is available from the British Library
Library of Congress Catalog Card Number
93-70495

Acknowledgements

Our thanks are due to Paul Branson Motorcycles of Yeovil who supplied the machines featured in this manual.

Brian Horsfall assisted with the stripdown and rebuilding, and devised the ingenious methods for overcoming the lack of manufacturer's service tools. Les Brazier took the photographs which accompany the text; Mansur Darlington edited the text.

Finally, we would like to thank the Avon Rubber Company, who kindly supplied information and technical assistance on tyre fitting; NGK Spark Plugs (UK) Ltd for information on sparking plug maintenance and electrode conditions, and Renold Ltd for advice on chain care and renewal.

About this manual

The purpose of this manual is to present the owner with a concise and graphic guide which will enable him to tackle any operation from basic routine maintenance to a major overhaul. It has been assumed that any work would be undertaken without the luxury of a well-equipped workshop and a range of manufacturer's service tools.

To this end, the machine featured in the manual was stripped and rebuilt in our own workshop, by a team comprising a mechanic, a photographer and the author. The resulting photographic sequence depicts events as they took place, the hands shown being those of the author and the mechanic.

The use of specialised, and expensive, service tools was avoided unless their use was considered to be essential due to risk of breakage or injury. There is usually some way of improvising a method of removing a stubborn component, providing that a suitable degree of care is exercised.

The author learnt his motorcycle mechanics over a number of years, faced with the same difficulties and using similar facilities to those encountered by most owners. It is hoped that this practical experience can be passed on through the pages of this manual.

Where possible, a well-used example of the machine is chosen for the workshop project, as this highlights any areas which might be particularly prone to giving rise to problems. In this way, any such difficulties are encountered and resolved before the text is written, and the techniques used to deal with them can be incorporated in the relevant section. Armed with a working knowledge of the machine, the author undertakes a considerable amount of research in order that the maximum amount of data can be included in the manual.

A comprehensive section, preceding the main part of the manual, describes procedures for carrying out the routine maintenance of the machine at intervals of time and mileage. This section is included particularly for those owners who wish to ensure the efficient day-to-day running of their motorcycle, but who choose not to undertake overhaul or renovation work.

Each Chapter is divided into numbered sections. Within these sections are numbered paragraphs. Cross reference throughout the manual is quite straightforward and logical. When reference is made 'See Section 6.10' it means Section 6, paragraph 10 in the same Chapter. If another Chapter were intended, the reference would read, for example, 'See Chapter 2, Section 6.10'. All the photographs are captioned with a section/paragraph number to which they refer and are relevant to the Chapter text adjacent.

Figures (usually line illustrations) appear in a logical but numerical order, within a given Chapter. Fig. 1.1 therefore refers to the first figure in Chapter 1.

Left-hand and right-hand descriptions of the machines and their components refer to the left and right of a given machine when the rider is seated normally.

Motorcycle manufacturers continually make changes to specifications and recommendations, and these, when notified, are incorporated into our manuals at the earliest opportunity.

We take great pride in the accuracy of information given in this manual, but motorcycle manufacturers make alterations and design changes during the production run of a particular motorcycle of which they do not inform us. No liability can be accepted by the authors or publishers for loss, damage or injury caused by any errors in, or omissions from, the information given.

Contents

Honda MB50

Close-up of MB50 engine

Honda MT50

Close-up of MT50 engine

Introduction to the Honda MB and MT50

The Honda MB50 currently sold in the US is an attempt by American Honda to capture the new younger generation of riders who do not wish to ride mopeds and yet are unable or unwilling to graduate to the larger machines. By giving the machine racer orientated styling with the maximum use of plastics in mudguards, chainguard and tail hump, Honda have produced a lightweight motorcycle with very good performance. This is backed up with the use of fully damped suspension front and rear, and with the use of Comstar wheels fitted with a hydraulic disc brake at the front and a drum brake of adequate size at the rear. These factors are combined to produce a lightweight motorcycle which is easy to handle by the novice rider, and which offers performance and handling similar to larger machines.

The models sold in the UK are directed at the 16-year old rider who, under the law currently in force, may not ride a moped with a design top speed of more than 30 mph. The two models offered are the MB50, which is a restricted version of the US model and is fitted with a small fairing and clip-on style handlebars to give the racer styling, and the MT50, which follows the current trail-bike styling, with a high-level exhaust pipe, high-mounted plastic mudguards and knobbly tyres. It is a credit to the machines that they can, under the restrictions imposed on them, present a sufficiently appealing package to attract the younger riders in quantity.

Later models, namely the MBX and MTX50, and the MT50 S-E/F, G, J and L, are covered in Chapter 7 of this manual.

Dimensions and weight

	MB50 (UK)	MB50 (US)	MT50
Overall length	1880 mm (74.0 in)	1880 mm (74.0 in)	1905 mm (75.0 in)
Overall width	655 mm (25.8 in)	705 mm (27.8 in)	780 mm (30.7 in)
Overall height	1160 mm (45.7 in)	1025 mm (40.4 in)	1055 mm (41.5 in)
Wheelbase	1225 mm (48.2 in)	1215 mm (47.8 in)	1240 mm (48.8 in)
Ground clearance	160 mm (6.3 in)	160 mm (6.3 in)	220 mm (8.7 in)
Dry weight	82 kg (181 lb)	79 kg (174 lb)	81 kg (179 lb)

Ordering spare parts

When ordering spare parts, it is advisable to deal direct with an official Honda agent, who will be able to supply many of the items required ex-stock. It is advisable to get acquainted with the local Honda agent, and to rely on his advice when purchasing spares. He is in a better position to specify exactly the parts required and to identify the relevant spare part numbers so that there is less chance of the wrong part being supplied by the manufacturer due to a vague or incomplete description.

When ordering spares, always quote the frame and engine numbers in full, together with any prefixes or suffixes in the form of letters.

The frame number is found stamped on the right-hand side of the steering head, parallel with the forks. The engine number is stamped on the left-hand side of the crankcase, just forward of the gearchange lever shaft.

Use only parts of genuine Honda manufacture. A few pattern parts are available, sometimes at cheaper prices, but there is no guarantee that they will give such good service as the originals they replace. Retain any worn or broken parts until the replacements have been obtained; they are sometimes needed as a pattern to help identify the correct replacement when design changes have been made during a production run.

Some of the more expendable parts such as sparking plugs, bulbs, tyres, oils and greases etc., can be obtained from accessory shops and motor factors, who have convenient opening hours, and can often be found not far from home. It is also possible to obtain parts on a Mail Order basis from a number of specialists who advertise regularly in the motorcycle magazines.

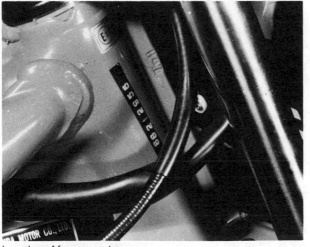

Location of frame number

Location of engine number

Safety first!

Professional motor mechanics are trained in safe working procedures. However enthusiastic you may be about getting on with the job in hand, do take the time to ensure that your safety is not put at risk. A moment's lack of attention can result in an accident, as can failure to observe certain elementary precautions.

There will always be new ways of having accidents, and the following points do not pretend to be a comprehensive list of all dangers; they are intended rather to make you aware of the risks and to encourage a safety-conscious approach to all work you carry out on your vehicle.

Essential DOs and DON'Ts

DON'T start the engine without first ascertaining that the transmission is in neutral.

DON'T suddenly remove the filler cap from a hot cooling system – cover it with a cloth and release the pressure gradually first, or you may get scalded by escaping coolant.

DON'T attempt to drain oil until you are sure it has cooled sufficiently to avoid scalding you.

DON'T grasp any part of the engine, exhaust or silencer without first ascertaining that it is sufficiently cool to avoid burning you.

DON'T allow brake fluid or antifreeze to contact the machine's paintwork or plastic components.

DON'T syphon toxic liquids such as fuel, brake fluid or antifreeze by mouth, or allow them to remain on your skin.

DON'T inhale dust – it may be injurious to health (see *Asbestos* heading).

DON'T allow any spilt oil or grease to remain on the floor – wipe it up straight away, before someone slips on it.

DON'T use ill-fitting spanners or other tools which may slip and cause injury.

DON'T attempt to lift a heavy component which may be beyond your capability – get assistance.

DON'T rush to finish a job, or take unverified short cuts.

DON'T allow children or animals in or around an unattended vehicle.

DON'T inflate a tyre to a pressure above the recommended maximum. Apart from overstressing the carcase and wheel rim, in extreme cases the tyre may blow off forcibly.

DO ensure that the machine is supported securely at all times. This is especially important when the machine is blocked up to aid wheel or fork removal.

DO take care when attempting to slacken a stubborn nut or bolt. It is generally better to pull on a spanner, rather than push, so that if slippage occurs you fall away from the machine rather than on to it.

DO wear eye protection when using power tools such as drill, sander, bench grinder etc.

DO use a barrier cream on your hands prior to undertaking dirty jobs – it will protect your skin from infection as well as making the dirt easier to remove afterwards; but make sure your hands aren't left slippery. Note that long-term contact with used engine oil can be a health hazard.

DO keep loose clothing (cuffs, tie etc) and long hair well out of the way of moving mechanical parts.

DO remove rings, wristwatch etc, before working on the vehicle – especially the electrical system.

DO keep your work area tidy – it is only too easy to fall over articles left lying around.

DO exercise caution when compressing springs for removal or installation. Ensure that the tension is applied and released in a controlled manner, using suitable tools which preclude the possibility of the spring escaping violently.

DO ensure that any lifting tackle used has a safe working load rating adequate for the job.

DO get someone to check periodically that all is well, when working alone on the vehicle.

DO carry out work in a logical sequence and check that everything is correctly assembled and tightened afterwards.

DO remember that your vehicle's safety affects that of yourself and others. If in doubt on any point, get specialist advice.

IF, in spite of following these precautions, you are unfortunate enough to injure yourself, seek medical attention as soon as possible.

Asbestos

Certain friction, insulating, sealing, and other products – such as brake linings, clutch linings, gaskets, etc – contain asbestos. *Extreme care must be taken to avoid inhalation of dust from such products since it is hazardous to health.* If in doubt, assume that they *do* contain asbestos.

Fire

Remember at all times that petrol (gasoline) is highly flammable. Never smoke, or have any kind of naked flame around, when working on the vehicle. But the risk does not end there – a spark caused by an electrical short-circuit, by two metal surfaces contacting each other, by careless use of tools, or even by static electricity built up in your body under certain conditions, can ignite petrol vapour, which in a confined space is highly explosive.

Always disconnect the battery earth (ground) terminal before working on any part of the fuel or electrical system, and never risk spilling fuel on to a hot engine or exhaust.

It is recommended that a fire extinguisher of a type suitable for fuel and electrical fires is kept handy in the garage or workplace at all times. Never try to extinguish a fuel or electrical fire with water.

Note: *Any reference to a 'torch' appearing in this manual should always be taken to mean a hand-held battery-operated electric lamp or flashlight. It does **not** mean a welding/gas torch or blowlamp.*

Fumes

Certain fumes are highly toxic and can quickly cause unconsciousness and even death if inhaled to any extent. Petrol (gasoline) vapour comes into this category, as do the vapours from certain solvents such as trichloroethylene. Any draining or pouring of such volatile fluids should be done in a well ventilated area.

When using cleaning fluids and solvents, read the instructions carefully. Never use materials from unmarked containers – they may give off poisonous vapours.

Never run the engine of a motor vehicle in an enclosed space such as a garage. Exhaust fumes contain carbon monoxide which is extremely poisonous; if you need to run the engine, always do so in the open air or at least have the rear of the vehicle outside the workplace.

The battery

Never cause a spark, or allow a naked light, near the vehicle's battery. It will normally be giving off a certain amount of hydrogen gas, which is highly explosive.

Always disconnect the battery earth (ground) terminal before working on the fuel or electrical systems.

If possible, loosen the filler plugs or cover when charging the battery from an external source. Do not charge at an excessive rate or the battery may burst.

Take care when topping up and when carrying the battery. The acid electrolyte, even when diluted, is very corrosive and should not be allowed to contact the eyes or skin.

If you ever need to prepare electrolyte yourself, always add the acid slowly to the water, and never the other way round. Protect against splashes by wearing rubber gloves and goggles.

Mains electricity and electrical equipment

When using an electric power tool, inspection light etc, always ensure that the appliance is correctly connected to its plug and that, where necessary, it is properly earthed (grounded). Do not use such appliances in damp conditions and, again, beware of creating a spark or applying excessive heat in the vicinity of fuel or fuel vapour. Also ensure that the appliances meet the relevant national safety standards.

Ignition HT voltage

A severe electric shock can result from touching certain parts of the ignition system, such as the HT leads, when the engine is running or being cranked, particularly if components are damp or the insulation is defective. Where an electronic ignition system is fitted, the HT voltage is much higher and could prove fatal.

Working conditions and tools

When a major overhaul is contemplated, it is important that a clean, well-lit working space is available, equipped with a workbench and vice, and with space for laying out or storing the dismantled assemblies in an orderly manner where they are unlikely to be disturbed. The use of a good workshop will give the satisfaction of work done in comfort and without haste, where there is little chance of the machine being dismantled and reassembled in anything other than clean surroundings. Unfortunately, these ideal working conditions are not always practicable and under these latter circumstances when improvisation is called for, extra care and time will be needed.

The other essential requirement is a comprehensive set of good quality tools. Quality is of prime importance since cheap tools will prove expensive in the long run if they slip or break when in use, causing personal injury or expensive damage to the component being worked on. A good quality tool will last a long time, and more than justify the cost.

For practically all tools, a tool factor is the best source since he will have a very comprehensive range compared with the average garage or accessory shop. Having said that, accessory shops often offer excellent quality tools at discount prices, so it pays to shop around. There are plenty of tools around at reasonable prices, but always aim to purchase items which meet the relevant national safety standards. If in doubt, seek the advice of the shop proprietor or manager before making a purchase.

The basis of any tool kit is a set of open-ended spanners, which can be used on almost any part of the machine to which there is reasonable access. A set of ring spanners makes a useful addition, since they can be used on nuts that are very tight or where access is restricted. Where the cost has to be kept within reasonable bounds, a compromise can be effected with a set of combination spanners – open-ended at one end and having a ring of the same size on the other end. Socket spanners may also be considered a good investment, a basic $3/8$ in or $1/2$ in drive kit comprising a ratchet handle and a small number of socket heads, if money is limited. Additional sockets can be purchased, as and when they are required. Provided they are slim in profile, sockets will reach nuts or bolts that are deeply recessed. When purchasing spanners of any kind, make sure the correct size standard is purchased. Almost all machines manufactured outside the UK and the USA have metric nuts and bolts, whilst those produced in Britain have BSF or BSW sizes. The standard used in USA is AF, which is also found on some of the later British machines. Others tools that should be included in the kit are a range of crosshead screwdrivers, a pair of pliers and a hammer.

When considering the purchase of tools, it should be remembered that by carrying out the work oneself, a large proportion of the normal repair cost, made up by labour charges, will be saved. The economy made on even a minor overhaul will go a long way towards the improvement of a toolkit.

In addition to the basic tool kit, certain additional tools can prove invaluable when they are close to hand, to help speed up a multitude of repetitive jobs. For example, an impact screwdriver will ease the removal of screws that have been tightened by a similar tool, during assembly, without a risk of damaging the screw heads. And, of course, it can be used again to retighten the screws, to ensure an oil or airtight seal results. Circlip pliers have their uses too, since gear pinions, shafts and similar components are frequently retained by circlips that are not too easily displaced by a screwdriver. There are two types of circlip pliers, one for internal and one for external circlips. They may also have straight or right-angled jaws.

One of the most useful of all tools is the torque wrench, a form of spanner that can be adjusted to slip when a measured amount of force is applied to any bolt or nut. Torque wrench settings are given in almost every modern workshop or service manual, where the extent to which a complex component, such as a cylinder head, can be tightened without fear of distortion or leakage. The tightening of bearing caps is yet another example. Overtightening will stretch or even break bolts, necessitating extra work to extract the broken portions.

As may be expected, the more sophisticated the machine, the greater is the number of tools likely to be required if it is to be kept in first class condition by the home mechanic. Unfortunately there are certain jobs which cannot be accomplished successfully without the correct equipment and although there is invariably a specialist who will undertake the work for a fee, the home mechanic will have to dig more deeply in his pocket for the purchase of similar equipment if he does not wish to employ the services of others. Here a word of caution is necessary, since some of these jobs are best left to the expert. Although an electrical multimeter of the AVO type will prove helpful in tracing electrical faults, in inexperienced hands it may irrevocably damage some of the electrical components if a test current is passed through them in the wrong direction. This can apply to the synchronisation of twin or multiple carburettors too, where a certain amount of expertise is needed when setting them up with vacuum gauges. These are, however, exceptions. Some instruments, such as a strobe lamp, are virtually essential when checking the timing of a machine powered by CDI ignition system. In short, do not purchase any of these special items unless you have the experience to use them correctly.

Although this manual shows how components can be removed and replaced without the use of special service tools (unless absolutely essential), it is worthwhile giving consideration to the purchase of the more commonly used tools if the machine is regarded as a long term purchase Whilst the alternative methods suggested will remove and replace parts without risk of damage, the use of the special tools recommended and sold by the manufacturer will invariably save time.

Fault diagnosis

Contents

1 Introduction

This Section provides an easy reference-guide to the more common ailments that are likely to afflict your machine. Obviously, the opportunities are almost limitless for faults to occur as a result of obscure failures, and to try and cover all eventualities would require a book. Indeed, a number have been written on the subject.

Successful fault diagnosis is not a mysterious 'black art' but the application of a bit of knowledge combined with a systematic and logical approach to the problem. Approach any fault diagnosis by first accurately identifying the symptom and then checking through the list of possibile causes, starting with the simplest or most obvious and progressing in stages to the most complex. Take nothing for granted, but above all apply liberal quantities of common sense.

The main symptom of a fault is given in the text as a major heading below which are listed, as Sections headings, the various systems or areas which may contain the fault. Details of each possible cause for a fault and the remedial action to be taken are given, in brief, in the paragraphs below each Section heading. Further information should be sought in the relevant Chapter.

Engine does not start when turned over

2 No fuel flow to carburettor

● Fuel tank empty or level too low. Check that the tap is turned to 'On' or 'Reserve' position as required. If in doubt, prise off the fuel feed pipe at the carburettor end and check that fuel runs from pipe when the tap is turned on.
● Tank filler cap vent obstructed. This can prevent fuel from flowing into the carburettor float bowl bcause air cannot enter the fuel tank to replace it. The problem is more likely to appear when the machine is being ridden. Check by listening close to the filler cap and releasing it. A hissing noise indicates that a blockage is present. Remove the cap and clear the vent hole with wire or by using an air line from the inside of the cap.
● Fuel tap or filter blocked. Blockage may be due to accumulation of rust or paint flakes from the tank's inner surface or of foreign matter from contaminated fuel. Remove the tap and clean it and the filter. Look also for water droplets in the fuel.
● Fuel line blocked. Blockage of the fuel line is more likely to result from a kink in the line rather than the accumulation of debris.

3 Fuel not reaching cylinder

● Float chamber not filling. Caused by float needle or floats sticking in up position. This may occur after the machine has been left standing for an extended length of time allowing the fuel to evaporate. When this occurs a gummy residue is often left which hardens to a varnish-like substance. This condition may be worsened by corrosion and crystalline deposits produced prior to the total evaporation of contaminated fuel. Sticking of the float needle may also be caused by wear. In any case removal of the float chamber will be necessary for inspection and cleaning.
● Blockage in starting circuit, slow running circuit or jets. Blockage of these items may be attributable to debris from the fuel tank by-passing the filter system or to gumming up as described in paragraph 1. Water droplets in the fuel will also block jets and passages. The carburettor should be dismantled for cleaning.
● Fuel level too low. The fuel level in the float chamber is controlled by float height. The fuel level may increase with wear or damage but will never reduce, thus a low fuel level is an inherent rather than developing condition. Check the float height, renewing the float or needle if required.
● Oil blockage in fuel system or carburettor (petroil lubricated engines only). May arise when the machine has been parked for long periods and the residual petrol has evaporated. To rectify, dismantle and clean the carburettor and tap, flush the tank and fill with fresh petroil mixed in the correct proportions. This problem can be avoided by running the float bowl dry before the machine is stored for long periods. Do not attempt to use fuel which has become stale.

4 Engine flooding

● Float valve needle worn or stuck open. A piece of rust or other debris can prevent correct seating of the needle against the valve seat thereby permitting an uncontrolled flow of fuel. Similarly, a worn needle or needle seat will prevent valve closure. Dismantle the carburettor float bowl for cleaning and, if necessary, renewal of the worn components.
● Fuel level too high. The fuel level is controlled by the float height which may increase due to wear of the float needle, pivot pin or operating tang. Check the float height, renewing the float or needle if required. A leaking float will cause an increase in fuel level, and thus should be renewed.
● Cold starting mechanism. Check the choke (starter mechanism) for correct operation. If the mechanism jams in the 'On' position subsequent starting of a hot engine will be difficult.
● Blocked air filter. A badly restricted air filter will cause flooding. Check the filter and clean or renew as required. A collapsed inlet hose will have a similar effect. Check that the air filter inlet has not become blocked by a rag or similar item.

5 No spark at plug

● Ignition switch not on.
● Engine stop switch off.
● Spark plug dirty, oiled or 'whiskered'. Because the induction mixture of a two-stroke engine is inclined to be of a rather oily nature it is comparatively easy to foul the plug electrodes, especially where there have been repeated attempts to start the engine. A machine used for short journeys will be more prone to fouling because the engine may never reach full operating temperature, and the deposits will not burn off. On rare occasions a change of plug grade may be required but the advice of a dealer should be sought before making such a change. 'Whiskering' is a comparatively rare occurrence on modern machines but may be encountered where pre-mixed petrol and oil (petroil) lubrication is employed. An electrode deposit in the form of a barely visible filament across the plug electrodes can short circuit the plug and prevent its sparking. On all two-stroke machines it is a sound precaution to carry a new spare spark plug for substitution in the event of fouling problems.
● Spark plug failure. Clean the spark plug thoroughly and reset the electrode gap. Refer to the spark plug section and the colour condition guide in Chapter 4. If the spark plug shorts internally or has sustained visible damage to the electrodes, core or ceramic insulator it should be renewed. On rare occasions a plug that appears to spark vigorously will fail to do so when refitted to the engine and subjected to the compression pressure in the cylinder.
● Spark plug cap or high tension (HT) lead faulty. Check condition and security. Replace if deterioration is evident. Most spark plugs have an internal resistor designed to inhibit electrical interference with radio and television sets. On rare occasions the resistor may break down, thus preventing sparking. If this is suspected, fit a new cap as a precaution.
● Spark plug cap loose. Check that the spark plug cap fits securely over the plug and, where fitted, the screwed terminal

on the plug end is secure.

● Shorting due to moisture. Certain parts of the ignition system are susceptible to shorting when the machine is ridden or parked in wet weather. Check particularly the area from the spark plug cap back to the ignition coil. A water dispersant spray may be used to dry out waterlogged components. Recurrence of the problem can be prevented by using an ignition sealant spray after drying out and cleaning.

● Ignition or stop switch shorted. May be caused by water corrosion or wear. Water dispersant and contact cleaning sprays may be used. If this fails to overcome the problem dismantling and visual inspection of the switches will be required.

● Shorting or open circuit in wiring. Failure in any wire connecting any of the ignition components will cause ignition malfunction. Check also that all connections are clean, dry and tight.

● Ignition coil failure. Check the coil, referring to Chapter 3.

● Pulser coil failure. Check coil for correct resistance.

● CDI unit faulty. See Chapter 3, Sections 2 and 6 for details.

6 Weak spark at plug

● Feeble sparking at the plug may be caused by any of the faults mentioned in the preceding Section other than those items in the first two paragraphs. Check first the spark plug, this being the most likely culprit.

7 Compression low

● Spark plug loose. This will be self-evident on inspection, and may be accompanied by a hissing noise when the engine is turned over. Remove the plug and check that the threads in the cylinder head are not damaged. Check also that the plug sealing washer is in good condition.

● Cylinder head gasket leaking. This condition is often accompanied by a high pitched squeak from around the cylinder head and oil loss, and may be caused by insufficiently tightened cylinder head fasteners, a warped cylinder head or mechanical failure of the gasket material. Re-torqueing the fasteners to the correct specification may seal the leak in some instances but if damage has occurred this course of action will provide, at best, only a temporary cure.

● Low crankcase compression. This can be caused by worn main bearings and seals and will upset the incoming fuel/air mixture. A good seal in these areas is essential on any two-stroke engine.

● Worn disc valve. Disc valve wear is not common, but will cause similar symptoms to those described above. Overhaul will be necessary.

● Piston rings sticking or broken. Sticking of the piston rings may be caused by seizure due to lack of lubrication or heating as a result of poor carburation or incorrect fuel type. Gumming of the rings may result from lack of use, or carbon deposits in the ring grooves. Broken rings result from over-revving, over-heating or general wear. In either case a top-end overhaul will be required.

Engine stalls after starting

8 General causes

● Improper cold start mechanism operation. Check that the operating controls function smoothly and, where applicable, are correctly adjusted. A cold engine may not require application of an enriched mixture to start initially but may baulk without choke once firing. Likewise a hot engine may start with an enriched mixture but will stop almost immediately if the choke is inadvertently in operation.

● Ignition malfunction. See Section 9. Weak spark at plug.

● Carburettor incorrectly adjusted. Maladjustment of the mixture strength or idle speed may cause the engine to stop immediately after starting. See Chapter 2.

● Fuel contamination. Check for filter blockage by debris or water which reduces, but does not completely stop, fuel flow, or blockage of the slow speed circuit in the carburettor by the same agents. If water is present it can often be seen as droplets in the bottom of the float bowl. Clean the filter and, where water is in evidence, drain and flush the fuel tank and float bowl.

● Intake air leak. Check for security of the carburettor mounting and hose connections, and for cracks or splits in the hoses. Check also that the carburettor top is secure and that the vacuum gauge adaptor plug (where fitted) is tight.

● Air filter blocked or omitted. A blocked filter will cause an over-rich mixture; the omission of a filter will cause an excessively weak mixture. Both conditions will have a detrimental affect on carburation. Clean or renew the filter as necessary.

● Fuel filler cap air vent blocked. Usually caused by dirt or water. Clean the vent orifice.

● Choked exhaust system. Caused by excessive carbon build-up in the system, particularly around the silencer baffles. In many cases these can be detached for cleaning, though mopeds have one-piece systems which require a rather different approach. Refer to Chapter 2 for further information.

● Excessive carbon build-up in the engine. This can result from failure to decarbonise the engine at the specified interval or through excessive oil consumption. On pump-fed engines check pump adjustment. On pre-mix (petroil) systems check that oil is mixed in the recommended ratio.

Poor running at idle and low speed

9 Weak spark at plug or erratic firing

● Spark plug fouled, faulty or incorrectly adjusted. See Section 4 or refer to Chapter 4.

● Spark plug cap or high tension lead shorting. Check the condition of both these items ensuring that they are in good condition and dry and that the cap is fitted correctly.

● Spark plug type incorrect. Fit plug of correct type and heat range as given in Specifications. In certain conditions a plug of hotter or colder type may be required for normal running.

● Pulser coil failure in generator. See test details in Chapter 3.

● Ignition timing incorrect. Check the ignition timing statically and dynamically, ensuring that the advance is functioning correctly.

● Faulty ignition coil. Partial failure of the coil internal insulation will diminish the performance of the coil. No repair is possible, a new component must be fitted.

● CDI unit faulty. See details in Chapter 3.

10 Fuel/air mixture incorrect

● Intake air leak. Check carburettor mountings and air cleaner hoses for security and signs of splitting. Ensure that carburettor top is tight and that the vacuum gauge take-off plug (where fitted) is tight.

● Mixture strength incorrect. Adjust slow running mixture strength using pilot adjustment screw.

● Carburettor synchronisation.

● Pilot jet or slow running circuit blocked. The carburettor should be removed and dismantled for thorough cleaning. Blow through all jets and air passages with compressed air to clear obstructions.

● Air cleaner clogged or omitted. Clean or fit air cleaner element as necessary. Check also that the element and air filter cover are correctly seated.

● Cold start mechanism in operation. Check that the choke has not been left on inadvertently and the operation is correct.

Where applicable check the operating cable free play.
● Fuel level too high or too low. Check the float height, renewing float or needle if required. See Section 3 or 4.
● Fuel tank air vent obstructed. Obstructions usually caused by dirt or water. Clean vent orifice.

11 Compression low

● See Section 7.

Acceleration poor

12 General causes

● All items as for previous Section.
● Choked air filter. Failure to keep the air filter element clean will allow the build-up of dirt with proportional loss of performance. In extreme cases of neglect acceleration will suffer.
● Choked exhaust system. This can result from failure to remove accumulations of carbon from the silencer baffles at the prescribed intervals. The increased back pressure will make the machine noticeably sluggish. Refer to Chapter 2 for further information on decarbonisation.
● Excessive carbon build-up in the engine. This can result from failure to decarbonise the engine at the specified interval or through excessive oil consumption. On pump-fed engines check pump adjustment. On pre-mix (petroil) systems check that oil is mixed in the recommended ratio.
● Ignition timing incorrect. Check the ignition timing as described in Chapter 4. Where no provision for adjustment exists, test the electronic ignition components and renew as required.
● Carburation fault. See Section 10.
● Mechanical resistance. Check that the brakes are not binding. On small machines in particular note that the increased rolling resistance caused by under-inflated tyres may impede acceleration.

Poor running or lack of power at high speeds

13 Weak spark at plug or erratic firing

● All items as for Section 9.
● HT lead insulation failure. Insulation failure of the HT lead and spark plug cap due to old age or damage can cause shorting when the engine is driven hard. This condition may be less noticeable, or not noticeable at all at lower engine speeds.

14 Fuel/air mixture incorrect

● All items as for Section 10, with the exception of items relative exclusively to low speed running.
● Main jet blocked. Debris from contaminated fuel, or from the fuel tank, and water in the fuel can block the main jet. Clean the fuel filter, the float bowl area, and if water is present, flush and refill the fuel tank.
● Main jet is the wrong size. The standard carburettor jetting is for sea level atmospheric pressure. For high altitudes, usually above 5000 ft, a smaller main jet will be required.
● Jet needle and needle jet worn. These can be renewed individually but should be renewed as a pair. Renewal of both items requires partial dismantling of the carburettor.
● Air bleed holes blocked. Dismantle carburettor and use compressed air to blow out all air passages.
● Reduced fuel flow. A reduction in the maximum fuel flow from the fuel tank to the carburettor will cause fuel starvation, proportionate to the engine speed. Check for blockages through debris or a kinked fuel line.

15 Compression low

● See Section 7.

Knocking or pinking

16 General causes

● Carbon build-up in combustion chamber. After high mileages have been covered large accumulation of carbon may occur. This may glow red hot and cause premature ignition of the fuel/air mixture, in advance of normal firing by the spark plug. Cylinder head removal will be required to allow inspection and cleaning.
● Fuel incorrect. A low grade fuel, or one of poor quality may result in compression induced detonation of the fuel resulting in knocking and pinking noises. Old fuel can cause similar problems. A too highly leaded fuel will reduce detonation but will accelerate deposit formation in the combustion chamber and may lead to early pre-ignition as described in item 1.
● Spark plug heat range incorrect. Uncontrolled pre-ignition can result from the use of a spark plug the heat range of which is too hot.
● Weak mixture. Overheating of the engine due to a weak mixture can result in pre-ignition occurring where it would not occur when engine temperature was within normal limits. Maladjustment, blocked jets or passages and air leaks can cause this condition.

Overheating

17 Firing incorrect

● Spark plug fouled, defective or maladjusted. See Section 5.
● Spark plug type incorrect. Refer to the Specifications and ensure that the correct plug type is fitted.
● Incorrect ignition timing. Timing that is far too much advanced or far too much retarded will cause overheating. Check the ignition timing is correct.

18 Fuel/air mixture incorrect

● Slow speed mixture strength incorrect. Adjust pilot air screw.
● Main jet wrong size. The carburettor is jetted for sea level atmospheric conditions. For high altitudes, usually above 5000 ft, a smaller main jet will be required.
● Air filter badly fitted or omitted. Check that the filter element is in place and that it and the air filter box cover are sealing correctly. Any leaks will cause a weak mixture.
● Induction air leaks. Check the security of the carburettor mountings and hose connections, and for cracks and splits in the hoses. Check also that the carburettor top is secure and that the vacuum gauge adaptor plug (where fitted) is tight.
● Fuel level too low. See Section 3.
● Fuel tank filler cap air vent obstructed. Clear blockage.

19 Lubrication inadequate

● Petrol/oil mixture incorrect. The proportion of oil mixed with the petrol in the tank is critical if the engine is to perform correctly. Too little oil will leave the reciprocating parts and bearings poorly lubricated and overheating will occur. In extreme case the engine will seize. Conversely, too much oil will effectively displace a similar amount of petrol. Though this does not often cause overheating in practice it is possible that the resultant weak mixture may cause overheating. It will inevitably cause a loss of power and excessive exhaust smoke.

● Oil pump settings incorrect. The oil pump settings are of great importance since the quantities of oil being injected are very small. Any variation in oil delivery will have a significant effect on the engine. Refer to Chapter 3 for further information.

● Oil tank empty or low. This will have disastrous consequences if left unnoticed. Check and replenish tank regularly.

● Transmission oil low or worn out. Check the level regularly and investigate any loss of oil. If the oil level drops with no sign of external leakage it is likely that the crankshaft main bearing oil seals are worn, allowing transmission oil to be drawn into the crankcase during induction.

20 Miscellaneous causes

● Engine fins clogged. A build-up of mud in the cylinder head and cylinder barrel cooling fins will decrease the cooling capabilities of the fins. Clean the fins as required.

Clutch operating problems

21 Clutch slip

● No clutch lever play. Adjust clutch lever end play according to the procedure in Chapter 1.

● Friction plates worn or warped. Overhaul clutch assembly, replacing plates out of specification.

● Steel plates worn or warped. Overhaul clutch assembly, replacing plates out of specification.

● Clutch spring broken or worn. Old or heat-damaged (from slipping clutch) springs should be replaced with new ones.

● Clutch inner cable snagging. Caused by a frayed cable or kinked outer cable. Replace the cable with a new one. Repair of a frayed cable is not advised.

● Clutch release mechanism defective. Worn or damaged parts in the clutch release mechanism could include the shaft, cam, actuating arm or pivot. Replace parts as necessary.

● Clutch hub and outer drum worn. Severe indentation by the clutch plate tangs of the channels in the hub and drum will cause snagging of the plates preventing correct engagement. If this damage occurs, renewal of the worn components is required.

● Lubricant incorrect. Use of a transmission lubricant other than that specified may allow the plates to slip.

22 Clutch drag

● Clutch lever excessive. Adjust lever at bars or at cable end if necessary.

● Clutch plates warped or damaged. This will cause a drag on the clutch, causing the machine to creep. Overhaul clutch assembly.

● Clutch spring tension uneven. Usually caused by a sagged or broken spring. Check and replace springs.

● Transmission oil deteriorated. Badly contaminated transmission oil and a heavy deposit of oil sludge on the plates will cause plate sticking. The oil recommended for this machine is of the detergent type, therefore it is unlikely that this problem will arise unless regular oil changes are neglected.

● Transmission oil viscosity too high. Drag in the plates will result from the use of an oil with too high a viscosity. In very cold weather clutch drag may occur until the engine has reached operating temperature.

● Clutch hub and outer drum worn. Indentation by the clutch plate tangs of the channels in the hub and drum will prevent easy plate disengagement. If the damage is light the affected areas may be dressed with a fine file. More pronounced damage will necessitate renewal of the components.

● Clutch housing seized to shaft. Lack of lubrication, severe wear or damage can cause the housing to seize to the shaft. Overhaul of the clutch, and perhaps the transmission, may be necessary to repair damage.

● Clutch release mechanism defective. Worn or damaged release mechanism parts can stick and fail to provide leverage. Overhaul clutch cover components.

● Broken or displaced clutch hub circlip. Causes drum and hub misalignment, putting a drag on the engine. Engagement adjustment continually varies. Overhaul clutch assembly.

Gear selection problems

23 Gear lever does not return

● Weak or broken centraliser spring. Renew the spring.

● Gearchange shaft bent or seized. Distortion of the gearchange shaft often occurs if the machine is dropped heavily on the gear lever. Provided that damage is not severe straightening of the shaft is permissible.

24 Gear selection difficult or impossible

● Clutch not disengaging fully. See Section 22.

● Gearchange shaft bent. This often occurs if the machine is dropped heavily on the gear lever. Straightening of the shaft is permissible if the damage is not too great.

● Gearchange arms, pawls or pins worn or damaged. Wear or breakage of any of these items may cause difficulty in selecting one or more gears. Overhaul the selector mechanism.

● Gearchange shaft centraliser spring maladjusted. This is often characterised by difficulties in changing up or down, but rarely in both directions. Adjust the centraliser anchor bolt as described in Chapter 1.

● Gearchange drum stopper cam or detent plunger damaged. Failure, rather than wear of these items may jam the drum thereby preventing gearchanging or causing false selection at high speed.

● Selector forks bent or seized. This can be caused by dropping the machine heavily on the gearchange lever or as a result of lack of lubrication. Though rare, bending of a shaft can result from a missed gearchange or false selection at high speed.

● Selector fork end and pin wear. Pronounced wear of these items and the grooves in the gearchange drum can lead to imprecise selection and, eventually, no selection. Renewal of the worn components will be required.

● Structural failure. Failure of any one component of the selector rod and change mechanism will result in improper or fouled gear selection.

25 Jumping out of gear

● Detent plunger assembly worn or damaged. Wear of the plunger and the cam with which it locates and breakage of the detent spring can cause imprecise gear selection resulting in jumping out of gear. Renew the damaged components.

● Gear pinion dogs worn or damaged. Rounding off the dog edges and the mating recesses in adjacent pinion can lead to jumping out of gear when under load. The gears should be inspected and renewed. Attempting to reprofile the dogs is not recommended.

● Selector forks, gearchange drum and pinion grooves worn. Extreme wear of these interconnected items can occur after high mileages especially when lubrication has been neglected. The worn components must be renewed.

● Gear pinions, bushes and shafts worn. Renew the worn components.

● Bent gearchange shaft. Often caused by dropping the

machine on the gear lever.
● Gear pinion tooth broken. Chipped teeth are unlikely to cause jumping out of gear once the gear has been selected fully; a tooth which is completely broken off, however, may cause problems in this respect and in any event will cause transmission noise.

26 Overselection

● Pawl spring weak or broken. Renew the spring.
● Detent plunger worn or broken. Renew the damaged items.
● Stopper arm spring worn or broken. Renew the spring.
● Gearchange arm stop pads worn. Repairs can be made by welding and reprofiling with a file.
● Selector limiter claw components (where fitted) worn or damaged. Renew the damaged items.

Abnormal engine noise

27 Knocking or pinking

● See Section 16.

28 Piston slap or rattling from cylinder

● Cylinder bore/piston clearance excessive. Resulting from wear, or partial seizure. This condition can often be heard as a high, rapid tapping noise when the engine is under little or no load, particularly when power is just beginning to be applied. Renewal of the piston only may be possible if cylinder wear is in limits. Failing this, renewal of piston and cylinder barrel will be required.
● Connecting rod bent. This can be caused by over-revving, trying to start a very badly flooded engine (resulting in a hydraulic lock in the cylinder) or by earlier mechanical failure. Attempts at straightening a bent connecting rod from a high performance engine are not recommended. Careful inspection of the crankshaft should be made before renewing the damaged connecting rod.
● Gudgeon pin, piston boss bore or small-end bearing wear or seizure. Excess clearance or partial seizure between normal moving parts of these items can cause continuous or intermittent tapping noises. Rapid wear or seizure is caused by lubrication starvation.
● Piston rings worn, broken or sticking. Renew the rings after careful inspection of the piston and bore.

29 Other noises

● Big-end bearing wear. A pronounced knock from within the crankcase which worsens rapidly is indicative of big-end bearing failure as a result of extreme normal wear or lubrication failure. Remedial action in the form of a bottom end overhaul should be taken; continuing to run the engine will lead to further damage including the possibility of connecting rod breakage.
● Main bearing failure. Extreme normal wear or failure of the main bearings is characteristically accompanied by a rumble from the crankcase and vibration felt through the frame and footrests. Renew the worn bearings and carry out a very careful examination of the crankshaft.
● Crankshaft (flywheel assembly) excessively out of true. A bent crank may result from over-revving or damage from an upper cylinder component or gearbox failure. Damage can also result from dropping the machine on either crankshaft end. Straightening of the crankshaft may be possible in certain circumstances.

● Engine mounting loose. Tighten all the engine mounting nuts and bolts.
● Cylinder head gasket leaking. The noise most often associated with a leaking head gasket is a high pitched squeaking, although any other noise consistent with gas being forced out under pressure from a small orifice can also be emitted. Gasket leakage is often accompanied by oil seepage from around the mating joint or from the cylinder head holding down bolts and nuts. Leakage results from insufficient or uneven tightening of the cylinder head fasteners, or from random mechanical failure. Retightening to the correct torque figure will, at best, only provide a temporary cure. The gasket should be renewed at the earliest opportunity.
● Exhaust system leakage. Popping or crackling in the exhaust system, particularly when it occurs with the engine on the overrun, indicates a poor joint either at the cylinder port or at the exhaust pipe/silencer connection. Failure of the gasket or looseness of the clamp should be looked for.

Abnormal transmission noise

30 Clutch noise

● Clutch outer drum/friction plate tang clearance excessive.
● Clutch outer drum/spacer clearance excessive.
● Clutch outer drum/thrust washer clearance excessive.
● Primary drive gear teeth worn or damaged.
● Clutch shock absorber assembly worn or damaged.

31 Transmission noise

● Bearing or bushes worn or damaged. Renew the affected components.
● Gear pinions worn or chipped. Renew the gear pinions.
● Metal chips jammed gear teeth. This can occur when pieces of metal from any failed component are picked up by a meshing pinion. The condition will lead to rapid bearing wear or early gear failure.
● Engine/transmission oil level too low. Top up immediately to prevent damage to gearbox and engine.
● Gearchange mechanism worn or damaged. Wear or failure of certain items in the selection and change components can induce mis-selection of gears (see Section 24) where incipient engagement of more than one gear set is promoted. Remedial action, by the overhaul of the gearbox, should be taken without delay.
● Chain snagging on cases or cycle parts. A badly worn chain or one that is excessively loose may snag or smack against adjacent components.

Exhaust smokes excessively

32 White/blue smoke (caused by oil burning)

● Piston rings worn or broken. Breakage or wear of any ring, but particularly the oil control ring, will allow engine oil past the piston into the combustion chamber. Examine and renew, where necessary, the cylinder barrel and piston.
● Cylinder cracked, worn or scored. These conditions may be caused by overheating, lack of lubrication, component failure or advanced normal wear. The cylinder barrel should be renewed and, if necessary, a new piston fitted.
● Petrol/oil ratio incorrect. Ensure that oil is mixed with the petrol in the correct ratio. The manufacturer's recommendation must be adhered to if excessive smoking or under-lubrication is to be avoided.
● Oil pump settings incorrect. Check and reset the oil pump as described in Chapter 2.
● Crankshaft main bearing oil seals worn. Wear in the main

bearing oil seals, often in conjunction with wear in the bearings themselves, can allow transmission oil to find its way into the crankcase and thence to the combustion chamber. This condition is often indicated by a mysterious drop in the transmission oil level with no sign of external leakage.

● Accumulated oil deposits in exhaust system. If the machine is used for short journeys only it is possible for the oil residue in the exhaust gases to condense in the relatively cool silencer. If the machine is then taken for a longer run in hot weather, the accumulated oil will burn off producing ominous smoke from the exhaust.

33 Black smoke (caused by over-rich mixture)

● Air filter element clogged. Clean or renew the element.
● Main jet loose or too large. Remove the float chamber to check for tightness of the jet. If the machine is used at high altitudes rejetting will be required to compensate for the lower atmospheric pressure.
● Cold start mechanism jammed on. Check that the mechanism works smoothly and correctly and that, where fitted, the operating cable is lubricated and not snagged.
● Fuel level too high. The fuel level is controlled by the float height which can increase as a result of wear or damage. Remove the float bowl and check the float height. Check also that floats have not punctured; a punctured float will lose buoyancy and allow an increased fuel level.
● Float valve needle stuck open. Caused by dirt or a worn valve. Clean the float chamber or renew the needle and, if necessary, the valve seat.

Poor handling or roadholding

34 Directional instability

● Steering head bearing adjustment too tight. This will cause rolling or weaving at low speeds. Re-adjust the bearings.
● Steering head bearing worn or damaged. Correct adjustment of the bearing will prove impossible to achieve if wear or damage has occurred. Inconsistent handling will occur including rolling or weaving at low speed and poor directional control at indeterminate higher speeds. The steering head bearing should be dismantled for inspection and renewed if required. Lubrication should also be carried out.
● Bearing races pitted or dented. Impact damage caused, perhaps, by an accident or riding over a pot-hole can cause indentation of the bearing, usually in one position. This should be noted as notchiness when the handlebars are turned. Renew and lubricate the bearings.
● Steering stem bent. This will occur only if the machine is subjected to a high impact such as hitting a curb or a pot-hole. The lower yoke/stem should be renewed; do not attempt to straighten the stem.
● Front or rear tyre pressures too low.
● Front or rear tyre worn. General instability, high speed wobbles and skipping over white lines indicates that tyre renewal may be required. Tyre induced problems, in some machine/tyre combinations, can occur even when the tyre in question is by no means fully worn.
● Swinging arm bearings worn. Difficulties in holding line, particularly when cornering or when changing power settings indicates wear in the swinging arm bearings. The swinging arm should be removed from the machine and the bearings renewed.
● Swinging arm flexing. The symptoms given in the preceding paragraph will also occur if the swinging arm fork flexes badly. This can be caused by structural weakness as a result of corrosion, fatigue or impact damage, or because the rear wheel spindle is slack.
● Wheel bearings worn. Renew the worn bearings.

● Loose wheel spokes. The spokes should be tightened evenly to maintain tension and trueness of the rim.
● Tyres unsuitable for machine. Not all available tyres will suit the characteristics of the frame and suspension, indeed, some tyres or tyre combinations may cause a transformation in the handling characteristics. If handling problems occur immediately after changing to a new tyre type or make, revert to the original tyres to see whether an improvement can be noted. In some instances a change to what are, in fact, suitable tyres may give rise to handling deficiences. In this case a thorough check should be made of all frame and suspension items which affect stability.

35 Steering bias to left or right

● Rear wheel out of alignment. Caused by uneven adjustment of chain tensioner adjusters allowing the wheel to be askew in the fork ends. A bent rear wheel spindle will also misalign the wheel in the swinging arm.
● Wheels out of alignment. This can be caused by impact damage to the frame, swinging arm, wheel spindles or front forks. Although occasionally a result of material failure or corrosion it is usually as a result of a crash.
● Front forks twisted in the steering yokes. A light impact, for instance with a pot-hole or low curb, can twist the fork legs in the steering yokes without causing structural damage to the fork legs or the yokes themselves. Re-alignment can be made by loosening the yoke pinch bolts, wheel spindle and mudguard bolts. Re-align the wheel with the handlebars and tighten the bolts working upwards from the wheel spindle. This action should be carried out only when there is no chance that structural damage has occurred.

36 Handlebar vibrates or oscillates

● Tyres worn or out of balance. Either condition, particularly in the front tyre, will promote shaking of the fork assembly and thus the handlebars. A sudden onset of shaking can result if a balance weight is displaced during use.
● Tyres badly positioned on the wheel rims. A moulded line on each wall of a tyre is provided to allow visual verification that the tyre is correctly positioned on the rim. A check can be made by rotating the tyre; any misalignment will be immediately obvious.
● Wheels rims warped or damaged. Inspect the wheels for runout as described in Chapter 6.
● Swinging arm bearings worn. Renew the bearings.
● Wheel bearings worn. Renew the bearings.
● Steering head bearings incorrectly adjusted. Vibration is more likely to result from bearings which are too loose rather than too tight. Re-adjust the bearings.
● Loosen fork component fasteners. Loose nuts and bolts holding the fork legs, wheel spindle, mudguards or steering stem can promote shaking at the handlebars. Fasteners on running gear such as the forks and suspension should be check tightened occasionally to prevent dangerous looseness of components occurring.
● Engine mounting bolts loose. Tighten all fasteners.

37 Poor front fork performance

● Damping fluid level incorrect. If the fluid level is too low poor suspension control will occur resulting in a general impairment of roadholding and early loss of tyre adhesion when cornering and braking. Too much oil is unlikely to change the fork characteristics unless severe overfilling occurs when the fork action will become stiffer and oil seal failure may occur.

● Damping oil viscosity incorrect. The damping action of the fork is directly related to the viscosity of the damping oil. The lighter the oil used, the less will be the damping action imparted. For general use, use the recommended viscosity of oil, changing to a slightly higher or heavier oil only when a change in damping characteristic is required. Overworked oil, or oil contaminated with water which has found its way past the seals, should be renewed to restore the correct damping performance and to prevent bottoming of the forks.

● Damping components worn or corroded. Advanced normal wear of the fork internals is unlikely to occur until a very high mileage has been covered. Continual use of the machine with damaged oil seals which allows the ingress of water, or neglect, will lead to rapid corrosion and wear. Dismantle the forks for inspection and overhaul.

● Weak fork springs. Progressive fatigue of the fork springs, resulting in a reduced spring free length, will occur after extensive use. This condition will promote excessive fork dive under braking, and in its advanced form will reduce the at-rest extended length of the forks and thus the fork geometry. Renewal of the springs as a pair is the only satisfactory course of action.

● Bent stanchions or corroded stanchions. Both conditions will prevent correct telescoping of the fork legs, and in an advanced state can cause sticking of the fork in one position. In a mild form corrosion will cause stiction of the fork thereby increasing the time the suspension takes to react to an uneven road surface. Bent fork stanchions should be attended to immediately because they indicate that impact damage has occurred, and there is a danger that the forks will fail with disastrous consequences.

38 Front fork judder when braking (see also Section 41)

● Wear between the fork stanchions and the fork legs. Renewal of the affected components is required.
● Slack steering head bearings. Re-adjust the bearings.
● Warped brake disc or drum. If irregular braking action occurs fork judder can be induced in what are normally serviceable forks. Renew the damaged brake components.

39 Poor rear suspension performance

● Rear suspension unit damper worn out or leaking. The damping performance of most rear suspension units falls off with age. This is a gradual process, and thus may not be immediately obvious. Indications of poor damping include hopping of the rear end when cornering or braking, and a general loss of positive stability.
● Weak rear springs. If the suspension unit springs fatigue they will promote excessive pitching of the machine and reduce the ground clearance when cornering. Although replacement springs are available separately from the rear suspension damper unit it is probable that if spring fatigue has occurred the damper units will also require renewal.
● Swinging arm flexing or bearings worn. See Sections 34 and 36.
● Bent suspension unit damper rod. This is likely to occur only if the machine is dropped or if seizure of the piston occurs. If either happens the suspension units should be renewed as a pair.

Abnormal frame and suspension noise

40 Front end noise

● Oil level low or too thin. This can cause a 'spurting' sound

and is usually accompanied by irregular fork action.
● Spring weak or broken. Makes a clicking or scraping sound. Fork oil will have a lot of metal particles in it.
● Steering head bearings loose or damaged. Clicks when braking. Check, adjust or replace.
● Fork clamps loose. Make sure all fork clamp pinch bolts are tight.
● Fork stanchion bent. Good possibility if machine has been dropped. Repair or replace tube.

41 Rear suspension noise

● Fluid level too low. Leakage of a suspension unit, usually evident by oil on the outer surfaces, can cause a spurting noise. The suspension units should be renewed as a pair.
● Defective rear suspension unit with internal damage. Renew the suspension units as a pair.

Brake problems

42 Brakes are spongy or ineffective – disc brakes

● Air in brake circuit. This is only likely to happen in service due to neglect in checking the fluid level or because a leak has developed. The problem should be identified and the brake system bled of air.
● Pad worn. Check the pad wear against the wear lines provided and renew the pads if necessary.
● Contaminated pads. Cleaning pads which have been contaminated with oil, grease or brake fluid is unlikely to prove successful; the pads should be renewed.
● Pads glazed. This is usually caused by overheating. The surface of the pads may be roughened using glass-paper or a fine file.
● Brake fluid deterioration. A brake which on initial operation is firm but rapidly becomes spongy in use may be failing due to water contamination of the fluid. The fluid should be drained and then the system refilled and bled.
● Master cylinder seal failure. Wear or damage of master cylinder internal parts will prevent pressurisation of the brake fluid. Overhaul the master cylinder unit.
● Caliper seal failure. This will almost certainly be obvious by loss of fluid, a lowering of fluid in the master cylinder reservoir and contamination of the brake pads and caliper. Overhaul the caliper assembly.
● Brake lever or pedal improperly adjusted. Adjust the clearance between the lever end and master cylinder plunger to take up lost motion, as recommended in Routine maintenance.

43 Brakes drag – disc brakes

● Disc warped. The disc must be renewed.
● Caliper piston, caliper or pads corroded. The brake caliper assembly is vulnerable to corrosion due to water and dirt, and unless cleaned at regular intervals and lubricated in the recommended manner, will become sticky in operation.
● Piston seal deteriorated. The seal is designed to return the piston in the caliper to the retracted position when the brake is released. Wear or old age can affect this function. The caliper should be overhauled if this occurs.
● Brake pad damaged. Pad material separating from the backing plate due to wear or faulty manufacture. Renew the pads. Faulty installation of a pad also will cause dragging.
● Wheel spindle bent. The spindle may be straightened if no structural damage has occurred.
● Brake lever or pedal not returning. Check that the lever or pedal works smoothly throughout its operating range and does not snag on any adjacent cycle parts. Lubricate the pivot if necessary.

● Twisted caliper support bracket. This is likely to occur only after impact in an accident. No attempt should be made to re-align the caliper; the bracket should be renewed.

44 Brake lever or pedal pulsates in operation – disc brakes

● Disc warped or irregularly worn. The disc must be renewed.
● Wheel spindle bent. The spindle may be straightened provided no structural damage has occurred.

45 Disc brake noise

● Brake squeal. This can be caused by the omission or incorrect installation of the anti-squeal shim fitted to the rear of one pad. The arrow on the shim should face the direction of wheel normal rotation. Squealing can also be caused by dust on the pads, usually in combination with glazed pads, or other contamination from oil, grease, brake fluid or corrosion. Persistent squealing which cannot be traced to any of the normal causes can often be cured by applying a thin layer of high temperature silicone grease to the rear of the pads. Make absolutely certain that no grease is allowed to contaminate the braking surface of the pads.
● Glazed pads. This is usually caused by high temperatures or contamination. The pad surfaces may be roughened using glass-paper or a fine file. If this approach does not effect a cure the pads should be renewed.
● Disc warped. This can cause a chattering, clicking or intermittent squeal and is usually accompanied by a pulsating brake lever or pedal or uneven braking. The disc must be renewed.
● Brake pads fitted incorrectly or undersize. Longitudinal play in the pads due to omission of the locating springs (where fitted) or because pads of the wrong size have been fitted will cause a single tapping noise every time the brake is operated. Inspect the pads for correct installation and security.

46 Brakes are spongy or ineffective – drum brakes

● Brake cable deterioration. Damage to the outer cable by stretching or being trapped will give a spongy feel to the brake lever. The cable should be renewed. A cable which has become corroded due to old age or neglect of lubrication will partially seize making operation very heavy. Lubrication at this stage may overcome the problem but the fitting of a new cable is recommended.
● Worn brake linings. Determine lining wear using the external brake wear indicator on the brake backplate, or by removing the wheel and withdrawing the brake backplate. Renew the shoe/lining units as a pair if the linings are worn below the recommended limit.
● Worn brake camshaft. Wear between the camshaft and the bearing surface will reduce brake feel and reduce operating efficiency. Renewal of one or both items will be required to rectify the fault.
● Worn brake cam and shoe ends. Renew the worn components.
● Linings contaminated with dust or grease. Any accumulations of dust should be cleaned from the brake assembly and drum using a petrol dampened cloth. Do not blow or brush off the dust because it is asbestos based and thus harmful if inhaled. Light contamination from grease can be removed from the surface of the brake linings using a solvent; attempts at removing heavier contamination are less likely to be successful because some of the lubricant will have been absorbed by the lining material which will severely reduce the braking performance.

47 Brake drag – drum brakes

● Incorrect adjustment. Re-adjust the brake operating mechanism.
● Drum warped or oval. This can result from overheating or impact or uneven tension of the wheel spokes. The condition is difficult to correct, although if slight ovality only occurs, skimming the surface of the brake drum can provide a cure. This is work for a specialist engineer. Renewal of the complete wheel hub is normally the only satisfactory solution.
● Weak brake shoe return springs. This will prevent the brake lining/shoe units from pulling away from the drum surface once the brake is released. The springs should be renewed.
● Brake camshaft, lever pivot or cable poorly lubricated. Failure to attend to regular lubrication of these areas will increase operating resistance which, when compounded, may cause tardy operation and poor release movement.

48 Brake lever or pedal pulsates in operation – drum brakes

● Drums warped or oval. This can result from overheating or impact or uneven spoke tension. This condition is difficult to correct, although if slight ovality only occurs skimming the surface of the drum can provide a cure. This is work for a specialist engineer. Renewal of the hub is normally the only satisfactory solution.

49 Drum brake noise

● Drum warped or oval. This can cause intermittent rubbing of the brake linings against the drum. See the preceding Section.
● Brake linings glazed. This condition, usually accompanied by heavy lining dust contamination, often induces brake squeal. The surface of the linings may be roughened using glass-paper or a fine file.

50 Brake induced fork judder

● Worn front fork stanchions and legs, or worn or badly adjusted steering head bearings. These conditions, combined with uneven or pulsating braking as described in Sections 44 and 48 will induce more or less judder when the brakes are applied, dependent on the degree of wear and poor brake operation. Attention should be given to both areas of malfunction. See the relevant Sections.

Electrical problems

51 Battery dead or weak

● Battery faulty. Battery life should not be expected to exceed 3 to 4 years, particularly where a starter motor is used regularly. Gradual sulphation of the plates and sediment deposits will reduce the battery performance. Plate and insulator damage can often occur as a result of vibration. Complete power failure, or intermittent failure, may be due to a broken battery terminal. Lack of electrolyte will prevent the battery maintaining charge.
● Battery leads making poor contact. Remove the battery leads and clean them and the terminals, removing all traces of corrosion and tarnish. Reconnect the leads and apply a coating of petroleum jelly to the terminals.
● Load excessive. If additional items such as spot lamps, are fitted, which increase the total electrical load above the maximum alternator output, the battery will fail to maintain full

charge. Reduce the electrical load to suit the electrical capacity.
● Rectifier or ballast resistor.
● Generator generating coils open-circuit or shorted.
● Charging circuit shorting or open circuit. This may be caused by frayed or broken wiring, dirty connectors or a faulty ignition switch. The system should be tested in a logical manner. See Section 54.

52 Battery overcharged

● Regulator or ballast resistor faulty. Overcharging is indicated if the battery becomes hot or it is noticed that the electrolyte level falls repeatedly between checks. In extreme cases the battery will boil causing corrosive gases and electrolyte to be emitted through the vent pipes.
● Battery wrongly matched to the electrical circuit. Ensure that the specified battery is fitted to the machine.

53 Total electrical failure

● Fuse blown. Check the main fuse. If a fault has occurred, it must be rectified before a new fuse is fitted.
● Battery faulty. See Section 51.
● Earth failure. Check that the frame main earth strap from the battery is securely affixed to the frame and is making a good contact.
● Ignition switch or power circuit failure. Check for current flow through the battery positive lead (red) to the ignition switch. Check the ignition switch for continuity.

54 Circuit failure

● Cable failure. Refer to the machine's wiring diagram and check the circuit for continuity. Open circuits are a result of loose or corroded connections, either at terminals or in-line connectors, or because of broken wires. Occasionally, the core of a wire will break without there being any apparent damage to the outer plastic cover.
● Switch failure. All switches may be checked for continuity in each switch position, after referring to the switch position boxes incorporated in the wiring diagram for the machine. Switch failure may be a result of mechanical breakage, corrosion or water.
● Fuse blown. Refer to the wiring diagram to check whether or not a circuit fuse is fitted. Replace the fuse, if blown, only after the fault has been identified and rectified.

55 Bulbs blowing repeatedly

● Vibration failure. This is often an inherent fault related to the natural vibration characteristics of the engine and frame and is, thus difficult to resolve. Modifications of the lamp mounting, to change the damping characteristics, may help.
● Intermittent earth. Repeated failure of one bulb, particularly where the bulb is fed directly from the generator, indicates that a poor earth exists somewhere in the circuit. Check that a good contact is available at each earthing point in the circuit.
● Reduced voltage. Where a quartz-halogen bulb is fitted the voltage to the bulb should be maintained or early failure of the bulb will occur. Do not overload the system with additional electrical equipment in excess of the system's power capacity and ensure that all circuit connections are maintained clean and tight.

HONDA MB/MT 50

Check list

Daily pre-riding check

1 Check the engine oil level
2 Check the level of petrol in the tank
3 Check the level of fluid in the master cylinder (MB models) and the correct operation of the brakes
4 Check the tyre pressures and tyre condition
5 Check that the final drive chain is correctly adjusted and adequately lubricated
6 Make a general safety check of all levers and controls
7 Check the operation of the lights and indicators

Weekly or every 150 miles (250 km)

1 Lubricate and adjust if necessary the final drive chain
2 Top up the master cylinder (MB models) and adjust the brake (drum)
3 Inspect the condition of the tyres and check the pressures
4 Check the operation of the front and rear suspension
5 Check the level of electrolyte in the battery
6 Check all nuts and bolts are tightened securely and lubricate lever pivots and exposed cables

Monthly or every 600 miles (1000 km)

1 Check the gearbox oil level
2 Remove and clean the sparking plug and check the gap

Three monthly or every 1800 miles (3000 km)

1 Remove and clean the air filter element
2 Check the operation of the throttle and lubricate the cable
3 Check the oil pump alignment marks and adjust if necessary
4 Inspect the wheels for damage and check for play in the bearings
5 Lubricate the speedometer and tachometer cables

Six monthly or every 3600 miles (6000 km)

1 Adjust the carburettor
2 Inspect the fuel delivery pipe for damage or deterioration
3 Adjust the clutch operating mechanism
4 Examine the brake shoes and pads, where fitted, for wear
5 Check for play in the steering head bearings
6 Decarbonize the engine
7 Check the operation of the sidestand and return spring – MT model

Nine monthly or every 5400 miles (9000 km)

1 Renew the sparking plug
2 Change the transmission oil
3 Decarbonize the exhaust silencer baffle

Annually or every 7200 miles (12 000 km)

1 Change the front fork oil
2 Overhaul the brakes

Additional routine maintenance

1 Clean the fuel and oil filters
2 Regrease the steering head bearings
3 Change the front brake hydraulic fluid – MB models
4 Clean the machine

Adjustment data

Tyre pressures

	Front	Rear
MB50 – solo	25 psi (1.75 kg/cm²)	32 psi (2.25 kg/cm²)
MB50 – pillion	25 psi (1.75 kg/cm²)	40 psi (2.80 kg/cm²)
MT50 – solo	21 psi (1.50 kg/cm²)	21 psi (1.50 kg/cm²)
MT50 – pillion	21 psi (1.50 kg/cm²)	40 psi (2.80 kg/cm²)

Sparking plug type
UK models   NGK BR7HS or ND W22FSR
US models   NGK BR8HS or ND W24FSR

Sparking plug gap   0.6 – 0.7 mm (0.024 – 0.028 in)

Ignition timing*
Initial   19° ± 3° BTDC @ 3000 rpm
Initial retard speed:
    UK models   5000 – 7000 rpm
    US model   3000 – 5000 rpm
Full retard:
    UK models   10° ± 5° BTDC @ 9000 rpm
    US model   10° ± 5° BTDC @ 7000 rpm
* Note: ignition timing retards as engine speed increases

Idle speed
UK models   1300 rpm
US model   1400 rpm

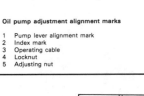

Oil pump adjustment alignment marks

1 Pump lever alignment mark
2 Index mark
3 Operating cable
4 Locknut
5 Adjusting nut

Recommended lubricants

Component	Quantity	Type/viscosity
① Engine:		Two-stroke engine oil
MB models	1.1 lit (2.0 Imp pt/ 2.4 US pt)	
MT model	1.5 lit (2.6 Imp pt)	
② Gearbox:		SAE 10W/40 SE engine oil
At oil change	0.9 lit (1.58 Imp pt/ 1.9 US pt)	
At engine rebuild	1.0 lit (1.76 Imp pt/ 2.2 US pt)	
③ Front forks:		Fork oil or ATF
MB models	72.5 – 77.5 cc (2.0 – 2.2/2.5 – 2.6 Imp/US fl oz)	
MT model	83 – 88 cc (2.3 – 2.5 Imp fl oz)	
④ Final drive chain	As required	Aerosol chain lubricant
⑤ Wheel bearings	As required	High melting-point grease
⑥ Swinging arm	As required	High melting point grease
⑦ Disc brake – MB models	As required	SAE J1703 or DOT 3 hydraulic brake fluid
⑧ Pivot points	As required	Multi-purpose grease
⑨ Control cables	As required	Light machine oil

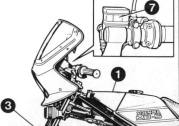

Brian Collins

ROUTINE MAINTENANCE GUIDE

Routine maintenance

For modifications and information relating to later models, see Chapter 7

Periodic routine maintenance is a continuous process which should commence immediately the machine is used. The object is to maintain all adjustments and to diagnose and rectify minor defects before they develop into more extensive, and often more expensive, problems.

It follows that if the machine is maintained properly, it will both run and perform with optimum efficiency, and be less prone to unexpected breakdowns. Regular inspection of the machine will show up any parts which are wearing, and with a little experience, it is possible to obtain the maximum life from any one component, renewing it when it becomes so worn that it is liable to fail.

Maintenance should, therefore, be regarded as an insurance policy to help keep the machine in peak condition and to ensure long, trouble-free service. It has the additional benefit of giving early warning of any faults that may develop and will act as a regular safety check, to the obvious advantage of both rider and machine alike.

Regular cleaning can be considered as important as mechanical maintenance. This will ensure that all the cycle parts are inspected regularly and are kept free from accumulations off road dirt and grime. Cleaning is especially important during the winter months, despite its appearance of being a thankless task which very soon seems pointless. On the contrary, it is during these months that the paintwork, chromium plating, and the alloy casings suffer the ravages of abrasive grit, rain and road salt. A couple of hours spent weekly on cleaning the machine will maintain its appearance and value, and highlight small points, like chipped paint, before they become a serious problem.

The various maintenance tasks are described under their respective mileage and calendar headings. Accompanying diagrams are provided where necessary. It should be remembered that the interval between the various maintenance tasks serves only as a guide. As the machine gets older or is used under particularly adverse conditions, it would be advisable to reduce the period between each check.

For ease of reference each service operation is described in detail under the relevant heading. However, if further general information is required, it can be found within the manual under the pertinent section heading in the relevant Chapter.

In order that the routine maintenance tasks are carried out with as much ease as possible, it is essential that a good selection of general workshop tools is available.

Included in the kit must be a range of metric ring or combination spanners and a selection of crosshead screwdrivers.

Additionally, owing to the extreme tightness of most casing screws on Japanese machines, an impact screwdriver, together with a choice of large and small crosshead screw bits, is absolutely indispensable. This is particularly so if the engine has not been dismantled since leaving the factory. Another tool which is essential for MT50 owners is a stand of some sort. A strong wooden box is normally recommended, but this is not always convenient for routine maintenance tasks, and so the purchase or fabrication of a metal stand, which will support the machine securely upright with enough height for either wheel to be removed, is advised. 'Paddock' type stands are frequently advertised in the national motorcycle press and are, in the author's view, well worth the money spent. MT50 owners should note that where a centre stand is mentioned in the following instructions, they must substitute their own stand.

Daily (pre-riding check)

Before taking the machine out on the road, there are certain checks which should be completed to ensure that it is in a safe and legal condition to be used.

1 Engine oil level

There is an oil level sight glass on the left-hand side of the machine. On MB50 models it is situated underneath the petrol tank, beside the cylinder head. On MT50 models it is at the rear, under the seat. The oil level should **Never** be allowed to drop below the lower mark, ie the centre of the sight glass. If it is, check the oil tank/oil pump feed pipe for air bubbles, and bleed the system if necessary. See Chapter 2, Section 21.

Use only two-stroke oil designed for motorcycle injection systems when topping up the tank, and only fill the tank to the bottom of the filler neck.

The engine oil level should be checked whenever the machine is refuelled and never allowed to run low. Remember, the first notice you will get of low oil if these precautions are not observed will be when the engine seizes up because of lack of oil.

Topping up oil tank – MB50

Topping up oil tank – MT50

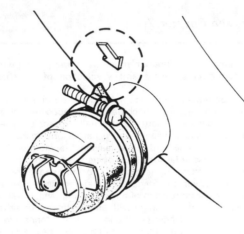

Oil level indicator

	Front	Rear
MB - solo	25 psi (1.75 kg/cm²)	32 psi (2.25 kg/cm²)
MT - solo	21 psi (1.50 kg/cm²)	21 psi (1.50 kg/cm²)
MB and MT - pillion	As solo	40 psi (2.80 kg/cm²)

At the same time as the tyre pressures are checked, examine the tyres themselves. Check them for damage, especially splitting of the sidewalls. Remove any small stones or other road debris caught between the treads. This is particularly important on the rear tyre, where rapid deflation due to penetration of the inner tube will almost certainly cause total loss of control. When checking the tyres for damage, they should be examined for tread depth in view of both the legal and safety aspects. It is vital to keep the tread depth within the UK legal limits of 1 mm of depth over three-quarters of the tread breadth around the entire circumference. Many riders, however, consider nearer 2 mm to be the limit for secure roadholding, traction, and braking, especially in adverse weather conditions.

2   Petrol level

Checking the petrol level may seem obvious, but it is all too easy to forget. Ensure that you have enough petrol to complete your journey, or at least to get you to the nearest petrol station.

3   Brakes

Check that the front and rear brakes work effectively and without binding. Ensure that the rod linkages and the cables, as applicable, are lubricated and properly adjusted. Check the fluid levels in the master cylinder reservoir of MB50 models, and ensure that there are no fluid leaks. Should topping-up be required, use only the recommended hydraulic fluid to specification SAE J1703 (UK) or DOT 3 (US).

4   Tyres

Check the tyre pressures with a gauge that is known to be accurate. It is worthwhile purchasing a pocket gauge for this purpose because the gauges on garage forecourt airlines are notoriously inaccurate. The pressures should be checked with the tyres cold. Even a few miles travelled will warm up the tyres to a point where pressures increase and an inaccurate reading will result. Tyre pressures for these models are:

Check tyre pressures using an accurate gauge

5 Final drive chain

Check that the final drive chain is properly lubricated and adjusted. Although it is not likely to be needed in the daily check, the full procedure is given here for easy reference. For any further details see Chapter 5, Section 17.

Lubrication is most effectively accomplished by the use of a special chain grease such as Linklyfe or Chainguard. This is, however, a long and potentially messy process which should be made at intervals of 500 - 1000 miles depending on the use to which the machine is put. A better solution for daily maintenance is the use of one of the many proprietary chain greases applied with an aerosol can. This can be applied very quickly, while the chain is in place on the machine, and makes very little mess. It should be applied at least once a week, and daily if the machine is used in wet weather conditions. If the roller surfaces look dry, then they need lubrication. Engine oil can be used for this task, but remember that it is flung off the chain far more easily than grease, thus making the rear end of the machine unnecessarily dirty, and requires more frequent application if it is to perform its task adequately. Also remember that surplus oil will eventually find its way on to the tyre, with quite disastrous consequences.

To adjust the chain, place the machine on its centre stand and check the tension midway between the sprockets on the lower run. Slowly turn the back wheel, testing the chain tension at points all along the chain's entire length until the tightest spot is found. This is necessary due to the fact that chains never wear evenly. Chain tension should be 10 - 20 mm ($\frac{3}{8}$ - $\frac{3}{4}$ in), with the chain at its tightest point, midway between the sprockets on the lower run. If adjustment is necessary, remove the split pin from the rear wheel spindle nut, slacken the nut, and draw the spindle back by means of the two drawbolt adjusters. Use the reference marks on the adjusters and the index marks on the swinging arm to ensure that the wheel spindle is pulled back by the same amount on both sides, thus preserving correct wheel alignment. Tighten the rear wheel nut to 5.5 - 6.5 kgf m (40 - 47 lbf ft) and fit a new spindle nut split pin, spreading its ends securely. Finally check the rear brake adjustment.

6 Controls

Check throttle, clutch, gear lever and footrests to ensure that they are securely fastened and working properly. If a bolt is going to work loose, or a cable snap, it is better that it does so with the machine at a standstill than when riding.

7 Lights and speedometer

Check that all lights, flashing indicators, horn and speedometer are working correctly to make sure that the machine complies with all legal requirements in this respect.

Weekly or every 150 miles (250 km)

This is where the proper procedure of routine maintenance begins. The daily checks serve to ensure that the machine is safe and legal to use, but contribute little to maintenance other than to give the owner an accurate picture of what item needs attention. However, if done conscientiously, they will give early warning, as has been stated, of any faults which are about to appear. When performing the following weekly maintenance tasks, therefore, carry out the daily checks first.

1 Final drive chain – adjustment and lubrication

Lubricate and check the adjustment, carrying out adjustment if necessary as described under the daily checks or in Chapter 5, Section 17. If Linklyfe, Chainguard, or similar is to be employed for regular lubrication, remove the chain by disconnecting it at its split link, wash it thoroughly in a petrol/paraffin mixture and allow it to dry. Heat the grease according to the manufacturer's instructions and immerse the chain in it. Swill

Clean chain and use aerosol lubricant regularly

Check chain tension midway between sprockets on the lower run

Use reference marks on both sides of swinging arm to ensure correct wheel alignment

the chain gently around to allow the grease fully to penetrate the rollers and withdraw it removing as much of the surplus as possible. When refitting the chain, ensure that the connecting link spring clip is replaced with its closed end facing the direction of normal travel of the chain. Note that this need only be done at intervals of 500 – 1000 miles, not every week. The actual interval is completely dependent on the use to which the machine is put, and the weather conditions in which it is used. If in doubt, remember that a tin of chain grease and some time spent applying it cost considerably less than a new chain and sprockets.

2 Adjusting the brakes

The hydraulic front brake of the MB50 model requires no adjustment. Check that the fluid level in the master cylinder reservoir is above the 'Lower' level mark. Remember that in a hydraulic brake, the level will sink only gradually, as the pads wear and more fluid is needed to maintain pressure.

A rapid drop in the fluid level is indicative of a leak somewhere in the system; immediate attention should be given to curing the leak. Refer to Chapter 5, Sections 5 – 10 as appropriate. For the purposes of routine maintenance, it will suffice to keep the fluid level topped up above the 'Lower' mark on the reservoir. Never overfill the reservoir, as fluid spillage will inevitably result. Top-up using only hydraulic fluid of the correct specification; this is SAE J1703 (UK) or DOT 3 (US). The drum brake fitted to the MT50 model is adjusted at the cable adjuster on the front wheel. Slacken the locknut and turn the adjuster nut as necessary to give 10 – 20 mm ($\frac{3}{8}$ – $\frac{3}{4}$in) free play at the brake lever tip.

The rear drum brake fitted to both models is adjusted by means of a single nut at the rear end of the brake operating rod. Turn the nut clockwise to reduce free play, if necessary, to measure 20 – 30 mm ($\frac{3}{4}$ – $1\frac{1}{4}$ in) at the brake pedal tip. Check that the rear wheel rotates freely and that the stop lamp is functioning properly. Remember that the stop lamp switch height must be adjusted every time the rear brake adjustment is altered. To adjust the switch height, turn its plastic sleeve nut as required until the stop lamp bulb lights when the brake pedal free play has been taken up and the rear brake shoes are just beginning to engage the brake drum.

Complete brake maintenance by oiling all lever pivot points, all exposed lengths of cable, cable nipples and the rear brake linkage with a few drops of oil from a can. Remember not to allow excessive oil on to the operating linkage, in case any surplus should find its way into the brake drum or on to the tyre.

3 Checking the tyres

The daily check should give you an accurate idea of the condition of the tyres, but they must still be checked thoroughly each week. Ensure that the pressures are correct as already mentioned and remove any foreign matter from the treads.

4 Checking the front and rear suspension

Ensure that the front forks operate smoothly and progressively by pumping them up and down whilst the front brake is held on. Any faults revealed by this check should be investigated further, because any deterioration in the handling of the machine can have serious consequences if left unremedied. Check the condition of the fork stanchions. As with most current production machines, the fork stanchions are left exposed in the interests of fashion, and are thus prone to damage from stone chips or abrasion. Any damage to the stanchions will lead to rapid wear of the fork seals and can only be cured by renewing the stanchions. This is both costly and time consuming, so it is worth checking that the area below each dust seal is kept clean and greased. Remove any abrasive grit which may have accumulated around the dust seal lip. The above problems can be eliminated by fitting fork gaiters, these being available from most accessory stockists.

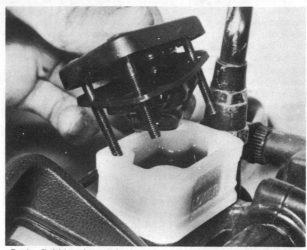

Brake fluid level must be kept between upper and lower lines

Adjust front brake by slackening locknuts and turning adjuster nut – MT50

Adjust rear brake by turning adjuster nut

The rear suspension can be checked with the machine on the centre stand. Check that all of the suspension components are securely attached to the frame. Check for free play in the swinging arm by pushing and pulling it horizontally.

5 Checking the battery

Remove the left-hand side panel and check that the electrolyte levels are between the level marks on the battery casing. Top up with distilled water to the upper level if necessary. Check that the connections are clean and tight and ensure that the battery breather pipe is free from kinks and blockages.

6 General checks and lubrication

Check around the machine, looking for loose nuts, bolts or screws, retightening them as necessary. Check the stand and lever pivots for security and lubricate them with light machine oil or engine oil. Make sure that the stand spring is is good condition.

It is advisable to lubricate the handlebar switches and stoplight switches with WD40 or similar water dispersant lubricant at regular intervals, and this is a convenient time to do it. This will keep the switches working properly and prolong their life especially if the machine is used in adverse weather conditions.

Monthly or every 600 miles (1000 km)

First complete the tasks listed under the two previous mileage/time headings and then carry out the following:

1 Checking the gearbox oil level

Before checking this, the machine must be run until it is warmed up to normal operating temperature. Place the machine on its stand so that it is upright on level ground. Withdraw the level plug which is situated in the right-hand engine cover, just in front of the kickstart shaft. Oil should slowly trickle out if the level is correct. Top up through the filler plug if necessary, but be careful not to overfill. If oil flows out in a steady stream, allow it to drain until the flow slows to a gentle trickle. Use a good quality SAE 10W/40 SE engine oil.

2 Cleaning and resetting the sparking plug

Detach the sparking plug cap, and using the correct spanner remove the sparking plug. Clean the electrodes using a wire brush followed by a strip of fine emery cloth or paper. Check the plug gap with a feeler gauge, adjusting it if necessary to within the range of 0.6 – 0.7 mm (0.024 – 0.028 in). Make adjustments by bending the outer electrode, never the inner (central) electrode.

Before fitting the sparking plug smear the threads with a graphited grease; this will aid subsequent removal.

Three monthly or every 1800 miles (3000 km)

First complete the tasks listed under the three previous mileage/time headings and then carry out the following:

1 Cleaning the air filter element

It is vitally important that the air filter element is kept clean and in good condition if the engine is to function properly. If the element becomes choked with dust it follows that the airflow to the engine will be impaired, leading to poor performance and high fuel consumption. Conversely, a damaged air filter will allow excessive amounts of unfiltered air to enter the engine,

Battery electrolyte level should be maintained between level marks

Oil should trickle from level plug orifice

Add engine oil via filler hole if necessary

which can result in an increased rate of wear and possibly damage due to the weak nature of the mixture. The interval specified above indicates the maximum time limit between each cleaning operation. Where the machine is used in particularly adverse conditions it is advised that cleaning takes place on a much more frequent basis.

Remove the right-hand side panel (MT50 only). Slacken and remove the three retaining screws and withdraw the air filter cover. Patience is required at this point as the cover is awkward to remove and to refit. Remove the metal supporting frame and withdraw the foam element.

The foam can be cleaned by washing in a high flash point solvent, such as white spirit. The use of petrol (gasoline) is not approved by the manufacturer in view of the potential fire risk. Allow the element to dry, then impregnate the foam with SAE 80 or 90 gear oil, removing any excess by squeezing it out. The element can now be reassembled and fitted.

If inspection has revealed any holes or tears, the element must be renewed immediately. On no account be tempted to omit the element in view of the damage that may ensue from the resulting weak mixture.

Remove metal frame and then the foam element

2 Checking the throttle operation and lubricating the cable

Open and close the throttle several times, allowing it to snap back under its own pressure. Ensure that it is able to shut off quickly and fully. Check that there is 2 – 6 mm (0.08 – 0.24 in) free play measured at the inner flange of the rubber twistgrip. If not, use the adjuster on the carburettor top to achieve the correct setting. See Chapter 2, Section 10 for full details. If there is any doubt at all about its condition, the throttle/oil pump cable must be thoroughly examined and lubricated. Check the outer cables for signs of damage, then examine the exposed portions of the inner cables. Any signs of kinking or fraying will indicate that renewal is required. To obtain maximum life and reliability from the cables they should be thoroughly lubricated. To do the job properly and quickly use one of the hydraulic cable oilers available from most motorcycle shops. Free one end of the cable and assemble the cable oiler as described by the manufacturer's instructions. Operate the oiler until oil emerges from the lower end, indicating that the cable is lubricated throughout its length. This process will expel any dirt or moisture and will prevent its subsequent ingress.

If a cable oiler is not available, an alternative is to remove the cable from the machine. Hang the cable upright and make up a small funnel arrangement using plasticene or by taping a plastic bag around the upper end. Fill the funnel with oil and leave it overnight to drain through. Note that where nylon-lined cables are fitted, they should be used dry or lubricated with a silicone-based lubricant suitable for this application. On no account use ordinary engine oil because this will cause the liner to swell, pinching the cable.

Check all pivots and control levers, cleaning and lubricating them to prevent wear or corrosion. Where necessary, dismantle and clean any moving part which may have become stiff in operation.

If cable removal is necessary for lubrication purposes, read Chapter 2 very carefully first, with especial reference to sections 10 and 20 regarding correct adjustment of carburettor and oil pump.

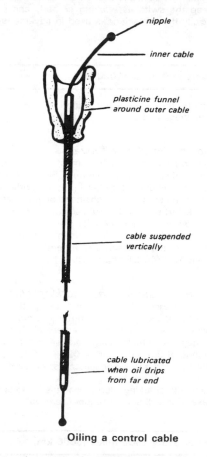
nipple
inner cable
plasticine funnel around outer cable
cable suspended vertically
cable lubricated when oil drips from far end

Oiling a control cable

3 Checking oil pump operation and adjustment

Check that the reference mark on the oil pump control lever lines up exactly with the index mark on the pump body with the throttle open fully. If adjustment is necessary, slacken the adjuster locknut and turn the adjusting nut until the marks line up exactly. Remember that the throttle must be fully open to align the marks. Note that the double line of the reference mark on the control lever allows more tolerance when aligning the marks. Always align the upper of the two lines, so that the pump delivery rate errs on the side of too much, rather than too little. Once the cable is adjusted correctly, tighten the adjuster

locknut and open the throttle fully two or three times to check the lever operation and to ensure that adjustment remains constant. Complete cable inspection and lubrication as outlined in the previous heading for the throttle cable.

The oil feed lines must be carefully inspected. Check for signs of leakage, tightening the clamps and unions where applicable, or replacing the tubing if necessary. If air bubbles or dirt are seen to be present in the transparent feed lines, the system must be cleaned or bled, as appropriate. Full details of filter cleaning and oil system bleeding will be found in Chapter 2.

Oil pump is adjusted by slackening the locknut and turning the adjuster nut

Adjust cable so that reference mark on the pump control lever is aligned with index mark on pump body

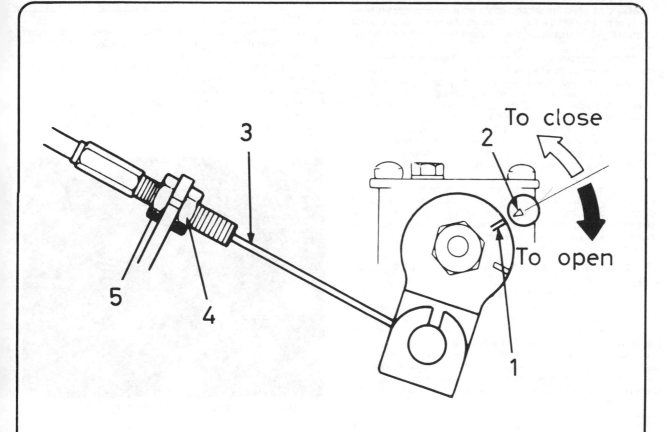

Oil pump adjustment alignment marks

1 *Pump lever alignment mark*
2 *Index mark*
3 *Operating cable*
4 *Locknut*
5 *Adjusting nut*

4   Checking the condition of the wheels and wheel bearings

Comstar wheels

Comstar wheels should be checked at regular intervals to prevent the sudden appearance of dangerous faults. Examine the rim alignment to ensure that the wheel is not distorted and check the spoke blades for cracking and security. It should be noted that while Honda recommend that the wheel is replaced if any fault appears, or if the rim is distorted by more than 2.0 mm (0.08 in) some private engineering firms offer a limited repair service. It must be stressed, however, that this is a job for the expert only and should on no account be undertaken by the private owner.

Wire-spoked wheels

Place the machine on the centre stand so that the front wheel is raised clear of the ground. Spin the wheel and check the rim alignment. Small irregularities can be corrected by tightening the spokes in the affected area although a certain amount of experience is necessary to prevent over-correction. Any flats in the wheel rim will be evident at the same time. These are more difficult to remove and in most cases it will be necessary to have the wheel rebuilt on a new rim. Apart from the effect on stability, a flat will expose the tyre bead and walls to greater risk of damage if the machine is run with a deformed wheel.

Check for loose and broken spokes. Tapping the spokes is the best guide to tension. A loose spoke will produce a quite different sound and should be tightened by turning the nipple in an anti-clockwise direction. Always check for run out by spinning the wheel again. If the spokes have to be tightened by an excessive amount, it is advisable to remove the tyre and tube as detailed in Chapter 5. This will enable the protruding ends of the spokes to be ground off, thus preventing them from chafing the inner tube and causing punctures. The condition of the rear wheel can be checked in exactly the same way as described above.

To check a wheel bearing condition, grasp the wheel at its rim and try to move it to and fro at right angles to the normal direction of rotation. If any play at all is felt, the wheel concerned must be removed, dismantled and its bearings examined and replaced if necessary.

5   Lubricating speedometer and tachometer cables

Each cable is secured at its upper mounting by a knurled, threaded ring and at its bottom mounting by a simple retaining screw or pinch bolt in the speedometer drive gearbox, front brake backplate, or right-hand outer cover, as appropriate. Remove the cable by using a pair of pliers to unscrew the knurled ring, and a screwdriver or spanner as necessary to slacken and remove the retaining screw. It should then be possible to withdraw the cable carefully from its mountings and remove it from the machine. Remove the inner cable by pulling it out from the bottom of the outer. Carefully examine the inner cable for signs of fraying, kinking, or for any shiny areas which will indicate tight spots, and the outer cable for signs of cracking, kinking or any other damage. Replace either cable if necessary. To lubricate the cable, smear a small quantity of grease on to the lower length only of the inner. Do not allow any grease on the top six inches of the cable as the grease will work its way rapidly up the length of the cable as it rotates and get into the instrument itself. This will rapidly ruin the instrument which will then have to be replaced. Insert the inner cable in the outer and replace the cable.

Six monthly or every 3600 miles (6000 km)

First carry out the tasks listed under the previous time/mileage headings and then carry out the following:

1   Carburettor adjustment

If rough running of the engine has developed, some adjustment of the carburettor pilot setting and tick-over speed may be required. If this is the case refer to Chapter 2, Section 10 for details. Do not make these adjustments unless they are obviously required, there is little to be gained by unwarranted attention to the carburettor.

Complete carburettor maintenance by slackening the drain screw on the float chamber, turning the petrol on, and allowing a small amount of fuel to drain through, thus flushing any water or dirt from the carburettor. Tighten the drain screw again.

2   Checking the fuel pipe condition

Give the pipe which connects the fuel tap and carburettor a close visual examination, checking for cracks or any signs of leakage. In time, the synthetic rubber pipe will tend to deteriorate, and will eventually leak. Apart from the obvious fire risk, the evaporating fuel will affect fuel economy. If the pipe is to be renewed, always use the correct replacement type to ensure a good leak-proof fit. Never use natural rubber tubing because this will tend to break up when in contact with petrol, and will obstruct the carburettor jets.

3   Clutch adjustment

Accurate adjustment of the clutch is necessary to ensure efficient operation of the unit. There is no provision for adjustment of the clutch itself.

Normal adjustment is made using the cable lower end adjuster, at the operating arm on the crankcase cover. Slacken the locknut and turn the adjuster nut. This tensions the inner cables and reduces the free play at the handlebar lever. When the free play at the handlebar lever is between 10 – 20 mm (0.4 – 0.8 in), the adjustment is correct. Retighten the lower end locknut.

Adjust the clutch cable by slackening the lock nut and turning the adjuster nut

4   Examination of brake pads and shoes

Close periodic inspection of the brake pads and shoes is necessary to ensure continued braking efficiency. The regular checks every week will ensure that the brakes are kept in proper adjustment but it is advisable to remove the wheels in the case of drum brakes, or the pads, in the case of discs, to check the amount of friction material left. It should be noted that wear limit indicators are provided so that inspection is greatly simplified. On brake pads these take the form of a red groove which, when worn away by the removal of friction material, indicates the need for immediate renewal of the pads. On drum brakes, a pointer on the brake operating arm should not move beyond an arrow stamped into the brake backplate when the brake is fully applied. These marks, however, only indicate the thickness of remaining friction material and it is advisable, especially if there is any doubt about the efficiency of the brakes, to remove the pads or drum brake shoes for cleaning and examination. See Chapter 5, Section 6 for the full pad removal and replacement procedure, and Sections 11 and 15 of the same Chapter for details of drum brake examination. Pay especial attention to cleaning any foreign material from pads or shoes if they are sufficiently unworn to be re-usable, and ensure that the brake cam is properly greased on drum brakes.

5 Checking the steering head bearings

Wear or play in the steering head bearings will cause imprecise handling and can be dangerous if allowed to develop unchecked. Test for play by pushing and pulling on the handlebars whilst holding the front brake on. Any wear in the head races will be seen as movement between the fork yokes and the steering lug.

Before carrying out adjustment, place a wooden crate or similar item beneath the crankcase so that the front wheel is raised clear of the ground. Check that the handlebars will turn smoothly and freely from lock to lock. If the steering feels notchy or jerky in operation it may be due to worn or damaged bearings. Should this be suspected it will be necessary to overhaul the steering head bearings as described in Chapter 4.

To adjust the steering head bearings, slacken the large steering stem nut at the centre of the top fork yoke, then use a C-spanner to tighten the slotted adjuster nut immediately below the top yoke. As a guide to adjustment, tighten the slotted nut until a light resistance is felt, then back it off by $\frac{1}{8}$ turn. The object is to remove all discernible play without applying any appreciable preload. It should be noted that it is possible to apply a loading of several tons on the small steering head bearings without this being obvious when turning the handlebars. This will cause an accelerated rate of wear, and thus must be avoided.

6 Decarbonising the engine

Due to the lubrication system employed on two-stroke engines, there is a surplus of oil in the combustion chamber which is not completely burned during combustion. This oil manifests itself as a relatively rapid build-up of carbon in the combustion chamber, exhaust port and exhaust system. Regular decarbonising of the engine is therefore necessary. Slacken and remove the two exhaust pipe front mounting nuts and single rear mounting bolt, and carefully remove the exhaust pipe. Note that removal of the seat will first be necessary on MT50 models. Slacken and remove the two carburettor securing nuts and very gently slide the carburettor back off its mounting studs. Slacken and remove the engine top mounting bolt and remove the sparking plug cap and sparking plug. Progressively slacken the four cylinder head nuts to ensure an even release of pressure, remove the nuts and withdraw the cylinder head and its gasket. Remove the oil feed pipe from the inlet stub and plug it using a bolt or screw of suitable size to prevent the loss of any oil and the entry of dirt or air. Turn the crankshaft using the kickstarter until the piston reaches the top of its stroke. Remove the cylinder barrel, noting that a few gentle taps with a soft-faced mallet around the area of the cylinder base may be necessary to free the joint. Before pulling the barrel clear of the piston, carefully pack the crankcase mouth with clean rag to prevent the entry of any dirt.

Using a blunt-edged scraping tool to prevent scratching the sofy alloy components, carefully remove all traces of carbon from the piston crown cylinder head combustion chamber and exhaust port. Finish off using a soft rag and metal polish to give a smooth, polished finish to these areas; this will reduce the ability of future carbon deposits to adhere so easily. Check that the piston rings are free in their grooves in the piston. If necessary, remove them carefully and clean the grooves using

Replace both brake pads when red groove is worn away (arrowed)

Mark on brake backplate indicates brake lining wear limit

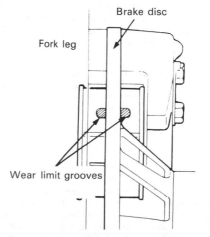

Brake disc

Fork leg

Wear limit grooves

Front brake pad wear limit – MB models

a section of broken piston ring to ensure that the grooves are not damaged. Carefully examine the rings as described in Section 20 of Chapter 1 and renew them if necessary.

Carefully clean the gasket surfaces of the crankcase, cylinder barrel; and cylinder head. Liberally oil the piston and rings, place a new cylinder base gasket in position, and replace the barrel, taking great care that the piston ring end gaps are correctly located at their respective pegs, and that the piston rings are not broken as the barrel is replaced. Use a new cylinder head gasket when replacing the cylinder head and tighten the four cylinder head nuts to the recommended torque setting of 1.8 – 2.2 kgf m (13 – 16 lbf ft). Replace the carburettor on its studs and securely tighten the retaining nuts. Unplug the oil feed line and replace it on the inlet stub union. If it has been properly plugged, bleeding of the oil injection system will not be necessary. If there is any doubt about this, carry out the bleeding operation described in Section 21 of Chapter 2. Tighten the engine top mounting bolt to 3.0 – 4.0 kgf m (22 – 29 lbf ft).

Using a longer scraping tool, remove all traces of carbon from the front length of the exhaust pipe. Carbon build-up in the pipe should not be very heavy, but this is a convenient time to perform this operation. Replace the exhaust pipe using a new exhaust gasket, replace the seat on MT50 models and fit the sparking plug and cap. Start the engine and carry out the bleeding operation if necessary. Note that it is necessary to allow the disturbed components time to settle down and so a period of approximately 50 – 100 miles running in is recommended.

7   Checking the sidestand – MT50 only
Honda recommend that the sidestand is cleaned and inspected at regular intervals, checking for cracks or damage to the stand and pivot, and for excessive wear in the return spring. Lubricate the pivot with grease or oil.

Nine monthly or every 5400 miles (9000 km)

First complete the tasks listed under the previous mileage/time headings, as appropriate, and then carry out the following:

1   Renewing the sparking plug
The manufacturer recommends that the sparking plug is renewed as a precautionary measure at this stage. Always ensure that a plug of the correct type and heat range is fitted, and that the gap is set to the prescribed 0.6 – 0.7 mm (0.024 – 0.028 in) prior to installation. If the old plug is in reasonable condition, it can be cleaned and re-gapped and carried as an emergency spare in the toolbox.

2   Changing the transmission oil
The engine must first be warmed up to normal operating temperature. This is ideally achieved by draining the oil immediately the machine is put away on the night before the maintenance tasks are to be carried out. In this way the oil will drain rapidly and completely, taking all the minute particles of metal and dirt with it, and making the oil change all the more effective. Failing this take the machine for a short run to warm it up. Place the machine on its stand, remove filler, level, and drain plugs and allow the oil to drain into a suitably-sized container. When the oil is completely drained, check that the drain plug sealing washer is in good condition and replace the drain plug, tightening it to a torque setting of 2.0 – 2.5 kgf m (14 – 18 lbf ft). Refill the gearbox with 0.9 lit (1.58/1.9 Imp/US pint) of good quality SAE 10W/40 SE engine oil. Replace filler and level plugs, start the engine and run it for a few minutes. Stop the engine and recheck the oil level, adding oil if necessary.

3   Decarbonising the silencer
The exhaust system on both MB50 and MT50 is fitted with a removable baffle tube secured by a single retaining bolt at the extreme rear of the silencer. Slacken and remove the retaining bolt and withdraw the baffle. If the deposits are of an oily nature only, it will usually suffice to scrub the baffle with a wire brush and a petrol/paraffin mixture. If however the carbon deposits are hard and dry, the use of a blow lamp is necessary to burn away the carbon. Whichever method is used, the holes in the baffle tube must be completely free before replacement.

The exhaust port end of the exhaust system should be checked when the exhaust pipe/silencer is removed at the six monthly/3600 mile check of the cylinder head and barrel. Deposits here can be scraped away with any suitably shaped tool. It should be noted that, with electronic ignition and oil pump injection, carbon build-up is not as severe a problem as with older two-strokes, and that the decarbonising intervals may be increased to once a year only (7200 miles, 12 000 km). This, however, is subject entirely to the use to which the machine is put and only experience will tell how often decarbonising is necessary.

Retaining bolt must be removed ...

... in order to remove exhaust baffle tube – MT50

Baffle tube – MB50

Annually or every 7200 miles (12 000 km)

Once a year the machine must be taken off the road for a major maintenance session. Complete all the tasks listed in the previous mileage/time headings and in addition, carry out the following:

1   Changing the fork oil

This is an important task which must be carried out to ensure the continuing stability and safety of the machine on the road. Fork oil gradually degenerates as it loses viscosity and is contaminated by water and dirt, which produces a very gradual loss of damping. This can occur over a long period of time, thus being completely unnoticed by the rider until the machine is in a dangerous condition. Regular changes of the fork oil will eliminate this possibility. Refer to Chapter 4, Sections 2 and 3 for details of fork leg removal. Unfortunately complete removal of each fork leg is necessary as there are no drain plugs fitted to the front forks on this model. The fork top bolt and spring must then be removed as described in Section 7 of Chapter 4 and the fork leg inverted to drain the oil. Pump the leg to complete the draining process. Now is a convenient moment to inspect the general condition of the front forks as described in Section 8 of Chapter 4, and to rectify any faults which may have appeared.

When draining and inspection are complete, reassemble the forks with the specified amount of oil. The oil recommended is ATF, but there are many proprietary brands of oil developed especially for use in front forks, which are available as alternatives. Refer to Sections 9 and 10 of Chapter 4 for details of reassembly.

2   Overhauling the brakes

If for any reason the brakes have not been stripped for examination, this must now be done. If no leaks are apparent in the hydraulic brake system of an MB50 then it will suffice to remove the pads for cleaning and examination, this procedure being described in Chapter 5, Section 6. Check that full lever pressure is maintained. If there appears to be some sponginess present the hydraulic system must first be bled to ensure that any air is removed. This procedure is fully described in Section 10 of Chapter 5. If it is necessary to bleed the system again after a short interval, this indicates that air is getting into the system somewhere. If this is not indicated by a fluid leak, the master cylinder must be overhauled, followed by the caliper if necessary. This is described in Sections 8 and 9 of Chapter 5.

Drum brake overhauling must be preceded by the removal of the wheel concerned. See Sections 3 and 13 which describe this. Sections 11 and 15 of Chapter 5 cover inspection and correct reassembly of the brake assembly.

Additional routine maintenance

Certain aspects of routine maintenance make it impossible to place operations under specific mileage or calendar headings, or may make necessary modification of the latter. A good example is the effect of a dusty environment on certain maintenance operations. In this case, the air cleaner element and chain maintenance intervals must be reduced considerably to prevent clogging of the former and accelerated wear of the latter. A similar example is engine decarbonising. An engine which is run at consistently low speeds, or on short journeys, will build up carbon deposits at a faster rate, and therefore need more frequent decarbonising, than an engine which is run at higher speeds or used for longer journeys. The problem of how to achieve the correct balance between too little maintenance, which will result in premature and expensive damage to the machine, and too much, is a delicate one which is unfortunately only resolved by personal experience. This experience is best gained by strict adherence to the specified mileage/time headings until the owner feels qualified to alter them to suit his own machine.

Some components will require inspection and attention at intervals dependent on usage rather than mileage or age. Three such tasks are given below:

1   Cleaning the fuel and oil filters

It should be necessary to attend to the filters only on rare occasions, for example when traces of dirt or water are found continually in the carburettor, or when dirt is seen in the oil tank or even in the oil tank/oil pump feed line. Carefully read Chapter 2, with especial reference to Sections 2, 3, 4 and 5, which are concerned with petrol tank and filter removal and cleaning, or Sections 16 and 17 which are concerned with oil tank removal and cleaning.

2   Greasing the steering head bearings

As already mentioned, the steering head bearings should be checked and adjusted at the six-monthly (3600 miles/6000 km) inspection. If, however, they are not dismantled during routine maintenance or for accident repair they should be dismantled for examination and greasing every two years. This would most conveniently fit in with the annual fork oil change, during which the front forks must be removed. Carefully read Chapter 4 with especial reference to Sections 4 and 5 which cover steering head removal and reassembly.

3   Changing the brake fluid

If the brake fluid is not completely changed during the course of routine maintenance, it should be changed at least every two years. Brake fluid is hygroscopic, which means that it absorbs moisture from the air. Although the system is sealed, the fluid will gradually deteriorate and must be renewed before contamination lowers its boiling point to an unsafe level.

Before starting work, obtain a full can of new DOT 3 or SAE J1703 hydraulic fluid and read Chapter 5, Section 10. Prepare the clear plastic tube and glass jar in the same way as for bleeding the hydraulic system, open the bleed nipple by unscrewing it $\frac{1}{4} - \frac{1}{2}$ a turn with a spanner and apply the front brake lever gently and repeatedly. This will pump out the old fluid. Keep the master cylinder reservoir topped up at all times, otherwise air may enter the system and greatly lengthen the operation. The old brake fluid is invariably much darker in colour than the new, making it easier to see when the old fluid is pumped out and the new fluid has completely replaced it.

When the new fluid appears in the clear plastic tubing completely uncontaminated by traces of old fluid, close the bleed nipple, remove the plastic tubing and replace the rubber cap on the nipple. Top the master cylindr reservoir up to the 'upper' level line and replace the cover. Wash away any surplus brake fluid and check that full braking pressure is maintained at the lever and that there are no fluid leaks.

4   Cleaning the machine

Keeping the motorcycle clean should be considered as an important part of the routine maintenance, to be carried out whenever the need arises. A machine cleaned regularly will not only succumb less speedily to the inevitable corrosion of external surfaces, and hence maintain its market value, but will be far more approachable when the time comes for maintenance or service work. Furthermore, loose or failing components are more readily spotted when not partially obscured by a mantle of road grime and oil.

Surface dirt should be removed using a sponge and warm, 'soapy water'; the latter being applied copiously to remove the particles of grit which might otherwise cause damage to the paintwork and polished surfaces.

Oil and grease is removed most easily by the application of a cleaning solvent such as 'Gunk' or 'Jizer'. The solvent should be applied when the parts are still dry and worked in with a stiff brush. Large quantities of water should be used when rinsing off, taking care that water does not enter the carburettors, air cleaners or electrics.

If desired a polish such as Solvol Autosol can be applied to the aluminium alloy parts to restore the original lustre. This does not apply in instances, much favoured by Japanese manufacturers, where the components are lacquered. Application of a wax polish to the cycle parts and a good chrome cleaner to the chrome parts will also give a good finish. Always wipe the machine down if used in the wet, and make sure the chain is well oiled. There is less chance of water getting into control cables if they are regularly lubricated, which will prevent stiffness of action.

Standard torque settings

Specific torque settings will be found at the end of the specifications section of each chapter. Where no figure is given, bolts should be secured according to the table below.

Fastener type (thread diameter)	kgf m	lbf ft
5 mm bolt or nut	0.45 – 0.6	3.5 – 4.5
6 mm bolt or nut	0.8 – 1.2	6 – 9
8 mm bolt or nut	1.8 – 2.5	13 – 18
10 mm bolt or nut	3.0 – 4.0	22 – 29
12 mm bolt or nut	5.0 – 6.0	36 – 43
5 mm screw	0.35 – 0.5	2.5 – 3.6
6 mm screw	0.7 – 1.1	5 – 8
6 mm flange bolt	1.0 – 1.4	7 – 10
8 mm flange bolt	2.4 – 3.0	17 – 22
10 mm flange bolt	3.0 – 4.0	22 – 29

Conversion factors

Length (distance)

Inches (in)	X	25.4	=	Millimetres (mm)	X	0.0394	= Inches (in)
Feet (ft)	X	0.305	=	Metres (m)	X	3.281	= Feet (ft)
Miles	X	1.609	=	Kilometres (km)	X	0.621	= Miles

Volume (capacity)

Cubic inches (cu in; in³)	X	16.387	=	Cubic centimetres (cc; cm³)	X	0.061	= Cubic inches (cu in; in³)
Imperial pints (Imp pt)	X	0.568	=	Litres (l)	X	1.76	= Imperial pints (Imp pt)
Imperial quarts (Imp qt)	X	1.137	=	Litres (l)	X	0.88	= Imperial quarts (Imp qt)
Imperial quarts (Imp qt)	X	1.201	=	US quarts (US qt)	X	0.833	= Imperial quarts (Imp qt)
US quarts (US qt)	X	0.946	=	Litres (l)	X	1.057	= US quarts (US qt)
Imperial gallons (Imp gal)	X	4.546	=	Litres (l)	X	0.22	= Imperial gallons (Imp gal)
Imperial gallons (Imp gal)	X	1.201	=	US gallons (US gal)	X	0.833	= Imperial gallons (Imp gal)
US gallons (US gal)	X	3.785	=	Litres (l)	X	0.264	= US gallons (US gal)

Mass (weight)

Ounces (oz)	X	28.35	=	Grams (g)	X	0.035	= Ounces (oz)
Pounds (lb)	X	0.454	=	Kilograms (kg)	X	2.205	= Pounds (lb)

Force

Ounces-force (ozf; oz)	X	0.278	=	Newtons (N)	X	3.6	= Ounces-force (ozf; oz)
Pounds-force (lbf; lb)	X	4.448	=	Newtons (N)	X	0.225	= Pounds-force (lbf; lb)
Newtons (N)	X	0.1	=	Kilograms-force (kgf; kg)	X	9.81	= Newtons (N)

Pressure

Pounds-force per square inch (psi; lbf/in²; lb/in²)	X	0.070	=	Kilograms-force per square centimetre (kgf/cm²; kg/cm²)	X	14.223	= Pounds-force per square inch (psi; lbf/in²; lb/in²)
Pounds-force per square inch (psi; lbf/in²; lb/in²)	X	0.068	=	Atmospheres (atm)	X	14.696	= Pounds-force per square inch (psi; lbf/in²; lb/in²)
Pounds-force per square inch (psi; lbf/in²; lb/in²)	X	0.069	=	Bars	X	14.5	= Pounds-force per square inch (psi; lbf/in²; lb/in²)
Pounds-force per square inch (psi; lbf/in²; lb/in²)	X	6.895	=	Kilopascals (kPa)	X	0.145	= Pounds-force per square inch (psi; lbf/in²; lb/in²)
Kilopascals (kPa)	X	0.01	=	Kilograms-force per square centimetre (kgf/cm²; kg/cm²)	X	98.1	= Kilopascals (kPa)
Millibar (mbar)	X	100	=	Pascals (Pa)	X	0.01	= Millibar (mbar)
Millibar (mbar)	X	0.0145	=	Pounds-force per square inch (psi; lbf/in²; lb/in²)	X	68.947	= Millibar (mbar)
Millibar (mbar)	X	0.75	=	Millimetres of mercury (mmHg)	X	1.333	= Millibar (mbar)
Millibar (mbar)	X	0.401	=	Inches of water (inH₂O)	X	2.491	= Millibar (mbar)
Millimetres of mercury (mmHg)	X	0.535	=	Inches of water (inH₂O)	X	1.868	= Millimetres of mercury (mmHg)
Inches of water (inH₂O)	X	0.036	=	Pounds-force per square inch (psi; lbf/in²; lb/in²)	X	27.68	= Inches of water (inH₂O)

Torque (moment of force)

Pounds-force inches (lbf in; lb in)	X	1.152	=	Kilograms-force centimetre (kgf cm; kg cm)	X	0.868	= Pounds-force inches (lbf in; lb in)
Pounds-force inches (lbf in; lb in)	X	0.113	=	Newton metres (Nm)	X	8.85	= Pounds-force inches (lbf in; lb in)
Pounds-force inches (lbf in; lb in)	X	0.083	=	Pounds-force feet (lbf ft; lb ft)	X	12	= Pounds-force inches (lbf in; lb in)
Pounds-force feet (lbf ft; lb ft)	X	0.138	=	Kilograms-force metres (kgf m; kg m)	X	7.233	= Pounds-force feet (lbf ft; lb ft)
Pounds-force feet (lbf ft; lb ft)	X	1.356	=	Newton metres (Nm)	X	0.738	= Pounds-force feet (lbf ft; lb ft)
Newton metres (Nm)	X	0.102	=	Kilograms-force metres (kgf m; kg m)	X	9.804	= Newton metres (Nm)

Power

Horsepower (hp)	X	745.7	=	Watts (W)	X	0.0013	= Horsepower (hp)

Velocity (speed)

Miles per hour (miles/hr; mph)	X	1.609	=	Kilometres per hour (km/hr; kph)	X	0.621	= Miles per hour (miles/hr; mph)

Fuel consumption*

Miles per gallon, Imperial (mpg)	X	0.354	=	Kilometres per litre (km/l)	X	2.825	= Miles per gallon, Imperial (mpg)
Miles per gallon, US (mpg)	X	0.425	=	Kilometres per litre (km/l)	X	2.352	= Miles per gallon, US (mpg)

Temperature

Degrees Fahrenheit = (°C x 1.8) + 32

Degrees Celsius (Degrees Centigrade; °C) = (°F - 32) x 0.56

*It is common practice to convert from miles per gallon (mpg) to litres/100 kilometres (l/100km), where mpg (Imperial) x l/100 km = 282 and mpg (US) x l/100 km = 235

Chapter 1 Engine, clutch and gearbox

For modifications and information relating to later models, see Chapter 7

Contents

Specifications

Engine

Type	Air-cooled, single cylinder two-stroke
Bore	39 mm (1.535 in)
Stroke	41.4 mm (1.630 in)
Capacity	49 cc (2.98 cu in)
Compression ratio:	
UK models	6.4 : 1
US models	7.6 : 1
Lubrication	Honda 2-stroke oil injection system
Compression pressure (at cranking speed)	130 kg/cm² (185 psi)

Piston

OD at skirt	38.955 – 38.970 mm (1.5337 – 1.5343 in)
Wear limit	38.920 mm (1.5323 in)
Gudgeon pin bore ID	12.002 – 12.008 mm (0.4725 – 0.4728 in)
Wear limit	12.030 mm (0.4736 in)
Gudgeon pin OD	11.994 – 12.000 mm (0.4722 – 0.4724 in)
Wear limit	11.980 mm (0.4717 in)
Piston ring end gap (installed):	
Top and second ring	0.10 – 0.25 mm (0.004 – 0.010 in)
Wear limit	0.35 mm (0.014 in)

Cylinder bore

Diameter	39.000 – 39.020 mm (1.5354 – 1.5362 in)
Wear limit	39.070 mm (1.5382 in)
Piston/cylinder clearance	0.030 – 0.060 mm (0.0012 – 0.0024 in)
Wear limit	0.150 mm (0.006 in)

Crankshaft

Small-end ID	17.005 – 17.017 mm (0.6695 – 0.6700 in)
Wear limit	17.030 mm (0.6705 in)
Big-end radial play (max)	0.05 mm (0.002 in)
Big-end side clearance	0.15 – 0.55 mm (0.006 – 0.022 in)
Wear limit	0.85 mm (0.033 in)
Run-out at journals (max)	0.10 mm (0.004 in)

Clutch

Type	Wet, multi-plate
Number of plates:	
Plain	2
Friction	3
Friction plate thickness	2.9 – 3.0 mm (0.114 – 0.118 in)
Wear limit	2.5 mm (0.098 in)
Plain plate warpage (max)	0.2 mm (0.008 in)
Clutch spring free length	30.2 mm (1.19 in)
Wear limit	28.5 mm (1.12 in)
Clutch outer drum bearing ID	17.000 – 17.018 mm (0.6693 – 0.6700 in)
Wear limit	17.060 mm (0.6717 in)

Primary transmission

Type	Gear
Reduction ratio	4.117 : 1 (70/17)

Gearbox

Type	Five-speed constant mesh
Ratios:	
1st	3.083 : 1 (37/12)
2nd	1.882 : 1 (32/17)
3rd	1.400 : 1 (28/20)
4th	1.130 : 1 (26/23)
5th	0.960 : 1 (24/25)
Kickstart spindle OD	11.966 – 11.984 mm (0.4711 – 0.4718 in)
Wear limit	11.950 mm (0.4704 in)
Kickstart pinion ID	12.016 – 12.034 mm (0.4731 – 0.4738 in)
Wear limit	12.070 mm (0.4752 in)
Kickstart idler gear (output) shaft OD	15.000 – 15.018 mm (0.5966 – 0.5913 in)
Wear limit	14.940 mm (0.5882 in)
Kickstart idler gear ID	15.032 – 15.050 mm (0.5918 – 0.5925 in)
Wear limit	15.100 mm (0.5945 in)
Oil pump driven gear shaft OD	9.965 – 9.987 mm (0.3923 – 0.3932 in)
Wear limit	9.930 mm (0.3909 in)
Balancer idler gear shaft OD	9.972 – 9.987 mm (0.3926 – 0.3932 in)
Wear limit	9.930 mm (0.3909 in)
Selector fork ID	10.000 – 10.018 mm (0.3937 – 0.3944 in)
Wear limit	10.05 mm (0.3957 in)
Selector fork claw thickness	4.93 – 5.00 mm (0.14 – 0.197 in)
Wear limit	4.50 mm (0.1772 in)
Selector fork shaft OD	9.972 – 9.987 mm (0.3926 – 0.3932 in)
Wear limit	9.95 mm (0.3917 in)
Selector drum OD:	
At 13 mm drum diameter	12.934 – 12.984 mm (0.5092 – 0.5112 in)
Wear limit	12.85 mm (0.5059 in)
At 36 mm drum diameter	35.950 – 35.975 mm (1.4154 – 1.4163 in)
Wear limit	35.90 mm (1.4134 in)

Gear pinion inside diameter:	
Input shaft 4th, 5th	17.016 – 17.034 mm (0.6699 – 0.6706 in)
Wear limit	17.10 mm (0.6732 in)
Output shaft 1st	16.522 – 16.543 mm (0.6505 – 0.6513 in)
Wear limit	16.60 mm (0.6535 in)
Output shaft 2nd	19.520 – 19.541 mm (0.7685 – 0.7693 in)
Wear limit	19.60 mm (0.7717 in)
Output shaft 3rd	19.020 – 19.041 mm (0.7488 – 0.7496 in)
Wear limit	19.10 mm (0.7520 in)
Input shaft OD at A	16.966 – 16.984 mm (0.6680 – 0.6687 in)
Wear limit	16.93 mm (0.6665 in)
Output shaft OD:	
At D	19.459 – 19.480 mm (0.7661 – 0.7669 in)
Wear limit	19.43 mm (0.7650 in)
At C	18.959 – 18.980 mm (0.7464 – 0.7472 in)
Wear limit	18.93 mm (0.7453 in)
At B	16.466 – 16.484 mm (0.6483 – 0.6490 in)
Wear limit	16.44 mm (0.6472 in)

Final drive

Type	Chain and sprocket
Reduction ratio:	
MB (UK)	3.750 : 1 (45/12)
MB (US)	3.307 : 1 (43/13)
MT	3.461 : 1 (45/13)

Torque wrench settings

Component	kgf m	lbf ft
Cylinder head nuts	1.8 – 2.2	13 – 16
Primary drive gear nut	4.5 – 5.5	33 – 40
Rotor centre nut	5.0 – 6.0	36 – 43
Crankcase bolts	1.0 – 1.4	7 – 10
Engine mounting bolts	3.0 – 4.0	22 – 29
Oil drain plug	2.0 – 2.5	14 – 18

1 General description

The Honda MB50 and MT50 models employ an air-cooled, single cylinder, two-stroke engine built in unit with the gearbox and clutch assemblies. This unit is common to both models with the exception that the MT50 model is not fitted with a tachometer, and its crankcase incorporates a front mounting lug, though this lug is not used.

The castings are of light alloy construction with a black painted finish. Although the cylinder barrel incorporates a steel liner, it should be noted that oversize pistons and rings are not available and, therefore, that reboring is not possible.

The crankshaft is of conventional construction, incorporating caged needle roller bearings at the small-end and big-end, with journal ball main bearings. Primary drive is direct from the crankshaft pinion to the clutch outer drum. To counter the imbalance inherent in all single cylinder engines a gear driven shaft primary balancer is used. This is driven through a balancer idler gear which incorporates an anti-backlash gear to minimise noise. Engine power is transmitted through the clutch to a five-speed constant mesh gearbox which is lubricated by splash from its own reservoir formed by the crankcase castings. The engine is lubricated by Honda's own two-stroke injection system in which a pump, driven from the clutch drum, feeds a metered amount of oil straight into the induction tract, thus eliminating the need for using petroil mixture. The oil pump is interconnected to the throttle cable, oil delivery being controlled by both throttle position and engine speed.

The US model is similar in general construction, differing only in those parts needed to achieve the higher power output allowed; ie, carburettor and reed valve assembly, piston, cylinder barrel, cylinder head and crankcase castings.

2 Operations with the engine/gearbox unit in the frame

1 The following items can be overhauled with the engine/gearbox unit installed in the frame:

a) Cylinder head
b) Cylinder barrel and piston
c) Clutch and primary drive
d) Kickstart mechanism
e) Gear selector mechanism
f) Oil pump and tachometer drive components
g) Final drive sprocket
h) Generator components

2 When several operations need to be undertaken simultaneously, it would probably be an advantage to remove the complete unit from the frame, a very simple operation which should take approximately half an hour. This will give the advantage of better access and more working space.

3 Operations with the engine/gearbox unit removed from the frame

1 It will necessary to remove the engine/gearbox unit from the frame to gain access to the following:

a) Crankshaft assembly
b) Balancer shaft
c) Gearbox components

4   Removing the engine/gearbox unit from the frame – MB models

1   Before commencing any dismantling work, it will be necessary to drain the gearbox oil. This is best done while the engine is still hot, so if time permits, drain the oil and leave the machine to cool down overnight before starting work. The drain plug is located centrally on the underside of the crankcase. The crankcase holds approximately 1 litre (1.76 pint) of oil, and a suitably sized drain tray should be placed to catch the old oil.

2   Place the machine securely on its centre stand ensuring that it is in no danger of falling off during dismantling. It is a good precaution to place wooden blocks against the front wheel to prevent the machine from rolling forward. It is helpful, though by no means essential, to raise the machine a few feet from the ground by placing it on a stout wooden bench or similar support.

3   Remove the left-hand side panel by pulling it free of the lower mounting grommet and displacing the two upper locating tabs. Disconnect the battery leads and remove the battery, placing it to one side to await reassembly. If it is anticipated that the machine is to be out of service for some time, arrangements should be made to give the battery a refresher charge every month or so, as detailed in Chapter 6. Trace the lead from the generator back up to its connector block, disconnect this and release any cable clips to free the lead from the frame. Remove the sparking plug cap and secure it clear of the engine.

4   Slacken and remove the pinch bolt which retains the gearchange lever and remove the lever. Marking the lever prior to removal will aid correct positioning on reassembly. Release the four bolts securing the left-hand engine cover and remove the cover. Slacken and remove the two sprocket mounting bolts, then turn the retainer plate until it can be pulled off the splines. Release the gearbox sprocket by sliding it clear of the shaft together with the drive chain. Disengage the sprocket from the drive chain, leaving the latter to hang around the swinging arm pivot. Should there not be enough slack in the drive chain to allow the sideways displacement of the sprocket, the chain must first be disconnected at its connecting link.

5   Remove the footrest bar by slackening and removing the two securing bolts. It should be noted that both bolts are removed from the left, and that one is hidden on the right-hand side underneath the crankcase, between the footrest bar and centre stand.

6   Disconnect the oil pump cable by slackening the two adjuster locknuts and sliding the cable clear of the adjuster bracket and the oil pump operating lever. Secure the cable clear of the engine. Disconnect the oil pump feed pipe, placing a finger over the end temporarily to stop the flow of oil. The pipe can then be plugged using a screw or bolt of suitable size. Care must be taken not to damage the end of the pipe. Tape the pipe to a convenient part of the frame with the end as high as possible to prevent loss of oil.

7   Moving round to the right-hand side of the machine, slacken and remove the pinch bolt securing the kickstart lever to its shaft, and remove the kickstart lever. Marking the lever positions prior to removal will aid correct positioning on reassembly. Remove the clutch cable by slackening the adjuster locknuts and sliding the cable clear of the adjuster bracket. The cable end nipple can now be disengaged from the operating arm on the engine casing. Tape the cable to the frame so that it is clear of the engine.

8   Remove the tachometer cable by slackening and removing the pinch bolt at its socket in the clutch cover, and then pulling the cable from its position in the casing. Replace the pinch bolt to avoid its loss and tape the tachometer cable alongside the clutch cable.

9   Slacken and remove the two nuts securing the exhaust pipe flange to the cylinder barrel. Support the weight of the exhaust system and remove the single bolt securing the exhaust pipe to the frame. Carefully remove the exhaust system from the machine. Replace the two nuts on their studs and the bolt in its position in the frame to prevent their loss.

10   Slacken and remove the two nuts securing the carburettor flange to the intake stub. When the engine is removed the carburettor will remain in place in the frame with the air filter and cable connections undisturbed. Slacken and remove the three nuts which fasten the engine mounting bolts.

11   The engine/gearbox unit is now ready to be removed, but it is possible that more clearance may be required to prevent the rear brake pedal fouling the engine. If this is necessary first disconnect the stop lamp switch by unhooking its spring from the pedal, and then slacken off the rear brake adjuster as required.

12   To remove the engine unit one person only is needed, but the assistance of a second person would be helpful. Push out first the engine bottom mounting bolt and then the upper rear mounting bolt, noting that the two spacers on the latter are retained by the air filter casing. Do not let the engine unit swing forward violently, instead ease it forward, supporting it with one hand and sliding the carburettor off its mounting studs with the other. Finally, holding the engine unit firmly with one hand, or supporting it with a wooden block, push out the top mounting bolt and remove the engine unit from the frame.

4.3 Disconnect leads and remove battery to a safe place

4.4a Note correct position of gear lever before removal

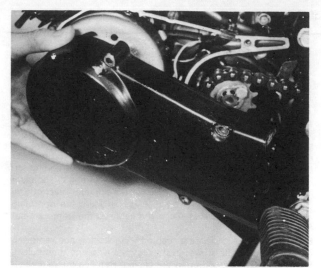
4.4b Slacken retaining bolts and remove left hand cover

4.5a Remove footrest mounting bolts – MB50 ...

4.5b ... noting that the right-hand bolt is well hidden

4.6 Disconnect and plug the oil line, placing it out of harm's way

4.7 Note correct position of kickstart lever before removal

4.8 Remove pinch bolt and withdraw tachometer cable – MB50

4.10a Slacken and remove the securing nuts on the engine top ...

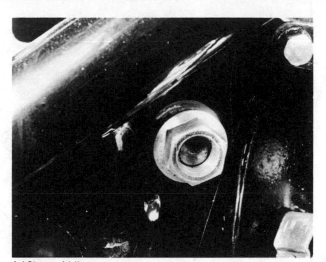

4.10b ... middle ...

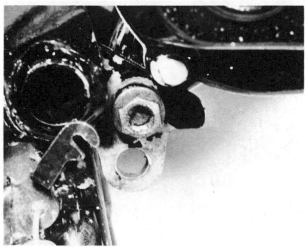

4.10c ... and bottom mounting bolts

3 There is of course, no tachometer fitted to this model and therefore no cable to remove.

4 Removing the exhaust pipe will require removal of the seat which is held by two bolts at the rear and by a hook under the tank. Seat removal exposes the two petrol tank mounting bolts, the right-hand one of which also secures an earth strap which must be released before removal of the exhaust pipe. To complete removal, slacken and remove the two nuts securing the exhaust pipe flange to the cylinder, and slide the exhaust pipe out forwards. Care must be exercised not to damage the paintwork on the exhaust or the frame. The rear section, complete with rubber joint, should be left in position unless it is wished to clean it out. It is advisable to replace the two nuts on their studs and to replace the seat with its mounting bolts to prevent loss or damage.

6 Dismantling the engine/gearbox unit: preliminaries

1 Before any dismantling work is undertaken, the external surfaces of the unit should be thoroughly cleaned and degreased. This will prevent the contamination of the engine internals, and will also make working a lot easier and cleaner. A high flash point solvent, such as paraffin (kerosene) can be used, or better still, a proprietary engine degreaser such as Gunk. Use old paintbrushes and toothbrushes to work the solvent into the various recesses of the engine castings. Take care to exclude solvent or water from the electrical components and inlet and exhaust ports. The use of petrol (gasoline) as a cleaning medium should be avoided, because the vapour is explosive and can be toxic if used in a confined space.

2 When clean and dry, arrange the unit on the workbench, leaving a suitable clear area for working. Gather a selection of small containers and plastic bags so that parts can be grouped together in an easily identifiable manner. Some paper and a pen should be on hand to permit notes to be made and labels attached where necessary. A supply of clean rag is also required.

3 Before commencing work, read through the appropriate section so that some ideas of the necessary procedure can be gained. When removing the various engine components it should be noted that great force is seldom required, unless specified. In many cases, a component's reluctance to be removed is indicative of an incorrect approach or removal method. If in any doubt, re-check with the text.

5 Removing the engine/gearbox unit from the frame – MT model

1 The removal procedure is essentially the same for both models; the following points, however, should be borne in mind when working on the MT model. Some method must be devised of holding the machine securely in the vertical position, preferably by means of a strong wooden box or some other stand placed under the swinging arm pivot. Failing this, the machine can be supported by its side stand, but care must be taken to ensure that it cannot move. This is even more important if it is raised on a bench as suggested in Section 4 of this Chapter. It should be noted that certain operations, such as draining and refilling the gearbox oil, cannot be properly carried out with the machine at an angle.

2 It is not necessary to remove the footrests in order to remove the engine unit because, although the engine bottom mounting bolt runs through the right-hand footrest, it is completely separate from the left-hand footrest. On this model both footrests are well clear of the engine unit.

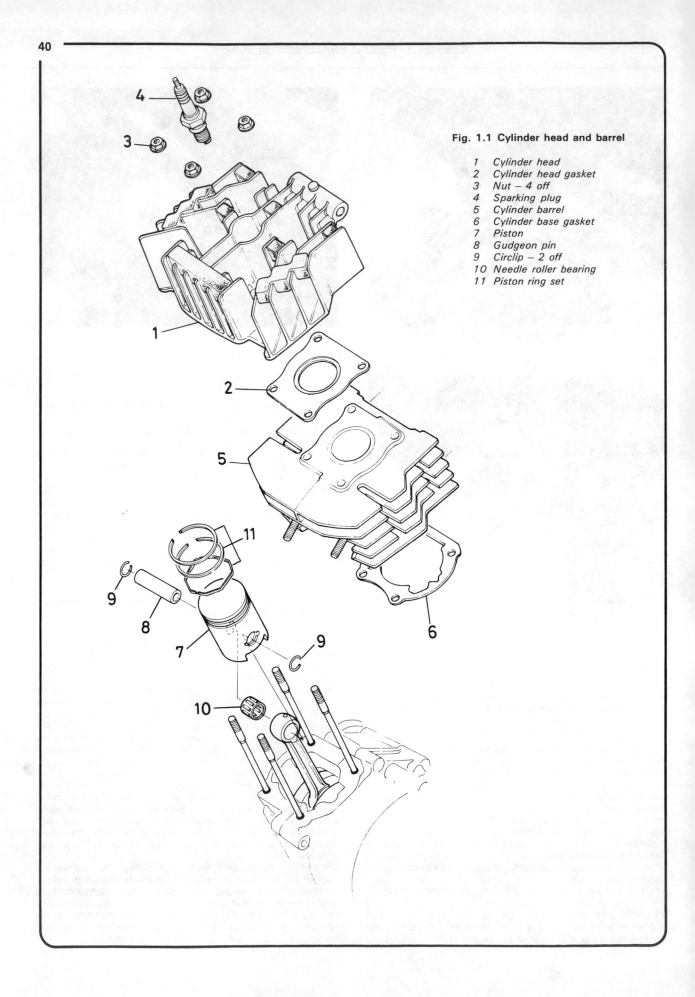

Fig. 1.1 Cylinder head and barrel

1 Cylinder head
2 Cylinder head gasket
3 Nut – 4 off
4 Sparking plug
5 Cylinder barrel
6 Cylinder base gasket
7 Piston
8 Gudgeon pin
9 Circlip – 2 off
10 Needle roller bearing
11 Piston ring set

7 Dismantling the engine/gearbox unit: removing the cylinder head barrel and piston

1   As mentioned earlier in this Chapter, removal of these components is possible with the engine/gearbox unit in or out of the frame.

2   Release the four cylinder head nuts. These should be slackened progressively by about one turn at a time, in a diagonal sequence. This will avoid any possibility of the cylinder head casting warping.

3   Remove the cylinder head and gasket. If, for any reason the joint will not free easily, do not use force to remove the cylinder head. Instead tap round the head with a soft-faced mallet to free the joint. Care must be taken not be damage the cooling fins which are brittle and easy to break. Do not risk damaging the gasket surfaces of the castings by levering the joint apart.

4   Remove the oil feed pipe from the inlet stub and plug it using a screw or bolt of suitable size. Turn the crankshaft until the piston reaches the top of its stroke. Gently ease the barrel along its studs, freeing the joints if necessary by tapping around the cylinder base with a soft-faced mallet. Before pulling the barrel clear of the piston, carefully pack the crankcase mouth with clean rag to catch any debris which might otherwise fall into the crankcase. Remove the cylinder barrel.

5   The reed valve/inlet stub assembly is removed by slackening the four retaining bolts in a diagonal sequence. Handle this assembly very carefully because the reed valve is easily damaged.

6   Prise out one of the gudgeon pin circlips using a small electrical screwdriver or similar tool in the slot provided. Support the piston and push the gudgeon pin out until the connecting rod is freed. The piston can now be lifted away. If the gudgeon pin is a tight fit, warm the piston crown with a rag soaked in boiling water, and tap the gudgeon pin out using a hammer and a soft metal drift of suitable size. Be very careful to support the piston and connecting rod during this operation and do not use excessive force, or there is a risk of bending the connecting rod. Remove the small-end bearing.

7   Place all the components on one side for further attention, but discard any circlips disturbed during dismantling. These should never be re-used; new ones must be obtained and fitted on reassembly.

8 Dismantling the engine/gearbox unit: removing the right-hand outer casing

1   The right-hand outer casing can be removed with the engine/gearbox unit in or out of the frame. In the former instance it will be necessary to carry out the following operations prior to removal.

  a)   Drain the gearbox oil
  b)   Remove the kickstart lever
  c)   Disconnect the clutch cable from the operating arm
  d)   Remove the tachometer cable (MB50 only)

These operations are described in Section 4 of this Chapter.

2   Slacken and remove the ten hexagon-headed screws from the periphery of the casing, then lift it away, taking care not to damage the kickstart shaft oil seal as it passes over the shaft splines. Be prepared to catch any residual oil left in the casing. There is a thrust washer on the kickstart shaft which may stick to the outer cover or fall clear. This should be replaced on the kickstart shaft for safekeeping.

9 Dismantling the engine/gearbox unit: removing the clutch and primary drive pinion

1   The clutch and primary drive can be removed with the engine/gearbox unit in or out of the frame. In either case it will

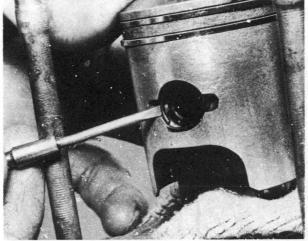

7.6 Prise out gudgeon pin circlips. Note clean rag packed in the crankcase mouth

be necessary to remove the right-hand outer casing as described in Section 8 of this Chapter.

2   Slacken and remove the four bolts securing the clutch lifter plate. This must be done progressively by about one turn at a time, in a diagonal sequence to release gradually the pressure of the four clutch springs under the lifter plate. Remove the lifter plate, bolts and springs.

3   Using a pair of circlip pliers, remove the circlip securing the clutch centre. Remove the clutch centre, the five clutch plates and the pressure plate. There should be a splined thrust washer between the pressure plate and the clutch outer. This should be removed with the clutch outer drum and kept with it to ensure its correct replacement.

4   To remove the primary drive pinion the crankshaft must be locked. If the cylinder head, barrel and piston have already been removed, push a smooth round metal bar through the small-end of the connecting rod and support it on two wooden blocks placed across the crankcase mouth. The metal bar must be a close fit in the connecting rod small-end to prevent damage occurring, and the two wooden blocks are essential to prevent damage to the crankcase mouth when using this method. Alternatively use a strap wrench or similar holding tool to lock the generator rotor. Having locked the crankshaft in position, slacken and remove the securing nut and slide off the lock washer, primary drive pinion and the spacer behind it. These should be put to one side for safe keeping.

9.2a Progressively slacken the four clutch bolts ...

9.2b .. and withdraw the clutch lifter and springs

10 Dismantling the engine/gearbox unit: removing the balancer idler pinion and oil pump drive pinion

1   Clutch removal is necessary to gain access to the balancer idler shaft and oil pump drive shaft and is described in full in Section 9 of this Chapter.

2   When the clutch has been removed, pull out the idler shaft complete with its integral double anti-backlash gear pinion, and the oil pump shaft complete with its integral nylon drive pinion. It should be noted that both are only available as complete assemblies and any attempt at further dismantling would be at least pointless and at worst it would risk severe engine damage due to the subsequent failure of either of these components.

11 Dismantling the engine/gearbox unit: removing the kickstart shaft assembly and idler gear

1   While the kickstart shaft assembly is easily accessible on removal of the right-hand outer cover, which is described in Section 8 of this Chapter, removal of the clutch is necessary before the kickstart idler gear can be withdrawn. Clutch removal is described in Section 9 of this Chapter.

2   Using a suitable pair of pliers, disengage the hooked arm of the kickstart return spring from its position on the ratchet guide plate, and allow it to unwind until the tension is released. Caution is required here as the spring is under some tension, and could do severe damage if allowed to fly off. The complete kickstart spindle assembly can then be withdrawn and put to one side if it requires no further attention. Do not forget the thrust washer on the outside next to the spring guide or the smaller thrust washer on the inside between the pinion gear and crankcase. These are very easy to lose if not kept with the kickstart assembly.

3   Dismantling of the kickstart shaft assembly need only be done if required. Remove the large thrust washer from the outer end of the shaft and use a suitable pair of pliers to remove the inner end of the kickstart return spring from its locating hole in the kickstart shaft. Withdraw the return spring, the nylon spring guide and the light coil spring from the outer end of the shaft, and the smaller thrust washer and pinion gear from the inner end. Slide off the kickstart ratchet. The individual components can then be inspected and replaced as necessary, but should be kept together in a suitable container to prevent their loss or damage until the time comes for reassembly.

4   Once the clutch and kickstarter shaft assembly have been removed, the kickstart idler gear can then be removed. Slacken and remove the two bolts which retain the ratchet guide plate and remove the plate, noting its correct position for reassembly. Withdraw the idler gear with the small thrust washer from the end of the output shaft. These components should be kept in a separate container to prevent their loss or confusion with other parts.

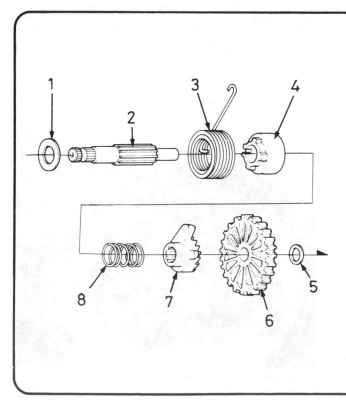

Fig. 1.2 Kickstart components

1   Thrust washer
2   Spindle
3   Return spring
4   Nylon collar
5   Thrust washer
6   Kickstart pinion
7   Ratchet
8   Spring

12 Dismantling the engine/gearbox unit: removing the gear selector mechanism

1 Prior to removal of the gear selector mechanism the right-hand outer cover, clutch assembly and kickstart assembly must first be removed as described in Section 8, 9 and 11 of this Chapter.

2 The components of the gear selector mechanism which can be reached outside the main crankcase consist of the gear selector shaft, incorporating the selector claw arm and pressure spring, return spring and detent stopper arm. These components act on the end of the selector drum with the stopper arm acting on notches in a camplate fixed to the end of the drum.

3 The detent stopper arm must be removed first by slackening and removing the single bolt which secures it. Care must be taken until the stopper arm spring pressure is released. The camplate securing bolt should now be removed. When removing the camplate the four pins are free to fall out and should therefore be removed with the plate and put to one side. All four are exactly the same, but are fitted into holes of different depths in the selector drum.

4 The selector shaft can then be withdrawn by easing it out of the main crankcase halves. Take care not to damage the oil seal on the left-hand side as the gear lever splines pass through it.

13 Dismantling the engine/gearbox unit: removing the flywheel generator

1 To carry out this operation first release the four bolts securing the left-hand outer cover and remove bolts and cover if this has not already been done.

2 The crankshaft must be locked before the rotor nut can be undone; if the engine/gearbox unit is in the frame when this is to be done, the simplest method is to select top gear and apply the back brake, thus locking the crankshaft through the gearbox. The alternatives if the engine/gearbox unit is removed from the frame, are to hold the flywheel with a strap wrench or similar holding tool, or to use a metal bar through the connecting rod small-end as described in Section 9 of this Chapter. Slacken and remove the nut and lock washer.

3 The method of rotor removal recommended is to use the manufacturer's special tool Part No 07733-0010000 or a pattern version of it which should be available at a much lower price at any good motorcycle dealer. To use this type of tool, fully unscrew the centre bolt and thread the tool body carefully into the rotor centre, noting that a left-hand thread is generally employed at this point. Once the tool body is screwed securely into the rotor as far as possible, tighten the centre bolt with a good quality ring spanner of the correct size, while holding the tool body with another spanner to prevent rotation. When the centre bolt is fully tightened on to the end of the crankshaft, tap the bolt smartly on its head with a hammer. This should immediately shock the rotor free. If it does not, tighten the tool centre bolt further and tap its head again. It should be noted that while this method often works well at the first attempt cases have been known of extreme stubbornness on the part of the rotor. If such a case is suspected, take the complete machine or engine/gearbox unit to an authorised Honda dealer for an expert opinion before any damage is done to the crankshaft or rotor due to inexpert or over-enthusiastic use of the rotor removal tool.

4 For those owners who are unwilling to purchase a tool which by the nature of the job it does, is unlikely to be used very often, or who do not have easy access to an authorised Honda dealer, an alternative method is given which uses a tool that is likely to be far more freely available. It must be stressed, however, that use of the special tool as previously described is the method recommended both by Honda and the author, this second method being for use only if no other option is open.

5 The operation of drawing the rotor from position may be accomplished with a conventional two-legged puller. Before placing the puller in position, refit the rotor securing nut on the crankshaft end so that the outer face of the nut is flush with the threaded end of the crankshaft. This will help prevent damage to the shaft. If the rotor refuses to release from the tapered shaft, do not continue tightening the puller centre screw; this will only damage the shaft. With the screw tightened down, strike firmly the screw head with a hammer. This should release the rotor. On no account strike the rotor itself to try and aid its removal; damage can easily result. Note that during this operation care must be taken not to damage any internal component or connections on the stator plate, when the legs of the puller are inserted through the openings in the rotor face. It follows, therefore, that the thinner the legs on the puller, the less likelihood of damage there is going to be. If the rotor proves particularly stubborn it is strongly recommended that no further attempts at removal using a two legged puller are made. The correct tool should be acquired or the machine should be taken to a service agent who will remove the rotor safely for a nominal sum.

6 After removing the rotor prise the Woodruff key from the tapered portion of the shaft and store it in safe place.

7 To remove the stator plate with the engine/gearbox unit still in the frame, trace the lead back up to its connector block, disconnect this, and unclip any cable ties which secure the lead to the frame. Remove the cover from the neutral indicator switch and pull out the switch wire which is retained by a spring clip. Slacken and remove the three stator plate securing bolts and pull away the stator.

13.4 Alternative method of removing flywheel (see text)

14 Dismantling the engine/gearbox unit: separating the crankcase halves and removing the crankshaft, balancer shaft and gear clusters

1 Crankcase separation is necessary to gain access to the crankshaft, balancer shaft and gearbox components. It can only be carried out after engine removal and preliminary dismantling as described in Sections 4 to 13 of this Chapter.

2 In addition to this the oil pump must be removed. Slacken and remove the two securing bolts and lift the pump away, complete with its feed pipe. Store the pump in an upright position to minimise oil leakage and to ease the task of bleeding on rebuilding.

3 Slacken and remove the eleven crankcase fastening bolts. As these are of varying lengths, the best method of keeping them is to mark a piece of thick cardboard with the position of

the bolts and then to push each bolt through the cardboard as it is removed. This ensures that each bolt is kept in the same relative position that it occupies in the crankcase and greatly simplifies the task of correctly rebuilding. Be careful to place the oil pump cable bracket and the two breather pipe clamps with their respective bolts on the cardboard.

4   Lay the crankcase on two wooden blocks so that the left-hand side is uppermost. To part the crankcases the use of the manufacturer's special tool Part No 07965-1660100 is rec-ommended. This is an extremely useful item at this stage of the operation as it is used for separating and rebuilding the crankcase halves and for removal and installation of the crankshaft itself. To use it, fit the short plain end of the tool against the crankshaft and bolt in place using three of the crankcase bolts. Tighten the tool on the crankshaft and carry on applying pressure while tapping lightly around the joint area with a soft-faced mallet. The left-hand crankcase should slide off the right-hand crankcase, leaving the crankshaft and gearbox components in the right-hand side.

5   An alternative to this method is to use a soft-faced mallet alone, tapping very carefully on the ends of the crankshaft and gearbox shafts, and round the joint area. This method requires extreme care with the use of the mallet or serious distortion of the shafts will result. With either method excessive force must not be used. If the crankcases are very reluctant to part, stop and find out why. Occasionally a particular shaft will stick in its bearing or the gasket will not free from the mating surface. If this should happen, gently free the part concerned and carry on. Never attempt to lever the crankcases apart with a screwdriver or similar tool. If there is any doubt whatever about this operation, the best course is to take the complete assembly to an authorised dfealer.

6   Once the cases have parted, lift the left-hand case clear and check that there are no thrust washers adhering to it or any other loose part such as a dowel pin which might be subse-quently lost. Any such part should be immediately replaced in the left-hand crankcase.

7   Carefully slide out the gearchange selector fork shaft and remove the three selector forks. These are all different and should be replaced immediately on the shaft in their correct relative positions to be placed to one side. It is useful to degrease each one and mark it with a spirit-based felt pen. This will prevent confusion on reassembly.

8   Remove the selector drum and balancer shaft. These are both easily lifted out of their bearings in the right-hand crankcase.

9   Remove the gear cluster. This is best done holding both shafts together and sliding them out as a complete unit. It will probably be necessary to use a soft-faced mallet, tapping gently on the shaft right-hand ends. Ensure that the thrust washers are kept in place on the left-hand end of their respective shafts.

10 Remove the crankshaft. The recommended method is to use the manufacturer's special tool, Part No 07965-1660100. If, however, this is not available, replace the primary drive gear nut on the crankshaft end to avoid damaging the thread and place the crankcase on two wooden blocks situated as close around the crankshaft as possible to give maximum support. The blocks should be of a size to hold the crankshaft far enough from the workbench top to allow the crankshaft to be removed. Using a soft-faced mallet with one hand, and supporting the crankshaft with the other, carefully tap the crankshaft out of its housing. Do not use excessive force and do not allow the crankshaft to drop away.

15 Dismantling the engine/gearbox unit: removal of ancillary components from the crankcase halves

1   If any work is to be done on the crankcase halves themselves, removal of additional items will be required.

2   All the oil seals must be removed and discarded. As a general rule they should be replaced whenever the crankcases

14.3 Do not forget the oil pump cable bracket and its mounting bolts when parting crankcases

are separated. To remove them, a screwdriver or similar tool with as few sharp edges as possible is required. Place the screwdriver end under one lip of the seal to be removed and lift that side of the seal out, pivoting the screwdriver if necessary on a piece of wood to prevent damage to the casting. Be careful that the screwdriver end does not scratch the seal housing. Once one side of the seal is levered from its position, it can be easily pulled away by hand. If there is no bearing behind the seal, and the seal is not retained by a lip in the casting, it can be driven out using a hammer and a socket or tubular drift of suitable size.

3   Press out the neutral indicator switch if necessary. This should be done using the bare minimum of force possible as the switch is only a light plastic moulding.

4   If any of the bearings are to be removed, the casting must first be heated. This is because the bearings are a tight press fit in their housings. The casting must be heated by a gradual application of heat over its entire surface to prevent the distortion which would result from a fierce local application of heat. An oven is, therefore, the best method of heating the casting to a temperature of approximately 100°C. An alterna-tive to this is to place the casting in a suitable metal container and to pour boiling water over it. It will be evident that great care must be employed when handling a casting heated by either of these methods. Do not use a welding torch or blowlamp for this operation as the even application of heat cannot be guaranteed by the inexperienced. When the casting has been heated to approximately 100°C, the higher coefficient of expansion of the aluminium alloy used in the casting will loosen the bearings to the point where they can be relatively easily drifted or pulled from their housings.

5   Bearings which are to be used again should be removed by tapping them out of their housings using a hammer and a socket or tubular drift which bears only on the outer race of the bearing concerned. If any other part of the bearing is used, unacceptably high side loadings will be placed on the balls or rollers and their cages, causing premature failure. If the entire outer race is not accessible, for instance where a bearing is in a blind housing, some other means of bearing removal will have to be found. The most widely used method is to prepare a clean, flat wooden surface, heat the crankcase casting as previously described and tap the casting on to the wooden surface hard enough to jar the bearings free. Great care must be taken to ensure that the crankcase half is tapped squarely on to a clean surface to avoid damage to the gasket surface. An alternative to this method is to heat the casting as previously described, place the casting on a clean wooden surface to support it evenly and

tap the casting directly behind the bearing with a soft-faced mallet, again with the object of jarring the bearing free. It must be stressed that tapping must be as gentle as possible to avoid damaging the casting. If either method fails, take the casting to an authorised Honda dealer for the bearings to be removed using a slide hammer with an internal puller attachment.

16 Examination and renovation: general

1   Before examining the parts of the dismantled engine unit for wear, it is essential that they should be cleaned thoroughly. Use a paraffin/petrol mix to remove all traces of old oil and sludge that may have accumulated within the engine.
2   Examine the crankcase castings for cracks or other signs of damage. If a crack is discovered, it will require professional repair.
3   Examine carefully each part to determine the extent of wear, if necessary checking with the tolerance figures listed in the Specifications Section of this Chapter, or accompanying the text.
4   Use a clean, lint-free rag for cleaning and drying the various components otherwise there is risk of small particles obstructing the internal oilways.
5   Should any studs or internal threads require repair, now is the appropriate time to attend to them. Where internal threads are stripped or badly worn, it is preferable to use a thread insert. The most common of these is the Helicoil type. The damaged thread is drilled oversize and then tapped to accept a diamond section wire thread insert. In most cases the original fastener can be used in the restored thread.

17 Examination and renovation: crankcase and fittings

1   The crankcase halves should be thoroughly degreased, using one of the proprietary water-soluble degreasing solutions such as Gunk. When clean and dry a careful examination should be made, looking for signs of cracks or other damage. Any such fault will probably require either professional repair or renewal of the crankcases as a pair. Note that any damage around the various bearing bosses will normally indicate that crankcase renewal is necessary, because a small discrepancy in these areas can result in serious mis-alignment of the shaft concerned. It is important to check crankcase condition at the earliest opportunity, because this will permit remedial action to be taken and any necessary machining or welding to be done whilst attention is turned to the remaining engine parts.
2   As mentioned previously, badly worn or damaged threads can be reclaimed by fitting a thread insert. This is a simple and inexpensive task, but one which requires the correct taps and fitting tools. It follows that the various threads should be checked and the cases taken to a local engineering works or motorcycle dealer offering this service so that repair can take place while the remaining engine parts are checked.

18 Examination and renovation: crankshaft assembly

1   Check the crankshaft assembly visually for damage, paying particular attention to the slot for the Woodruff key and to the threads at each end of the mainshaft. Should these have become damaged specialist help will be needed to reclaim them.

15.3 Handle the neutral light switch very carefully

2   The connecting rod should be checked for big-end bearing play. A small amount of end float is normal, but any up and down movement will necessitate renewal.
3   Grasp the connecting rod and pull it firmly up and down. Any movement will soon become evident. Be careful that endfloat is not mistaken for wear. Should the big-end bearing be worn it will be necessary to consult an expert for advice as to whether repair is possible or if the purchase of a new crankshaft assembly is advisable.
4   Assuming that the big-end bearing is in good order, attention should be turned to the rest of the connecting rod. Visually check the rod for straightness, particularly if the engine is being rebuilt after a seizure or other catastrophe. Look also for signs of cracking. This is extremely unlikely, but worthwhile checking. Spotting a hairline crack at this stage may save the engine from an untimely end.
5   If measuring facilities are available, set the crankshaft in V-blocks and check the big-end bearing radial clearance using a dial gauge mounted on a suitable stand. Check crankshaft run-out in the same way. Big-end axial clearance (endfloat) is measured with feeler gauges of the correct thickness which should be a firm sliding fit between the thrust washer next to the big-end eye and the machined shoulder on the flywheel. If any clearance exceeds the wear limits given in the specifications Section of this Chapter the crankshaft should be taken to an authorised Honda dealer or similar repair agent for repair or replacement.
6   It should be noted that crankshaft repair work is of a highly specialised nature and requires the use of equipment and skills not likely to be available to the average private owner. Such work should not be attempted by anyone without this equipment and the skill to use it.
7   A caged needle roller bearing is employed as the small-end bearing. This bearing can be removed quite easily for examination. Check the rollers for any imperfection, renewing the bearing if less than perfect. The gudgeon pin and a small-end eye should be checked whether the rollers bear upon them, and remedial action taken where the surface(s) are marked. Assemble the small-end bearing and gudgeon pin in the connecting rod eye, and check for radial play. If any movement is found, renew the bearing, particularly if the engine has produced a characteristic rattle in the past, indicating that all might not be well with this bearing.

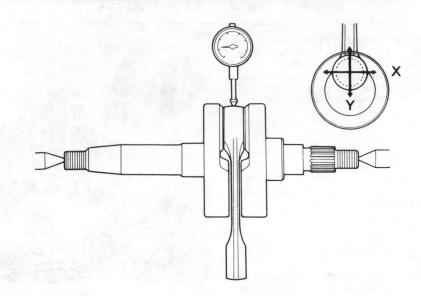

Fig. 1.3 Big-end bearing radial clearance measurement

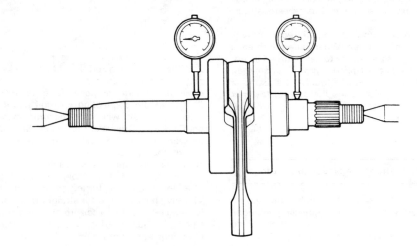

Fig. 1.4 Crankshaft run-out check

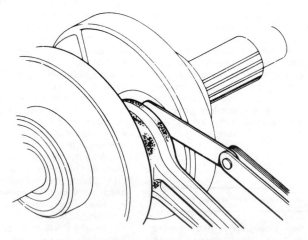

Fig. 1.5 Big-end bearing end float measurement

19 Examination and renovation: main bearings and seals

1 These components, particularly the left-hand main bearing, are of particular concern to owners of UK market machines. Premature failures of this bearing have occurred, and are cured, at the time of writing, by the use of a modified bearing which is incorporated as standard in US market machines. In view of this, particular care is needed in working on these parts.

2 To remove the seals a suitably-sized screwdriver should be used. Be careful when prising them out not to damage the crankcase edges. Once the seals have been disturbed, discard them. They are essential to the performance and reliability of the engine and should be renewed if there is any doubt at all about their condition. As a general rule, the seals should be renewed as a matter of course whenever the crankcases have been separated.

3 The bearings usually remain in place in the crankcase halves on removal of the crankshaft, in which case removal is as described in Section 15 of this Chapter. If, however, they stick on the crankshaft, a conventional knife-edged bearing puller is the safest and easiest method of removing them.

4 They should be washed in clean petrol and checked for play. Spinning the bearing will highlight any rough spots, producing obviously excessive amounts of noise once the lubricating film has been removed. Any signs of pitting or scoring of the bearing tracks or balls indicates the need for renewal. If there is any doubt as to their condition, replace them.

20 Examination and renovation: piston and piston rings

1 Before attending to these components it should be noted that there are no oversized parts available and that reboring, therefore, is not possible. It follows that greater care must be taken than is normal in assessing the condition of the piston and the piston rings if they are to be used to the full before renewal of both them and the cylinder barrel is necessary.

2 Examine the piston and rings. Any obvious wear or damage, such as heavy scoring of the piston skirt or broken piston rings will mean that the part concerned will have to be replaced anyway. No further time should be wasted on it. If discoloured areas are visible on the piston rings they should be discarded, as these areas indicate the blow-by of gas which means that the ring is not doing its job. If the piston is similarly discoloured it should be measured very carefully, if not by the owner then by an authorised Honda dealer or similar expert who will be able to judge whether the piston is re-usable.

3 Assuming that the piston and piston rings pass this preliminary inspection they must now be cleaned and examined very closely. Remove the piston rings by pushing the ends apart with the thumbs whilst gently easing the ring from its groove. Great care is necessary throughout this operation as the rings are brittle and will break easily if overstressed. If the rings are gummed in their grooves, three strips of tin can be used to ease them free as shown in the accompanying illustration. The expander ring in the lower ring groove is much less brittle, but is easy to damage as it is so thin. Pick it out with great care. Remove all traces of carbon from the piston and piston rings. Use a soft metal or hard wood scraper on the piston to ensure that it is not scratched. Finish off with metal polish to obtain a highly polished finish as carbon will adhere much less readily to a polished surface. Note that emery cloth should not be used as it leaves small particles behind, embedded in the soft alloy, which will cause rapidly accelerated wear.

4 If measuring equipment is not available, the piston must now be taken to an authorised Honda dealer or similar expert for accurate measurement. Piston wear usually occurs at the skirt or lower end of the piston and takes the form of vertical streaks or score marks on the thrust side. There may also be some variation in skirt thickness. This wear is measured at a point 10 mm ($\frac{3}{8}$ in) from the base of the skirt at right angles to

19.2a Renew main bearing oil seals as a matter of course ...

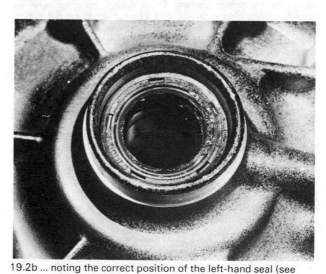

19.2b ... noting the correct position of the left-hand seal (see text)

19.4 Replace main bearings if there is any doubt at all about their condition

the gudgeon pin axis. This gives the overall diameter of the skirt. The measured figure must be compared with that given in the specifications Section of this Chapter. If the figure measured is less than the wear limit given, the piston must be renewed. If, however, the figure measured is higher than the wear limit, that aspect of piston condition is still good, and measurement of the remainder can proceed. Measure the internal diameter (ID) of the gudgeon pin bore, and the outside diameter (OD) of the gudgeon pin itself. Compare these figures with the wear limits set and renew the piston or gudgeon pin if necessary. If no measuring equipment is available, the gudgeon pin/piston clearances can be assumed to be good if the gudgeon pin is a tight push fit in the piston and if there is no discernible play when the gudgeon pin is in the installed position. Use a length of broken piston ring to clean the piston ring grooves without enlarging them. Once all traces of carbon are removed, carefully examine the grooves. Unfortunately no piston ring/ring groove clearance figure is given by the manufacturer and so assessment of this aspect of piston condition is largely a matter of experience. Carefully examine the piston ring upper and lower surfaces. If signs of wear are present, a new set of rings must be purchased and fitted. If up and down movement seems excessive, take the piston and rings to an authorised Honda dealer for an expert opinion. Great care is required here, as excessive side clearance will put a great strain on the piston rings, eventually causing them to break. This will almost certainly damage the cylinder bore to the extent that renewal is necessary. Check that the ring locating pegs in each ring groove are firmly fixed.

5   Once the piston has been measured and either found unworn or renewed, the piston rings must be examined. As already mentioned, the working surfaces must be clean and polished throughout, any discolouration showing that the rings have not been sealing against the bore surface. Also the upper and lower sides must be clean and unworn. If the rings pass this inspection insert them one at a time into the bore, using the piston crown to push them squarely down to a depth of approximately 1½ inches from the top of the bore. Using feeler gauges of appropriate thickness, measure the piston ring end gap. If the figure measured is more than that given in the specifications Section, the piston rings must be renewed. Note that if new piston rings are to be fitted, the cylinder bore must be very lightly honed to remove the glazed bore surface. Failure to do this will prevent correct and speedy bedding in of the rings. This operation should be carried out by a motorcycle dealer who has the necessary honing equipment. If this is not available, use fine wet and dry paper to achieve the same result. Remember that it must be used very lightly to produce a finely cross-hatched finish to the bore and that sandpaper or emery cloth should not be used for reasons already mentioned.

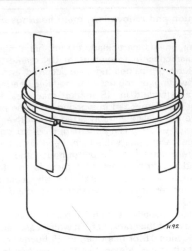

Fig. 1.6 Method of removing and replacing piston rings

21 Examination and renovation: cylinder barrel

1   Carefully remove all traces of old gasket cement, dirt, oil and grease from the barrel. Do not forget to clean the fins. Dry the bore with a clean rag and examine the surface for signs of wear or damage.

2   A small ridge may be in evidence near the top of the bore. This marks the extent of travel of the top piston ring and will probably be more pronounced at the thrust face than at any time. If this is barely perceptible, and the bore is otherwise undamaged, it will probably be safe to use it again. Take the barrel, piston and rings to an authorised Honda dealer for checking.

3   For those owners who have access to the correct equipment the condition of the bore may be checked by direct measurement. The bore should be measured at a point 15 mm (0.60 in) below the top edge of the cylinder both along the axis of the gudgeon pin and at right angles to it. Similar measurements should be made in the middle and at the bottom of the bore, avoiding the port areas. The minimum figure taken determines the amount of bore wear; this should not exceed the figure given in the specifications Section.

4   An alternative method can be used if, as is likely, an internal micrometer is not available. This requires a new piston, or one that is known to be within the specified wear limits. Place the bare piston in the bore in its correct position, ie with the 'In'

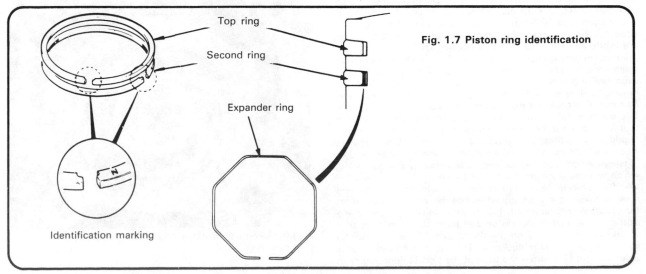

Top ring

Second ring

Expander ring

Identification marking

Fig. 1.7 Piston ring identification

mark facing the inlet port. Using feeler gauges, measure the amount of clearance between the piston and bore at the part which has the highest wear, ie at the front of the bore, 15 mm below its top edge. This clearance should not exceed the wear limit given for piston/cylinder clearance in the specifications Section. If it does, you will have a reasonably accurate indication of the fact that the bore is worn out. Due to the fact that reboring is not possible on this type of machine, a new barrel, complete with new piston, piston rings and circlips, must be purchased. To avoid unnecessary expense take the barrel and piston to an authorised Honda dealer for more accurate checking. He can only confirm your worst fears, and might even be able to point out that the barrel is still within tolerances when accurately measured, thus allowing further use of the barrel.

5 Clean all carbon deposits from the exhaust ports using a blunt ended scraper. It is important that all ports should have a clean, smooth appearance because this will have the dual benefit of improving gas flow and making it less easy for carbon to adhere in the future. Finish off with metal polish, to heighten the polishing effect.

6 Do not under any circumstances enlarge or alter the shape of the ports under the mistaken belief that improved performance will result. The size and position of the ports predetermines the characteristics of the engine and unwarranted tampering can produce adverse effects.

22 Examination and renovation: cylinder head

1 It is unlikely that the cylinder head will require any special attention apart from removing the carbon deposit from the combustion chamber. Finish off with metal polish; the polished surface will help improve gas flow and reduce the tendency of future carbon deposits to adhere so easily.

2 Check that the cooling fins are clean and unobstructed, so that they receive the full air flow.

3 Check the condition of the thread within the sparking plug hole. The thread is easily damaged if the sparking plug is overtightened. If necessary, a damaged thread can be reclaimed by fitting a Helicoil thread insert.

4 If there has been evidence of oil seepage from the cylinder head joint when the machine was in use, check whether the cylinder head is distorted by laying it out on a sheet of plate glass. Severe distortion will necessitate renewal of the cylinder head but if distortion is only slight, the head can be reclaimed by wrapping a sheet of emery paper (No 600) around the glass and using it as the surface on which to run down the head with a rotary motion, until it is once again flat. The usual cause of distortion is failure to tighten down the cylinder head nuts evenly, in a diagonal sequence.

23 Examination and renovation: gearbox components

1 Examine each of the gear pinions to ensure that there are no chipped or broken teeth and that the dogs on the end of the pinions are not rounded. Gear pinions with any of these defects must be renewed; there is no satisfactory method of reclaiming them.

2 The gearbox bearings must be free from play and show no signs of roughness when they are rotated. The bearings should first be washed in petrol and then dried. Check for pitting on the roller tracks.

3 Gearbox oil seals should be renewed irrespective of their condition. Remove them as described in Section 13 but only replace them when the crankcases have been reassembled.

4 Check the gear selector fork shaft for straightness by rolling it on a sheet of plate glass. If measuring equipment is available, compare the measured outside diameter of the shaft with that given in the specifications Section of this Chapter. If worn beyond the set limit, it must be replaced. If bent, it may be

possible to straighten the shaft, but this task must be carried out by an expert.

5 The selector forks should be examined closely to ensure that they are not bent or badly worn. If measuring equipment is available, check the dimensions against those given in the specifications Section. Selector fork wear is normally restricted to the fork claw ends and will be readily apparent, especially if the fork is bent, due to the blueing of the claw end which is caused by constant excessive pressure on the rotating gear pinions. If trouble has been experienced with gear selection or jumping out of gear, the selector forks should be very carefully examined.

6 If measuring equipment is available, carefully measure the outside diameter of the two bearing surfaces of the selector drum and compare the figures taken with those given in the specifications Section. Refer to the accompanying illustration to ensure that measurements are made at the correct place. The tracks in the selector drum should be checked for signs of excessive wear but it should be noted that this is extremely rare unless neglect has led to under lubrication of the gearbox. Also check the gearchange shaft, claw arm, and drum stopper arm springs for tension. Any weakness in these springs will contribute towards imprecise gear selection. Carefully examine the gearchange shaft assembly, drum stopper arm, camplate and the selector drum/camplate pins. Wear in any of these items will mean that a replacement part should be purchased before reassembly.

7 The gearbox shafts should be examined carefully. If the shafts are bent or their splines and circlip grooves are badly worn, then they must be replaced. Refer to the accompanying illustration which shows in detail at which points the outside diameters of the shafts are to be measured. These are the points at which the gear pinions rotate on the shaft instead of being fixed by splines. Compare the figures taken very carefully with those given in the specifications Section, and replace any shaft or corresponding gear pinion which is worn beyond the set limit. Excessive clearance between the shafts and their corresponding gear pinions will produce a disproportionate level of noise and will promote rapid and severe gearbox wear if not corrected during rebuilding. Refer to the accompanying line drawing and photographic sequence when fitting the gear pinions to the shafts and note that it is advisable to use new thrust washers and circlips throughout. The new parts should be obtained with the new seals and gaskets required for reassembly.

8 Check the condition of the kickstart components. If slipping has been encountered a worn ratchet and pawl will invariably be traced as the cause. Any other damage or wear to the components will be self-evident. If either the ratchet or pawl is found to be faulty, both components must be replaced as a pair. Examine the kickstart return spring which should be renewed if there is any doubt about its condition.

23.2a Examine all gearbox bearings ...

23.2b ... as described in the text ...

23.2c ... and renew them if necessary

23.3a Renew all gearbox oil seals ...

23.3b ... as a matter of course

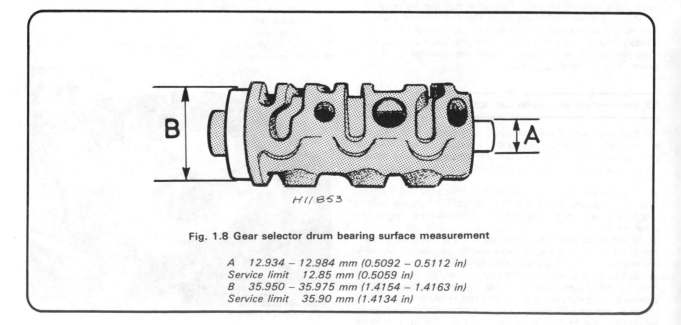

H11853

Fig. 1.8 Gear selector drum bearing surface measurement

A   12.934 – 12.984 mm (0.5092 – 0.5112 in)
Service limit   12.85 mm (0.5059 in)
B   35.950 – 35.975 mm (1.4154 – 1.4163 in)
Service limit   35.90 mm (1.4134 in)

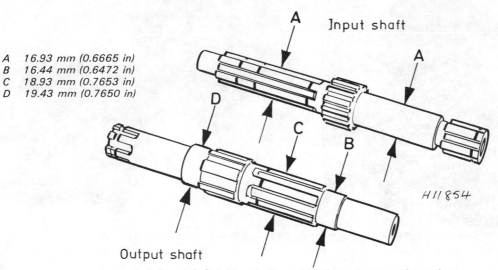

A 16.93 mm (0.6665 in)
B 16.44 mm (0.6472 in)
C 18.93 mm (0.7653 in)
D 19.43 mm (0.7650 in)

Input shaft

Output shaft

Fig. 1.9 Gearbox shaft outside diameter measuring points

24 Examination and renovation: clutch assembly

1   After an extended period of service the clutch friction plates will wear and promote clutch slip. Each plate should be measured for thickness and the measurement compared with the wear limit given in the specifications. When the wear limit is reached, the plates must be renewed, preferably as a complete set.

2   The two plain plates should not show any excess heating (blueing). Check the warpage of each plate using plate glass or a surface plate and a feeler gauge. The maximum allowed is given in the specifications Section.

3   The clutch springs will lose tension after a period of use, and should be renewed as a precaution if clutch slip has been evident and the friction plates are within limits. The free length of the clutch springs gives a good indication of condition, and this should be checked and compared with the figures given in the specifications Section.

4   Examine the clutch assembly for burrs or indentations on the edges of the protruding tongues of the friction plates and/or slots worn in the edges of the outer drum with which they engage. Similar wear can occur between the inner tongues of the plain clutch plates and the slots in the clutch inner drum. Wear of this nature will cause clutch drag and slow disengagement during gear changes, since the parts will become trapped and will not free fully when the clutch is withdrawn. A small amount of wear can be corrected by dressing with a fine file; more extensive wear will necessitate renewal of the worn parts.

5   The clutch release mechanism takes the form of a spindle running the right-hand outer casing, the shaped end of which bears on the clutch release pushrod when the handlebar lever is operated. The mechanism is of robust construction and requires no attention during normal maintenance or overhauls.

25 Engine and gearbox reassembly: general

1   Before reassembly of the engine/gear unit is commenced, the various component parts should be cleaned thoroughly and placed on a sheet of clean paper, close to the working area.

2   Make sure all traces of old gaskets have been removed and that the mating surfaces are clean and undamaged. One of the best ways to remove old gasket cement is to apply a rag soaked in methylated spirit. This acts as a solvent and will ensure that the cement is removed without resort to scraping and the consequent risk of damage.

3   Gather together all of the necessary tools and have avail-

able an oil can filled with clean engine oil. Make sure all new gaskets and oil seals are to hand, also all replacement parts required. Nothing is more frustrating than having to stop in the middle of a reassembly sequence because a vital gasket or replacement has been overlooked.

4   Make sure that the reassembly area is clean and that there is adequate working space. Refer to the torque and clearance settings wherever they are given. Many of the smaller bolts are easily sheared if over-tightened. Always use the correct size screwdriver bit for the crosshead screws and never an ordinary screwdriver or punch.

26 Engine and gearbox reassembly: rebuilding the gearbox clusters

1   If the gearbox components have been dismantled for examination and renewal, it is essential that they are rebuilt in the correct order to ensure proper operation of the gearbox. Use the accompanying photographic sequence and line drawing as aids to the identification of components and their correct relative positions.

2   Take the output shaft and slide the 3rd gear pinion on to its right-hand end with the selector dog holes facing outwards. Secure with a splined thrust washer and circlip. Slide on the 4th gear pinion with its selector fork groove towards the 3rd gear. Follow this with the 1st gear pinion which is fitted with the recessed side inwards. The last item to be fitted on the right-hand end is a thrust washer.

3   Turning to the left-hand end of the shaft, first slide on the 5th gear pinion with its selector fork groove inwards. This is followed by the 2nd gear pinion which is fitted with its blank non-drilled face outwards. This is followed by a thick spacer. Put the completed output shaft assembly to one side, ready for installation in the crankcases. Be careful not to lose the thrust washer and spacer on the ends.

4   Turning to the input shaft, first of all fit the thrust washer which butts up against the integral 1st gear. This is followed by the 4th gear pinion, which is fitted with the selector dogs facing the left-hand end of the shaft. Secure this by fitting first a splined thrust washer and then a circlip.

5   Next is 3rd gear, which is fitted with its selector fork groove inwards, adjoining the 4th gear. Secure this with a circlip. Slide another splined thrust washer along the shaft until it butts against the circlip. The 5th gear pinion is then fitted with its drilled face inwards to mate with the selector dogs on the 3rd gear pinion. Last is the 2nd gear pinion followed by a thick spacer. Put the completed input shaft assembly to one side.

26.2a Fit the output shaft 3rd gear pinion and secure it with a splined washer and circlip ...

26.2b ... followed by the 4th gear pinion ...

26.2c ... 1st gear pinion ...

26.2d ... and the thrust washer

26.3a Fit the 5th gear pinion over the left-hand end of the shaft

26.3b ... followed by the 2nd gear pinion

26.3c ... and the thick spacer

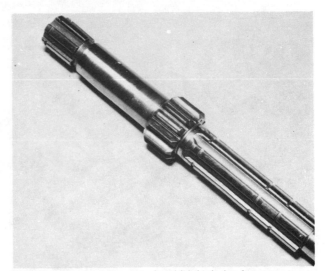

26.4a Take the bare input shaft, which includes 1st gear ...

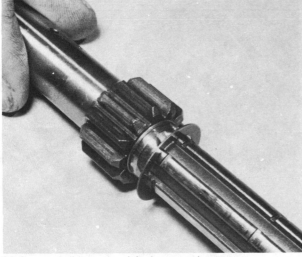

26.4b ... and slide on the plain thrust washer ...

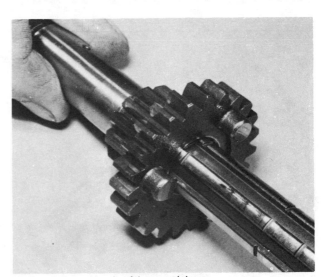

26.4c ... followed by the 4th gear pinion ...

26.4d ... which is retained by a splined thrust washer ...

26.4e ... and a circlip

26.5a Slide on the 3rd gear pinion ...

26.5b ... and secure with a circlip ...

26.5c ... followed by a splined thrust washer ...

26.5d ... and the 5th gear pinion

26.5e Lastly fit the 2nd gear pinion ...

26.5f ... and the thick spacer

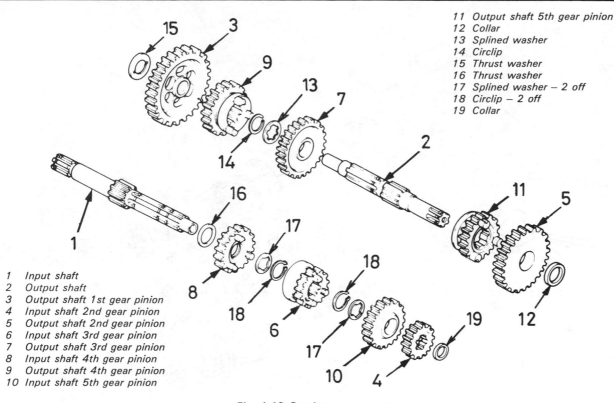

11 Output shaft 5th gear pinion
12 Collar
13 Splined washer
14 Circlip
15 Thrust washer
16 Thrust washer
17 Splined washer – 2 off
18 Circlip – 2 off
19 Collar

1   Input shaft
2   Output shaft
3   Output shaft 1st gear pinion
4   Input shaft 2nd gear pinion
5   Output shaft 2nd gear pinion
6   Input shaft 3rd gear pinion
7   Output shaft 3rd gear pinion
8   Input shaft 4th gear pinion
9   Output shaft 4th gear pinion
10 Input shaft 5th gear pinion

Fig. 1.10 Gearbox components

27 Engine and gearbox reassembly: preparing the crankcases and fitting the main bearings

1   The crankcases should be completely clean and dry at this stage. If any bearings are to be replaced, heat the crankcase as described in Section 15 of this Chapter. Tap the bearing gently and squarely into place using a hammer and a tubular drift or socket spanner. The drift must bear on the outer race of the bearing to ensure that it is fitted squarely in its machined recess without damage to bearing or crankcase.

2   The right-hand main bearing should be fitted in this way and lubricated, once the crankcase has cooled, with the recommended gearbox oil. The right-hand oil seal should then be tapped into place using a hammer and tubular drift or socket spanner which fits on its outside diameter. An application of grease around the outside of the seal will help this task.

3   The left-hand main bearing, if renewed, must be fitted on the crankshaft. Warm it slightly in an oven and tap it on to the crankshaft using a hammer and a tubular drift which bears on the inner race of the bearing. Be careful to support only the left-hand flywheel of the crankshaft in this operation. This will prevent the shock forces being passed through the crankpin, which might cause crankshaft misalignment.

4   Ensure that all bearings are in position in the crankcases and that the neutral indicator switch and the two locating dowel pins (if disturbed) are also in place.

28 Engine and gearbox reassembly: fitting the crankshaft

1   Using the manufacturer's tool Part No 07965-1660100 draw the crankshaft complete with left-hand main bearing into the crankcase half, until the bearing seats securely in place. It is recommended that the service tool is used if possible for this operation to ensure correct installation and the minimum strain

on the parts concerned.

2   If, as is likely, the service tool is not available the following method can be used, but great care must be taken. Insert the crankshaft into the right-hand main bearing ensuring that it is absolutely square to the crankcase and tap it into position, using a soft-faced mallet. Be very careful to hold the crankshaft exactly vertical to the crankcase while it is being replaced, and to use the bare minimum of force necessary to complete the task.

3   Lubricate the left-hand main bearing and big-end bearing with two stroke oil. Ensure that the crankshaft revolves easily and freely.

28.2 Ensure crankshaft is exactly vertical to crankcase on refitting

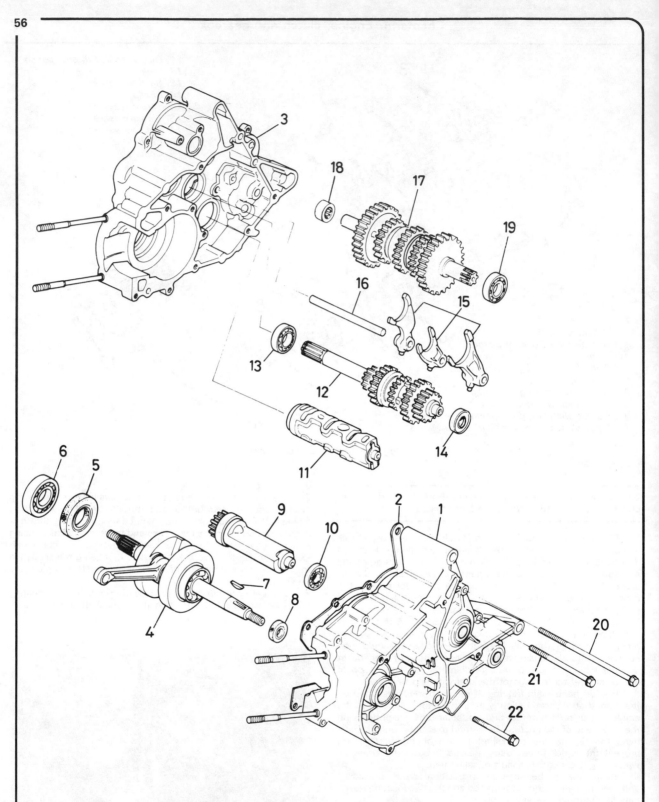

Fig. 1.11 Crankcase assembly

1	Left-hand crankcase half	7	Woodruff key	13	Right-hand bearing	18	Right-hand bearing
2	Gasket	8	Left-hand oil seal	14	Left-hand bearing	19	Left-hand bearing
3	Right-hand crankcase half	9	Balancer shaft	15	Selector forks	20	Bolt
4	Crankshaft	10	Bearing	16	Selector fork shaft	21	Bolt
5	Right-hand oil seal	11	Selector drum	17	Output shaft	22	Bolt
6	Right-hand bearing	12	Input shaft				

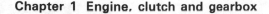

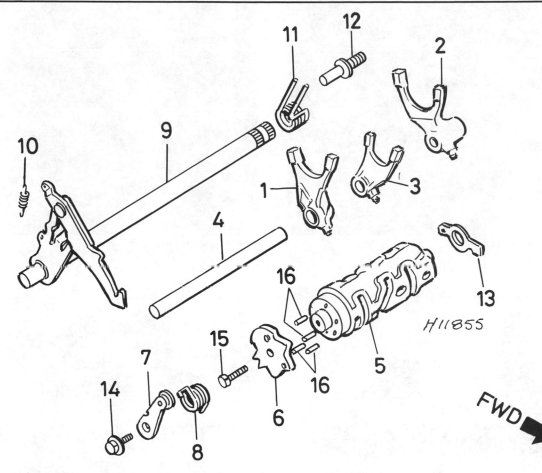

Fig. 1.12 Gearchange mechanism

1	Right-hand selector fork	5	Selector drum
2	Left-hand selector fork	6	Camplate
3	Centre selector fork	7	Detent stopper arm
4	Selector fork shaft	8	Return spring
9	Gearchange shaft	13	Neutral switch contact
10	Claw arm return spring	14	Bolt
11	Shaft return spring	15	Bolt
12	Locating peg	16	Pin – 4 off

29 Engine and gearbox reassembly: fitting the gearbox components

1   With the right-hand crankcase half lying on two wooden blocks to support it, lubricate lightly the gearbox bearings and bearing surfaces.

2   Take the two gearbox shaft assemblies and match them together with the gears in their correct relative positions. Carefully slide them into the crankcase; do not omit the thick spacers on the left-hand end of each shaft. It may be necessary to tap the left-hand end of the shafts while supporting the cluster with the other hand. Lightly lubricate the bearing surfaces of the shafts and their respective pinions and ensure that they revolve freely. Check that the sliding gears are free to move.

3   Lubricate both bearings of the balancer shaft and replace it. Check that the neutral switch blade is correctly fitted on the left-hand end of the selector drum and fit the drum into the right-hand crankcase. Line up the neutral switch blade with the neutral switch.

4   Replace the selector forks. Lightly oil each one before installation. The left-hand one operates on the output shaft 5th gear pinion, the centre one operates on the input shaft 3rd gear pinion and the right-hand one operates on the output shaft 4th gear pinion. Lightly oil the selector fork shaft and slide it through the forks into its housing in the right-hand crankcase.

5   Carefully check that the bearing surfaces of any moving parts are properly lubricated and ensure that all four shafts are quite free to rotate. Check that no parts have been left out.

29.2 Fit the two gearbox shafts as a complete unit

29.3a Fit the balancer shaft ...

29.3b ... and then the selector drum

29.4a Selector forks shown in correct relative positions

29.4b Selector forks shown in situ

29.4c Fit selector forks separately ...

29.4d ... aligning each one ...

29.4e ... with its track in the selector drum

29.4f Lightly oil selector fork shaft before fitting

30 Engine and gearbox reassembly: fitting the left-hand crankcase

1   Lightly smear a new crankcase centre gasket with grease and place it in position on the right-hand crankcase. Lubricate all bearings or bearing surfaces in the left-hand crankcase and lower it carefully into position. Using a soft-faced mallet gently tap it down over the shafts. Never use excessive force if it appears difficult to move. Instead check carefully that all the shafts are in correct alignment and then carry on. Be sure that the two locating dowels match their respective holes correctly.

2   Once the left-hand crankcase is firmly in position check that all the shafts are free to rotate easily. If not, the reason must be discovered before work goes any further. Occasionally a light tap on the end of a shaft is required to centralize it properly in its bearings, but this should not be necessary at this stage. Rotate the selector drum to check for correct gear selection.

3   Once it is established that the crankshaft and gearbox components are properly in place, refit the crankcase securing bolts in their correct positions and tighten them down to the specified torque setting working in a diagonal sequence from the centre outwards. Tighten the bolts in two stages to ensure an even application of pressure.

4   Lubricate the left-hand main bearing with two stroke oil and use a hammer and suitably-sized tubular drift to tap a new crankcase oil seal into position. It should be tapped in to the crankcase to a depth of 9 mm from the outside edge of the raised boss on the crankcase at this point. Grease applied to the inner and outer diameters of the seal will prevent damage to the sealing lips and ease the task of fitting it. The output shaft and gearchange shaft oil seals should now be fitted. Check that the left-hand bearing is lubricated with gearbox oil and tap the fresh oil seals into place as previously described. These seals fit flush with the edge of the crankcase.

5   Ensure that the gearbox drain plug is correctly fitted and fully tightened to the specified torque setting of 2.0 – 2.5 kgf m (14 – 18 lbf ft). Pack the crankcase mouth with clean rag to prevent the entry of dirt or debris during reassembly.

30.1a Always use a new gasket. Note position of locating dowels (arrowed)

30.1b Check all components are in place and oil bearing surfaces before refitting crankcase upper half

30.3 Note correct position of breather tube clamps

31.1a Align timing marks (arrowed) exactly

31 Engine and gearbox reassembly: fitting the flywheel generator

1　Fit the generator stator with the line scribed next to one of the mounting bolt holes lined up exactly with the index mark on the crankcase. Tighten the three mounting bolts. Using a suitably-sized pair of pliers, press down on the neutral indicator switch terminal and fit the switch wire through the hole thus exposed. Replace the switch cover and ensure that the wire is located in the retaining lugs in the crankcase.

2　Tap the Woodruff key into position in the crankshaft keyway and carefully replace the rotor. Replace the nut and lock washer.

3　Lock the crankshaft as described in Section 9 of this Chapter. Tighten the rotor nut to the specified torque setting of 5.0 – 6.0 kgf m (36 – 43 lbf ft).

32 Engine and gearbox reassembly: fitting the gear selector mechanism

1　Lightly oil the gear selector shaft and slide it through the crankcase halves. Take care not to damage the oil seal on the left-hand side as the gear lever splines pass through it.

2　Again support the engine/gearbox unit on two wooden blocks with the right-hand side uppermost. Replace the clean rag in the crankcase mouth to prevent the entry of dirt.

3　Slide the selector shaft fully into position ensuring that the selector claw arm fits next to the selector drum and that the selector shaft return spring is correctly engaged on its locating peg.

4　Fit the four camplate locating pins in their holes in the end of the selector drum. Engage the selector claw arm against the bottom pin. Fit the camplate, noting that the two raised pins fit into two holes in its underside. Use a thread locking cement on the securing bolt, which should then be tightened down.

5　Apply thread locking cement to the detent stopper arm bolt and fit the stopper arm assembly in position. Screw the bolt down lightly then ensure that the spring is located correctly, with its hooked end in the groove on the stopper arm and with its straight end butting against the crankcase bottom wall. Push the stopper arm against spring pressure and engage the roller in its notch in the camplate. Tighten down the securing bolt.

31.1b Connect neutral light switch wire

31.2a Replace Woodruff key

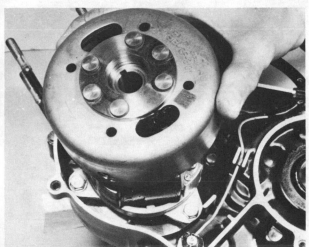

31.2b Ensure keyway in flywheel is correctly aligned with the key

32.4a Fit selector drum pins, noting that the two raised pins locate ...

32.4b ... the camplate. Use thread locking cement on the camplate retaining bolt (selector shaft removed for clarity)

32.5 Partially tighten stopper arm bolt with spring relaxed to avoid damage

33 Engine and gearbox reassembly: fitting the kickstart mechanism

1   Slide the kickstart pinion gear on to the kickstart spindle with the ratchet teeth facing the splined end of the spindle. Fit the smaller thrust washer behind it and locate the spindle in its machined boss in the crankcase.
2   Fit the thrust washer over the end of the output shaft, lightly lubricate the shaft, and place the idler gear in position. Apply thread locking cement to the two bolts securing the ratchet guide plate, place the guide plate in position and tighten down the two bolts. Ensure that the two gears revolve freely.
3   Slide the kickstart ratchet over the kickstart spindle so that the punch mark on the ratchet lines up with the spring hole in the spindle. Then fit the light coil spring and the nylon collar. Turn the spindle so that the ratchet arm locates against the ratchet guide plate.
4   Fit the kickstart return spring with its inner end located in the spring hole in the spindle, and with the notch in the nylon collar located around the spring inner end. Using a suitable pair of pliers, tension the kickstart return spring by moving the long hooked end clockwise until it can be engaged on the ratchet guide plate. Be careful to support the kickstart spindle assembly with the other hand during this operation. Slide the kickstart lever lightly into place and move it gently to check that all is free to move and working properly. Remove the kickstart lever and fit the large thrust washer over the end of the spindle.

34 Engine and gearbox reassembly: fitting the primary drive gear and oil pump

1   Lock the crankshaft as described in Section 9 of this Chapter. Fit the primary drive pinion spacer on to the right-hand end of the crankshaft. This is followed by the pinion itself which has a punch mark on its outer face. Align this exactly with the punch mark in the crankshaft end. Fit the lock washer and nut. Tighten the nut down to the specified torque setting of 4.5 – 5.5 kgf m (33 – 40 lbf ft).
2   Lightly oil the balancer idler gear and slide it into position. Make sure that both sets of the inner pair of gears line up properly with the teeth on the balancer shaft gear.
3   Check the condition of the O-ring on the oil pump spigot and renew the O-ring if necessary. Lightly grease the O-ring to aid fitting and slide the oil pump into place. Tighten down the two mounting bolts. Fit the oil pump drive gear aligning the slot in the gear shaft with the blade in the pump. Locate the oil pump feed pipe in its bracket on the crankcase.

33.1 Fit kickstarter spindle and pinion. Note correct position of thrust washer

33.2a Fit thrust washer and kickstart idler gear over output shaft

33.2b Use thread locking cement on ratchet guide plate bolts

33.3a Fit kickstart ratchet over kickstart spindle so that ...

33.3b ... punch mark on ratchet (arrrowed) lines up with spring hole in spindle

33.3c Fit light coil spring and spring guide

33.4a Install kickstart return spring

33.4b Tension kickstart spring with great care

33.4c Do not omit the large thrust washer

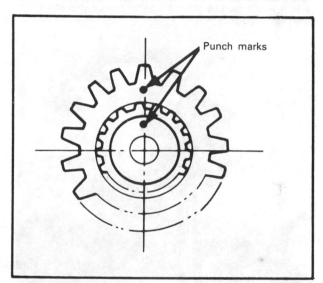
Punch marks

Fig. 1.13 Primary drive pinion alignment punch marks

34.1a Install primary drive pinion spacer ...

34.1b ... followed by the pinion, which has a punch mark ...

34.1c ... which must be aligned with the mark on the end of the crankshaft (arrowed)

34.1d Lock crankshaft to tighten primary drive gear nut

34.2 Ensure that anti-backlash gears line up correctly

34.3a Install oil pump first ...

34.3b ... followed by the oil pump drive gear

35 Engine and gearbox reassembly: fitting the clutch assembly

1   Carefully align the marks on the primary drive pinion and balancer shaft gear with their respective index marks on the crankcase (see illustration Fig. 1.14). Lightly oil the bush in the clutch outer drum. Slide the clutch outer drum into position on the input shaft, ensuring that the alignment of the marks is not disturbed and that both sets of the outer pair of gears on the balancer idler shaft line up correctly with the teeth on the clutch outer drum. Fit the splined thrust washer with its rounded surface outwards.
2   For ease of assembly, the clutch plates should be fitted on to the clutch centre. Start with a friction plate and continue assembly, fitting plain and friction plates alternately. Note that where new friction plates are fitted, these should be coated with gearbox oil before assembly. Fit the clutch pressure plate, passing the four projecting pillars through the corresponding holes in the clutch centre. Carefully align the projecting tongues on the friction plates. This is important to ensure that the

assembly will slide easily into the clutch outer drum.

3   Fit the whole pressure plate/clutch centre assembly into the clutch outer drum and secure it with a new circlip on the input shaft. Never re-use this circlip.

4   Place the four clutch springs in place over the corresponding pillars and then fit the lifter plate complete with its ball bearing, tightening the four bolts by hand alone at first. Complete the tightening with a spanner by about one turn at a time and in a diagonal sequence. This ensures the progressive and even application of spring pressure.

36 Engine and gearbox reassembly: fitting the right-hand outer cover

1   Check that the two dowel pins are in position in the crankcase and place a new gasket over them. Lightly grease the gasket to help it seat properly. Grease the kickstart spindle splines.

2   Carefully lower the right-hand outer cover into position. Take care not to damage the kickstart shaft oil seal as it passes over the shaft splines. Fit the ten hexagon-headed screws in their corresponding positions, not forgetting the clutch cable bracket. Tighten them down in a diagonal sequence starting from the centre. Check that the clutch operating arm is correctly positioned and moves freely.

3   Refill the gearbox with 1.0 litre (1.76/2.2 Imp/US pint) of gearbox oil. Remember to check the level after the engine has first been run. Check the tightness of the filler cap and drain plug.

37 Engine and gearbox reassembly: fitting the piston, cylinder barrel and cylinder head

1   Fit the piston rings to the piston. Note that the thin expander ring fits in the lower ring groove. The two compression rings are interchangeable but must be fitted the correct way up. It will be seen that there is a small mark, usually the letter N, stamped or etched on one surface of each ring in the vicinity of the ring gap. This mark must face towards the top of the piston. Check that the ring gaps are correctly aligned with

the locating peg in each groove on the piston.

2   Check that the clean rag is still in place in the crankcase mouth. Oil the small-end bearing and place it in the connecting rod. Position the piston over the connecting rod with the 'IN' marking facing the inlet side ie, to the rear of the engine. The gudgeon pin should be lightly oiled and then pushed through the piston and small-end bearing. If it is difficult to do this, warm the piston with a rag soaked in hot water. Secure the gudgeon pin with two new circlips and ensure that these are seated firmly in their grooves.

3   Lightly grease a new cylinder base gasket and slide it over the cylinder stuck into position on the crankcase mouth. It should be noted that, due to the shape of the ports and the offset position of the studs, there is only one way this gasket will fit properly. Check this carefully before damage is done to the gasket. Position the piston at TDC.

4   Lubricate the cylinder bore with two stroke oil and lower it over the studs down on to the piston. Due to the low weight and small size of the parts concerned this operation should be easily completed by one person. Compress the top piston ring by hand and gently push the barrel down over it. The lead in or chamfer at the bottom of the bore makes this a relatively easy task. If there is any sign of sticking check that the piston is entering squarely into the bore and that the ring gaps are correctly located at their respective pegs. Repeat the procedure with the second ring. When both rings have engaged the bore remove the rag from the crankcase mouth. Push the barrel gently down to rest firmly on the crankcase.

5   Lightly grease a new head gasket and place it in position on the cylinder, noting that the arrow marking must be upwards and facing the front (exhaust port). Lower the cylinder head into place and hand tighten the four nuts which secure it.

6   Using a torque wrench, tighten the four nuts in two stages to 1.8 – 2.2 kgf m (13 – 16 lbf ft). Tighten the nuts in a diagonal sequence to ensure a progressive and even application of pressure.

7   Lightly grease the new reed valve gasket and fit the reed valve assembly to the cylinder, followed by the inlet stub gasket and inlet stub. Tighten down the four securing bolts progressively and evenly. Do not overtighten.

8   Fit the sparking plug and tighten down to prevent the entry of dirt. Temporarily unplug the end of the oil feed pipe and push it over the union on the inlet stub.

35.1a Balancer timing marks aligned at crankshaft (arrowed)

35.1b Balancer timing marks aligned at balancer shaft (arrowed)

35.1c Ensure all gears mesh on installing clutch outer drum

35.1d Splined thrust washer fits with rounded surface outwards

35.2a Rebuild clutch plates on clutch centre, starting with a friction plate ...

35.2b ... then a plain plate

35.2c Finally fit the pressure plate

35.3a Fit the pressure plate/clutch centre assembly ...

35.3b ... and secure with a circlip

35.4 Replace the clutch springs and clutch lifter plate

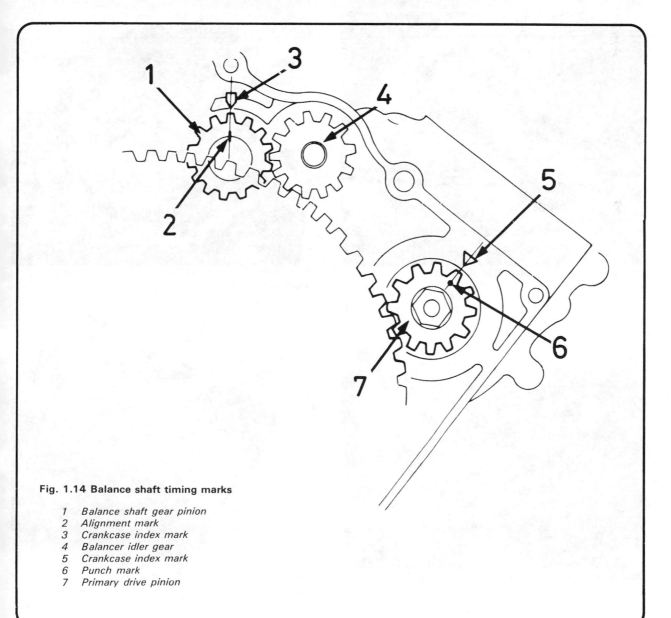

Fig. 1.14 Balance shaft timing marks

1 Balance shaft gear pinion
2 Alignment mark
3 Crankcase index mark
4 Balancer idler gear
5 Crankcase index mark
6 Punch mark
7 Primary drive pinion

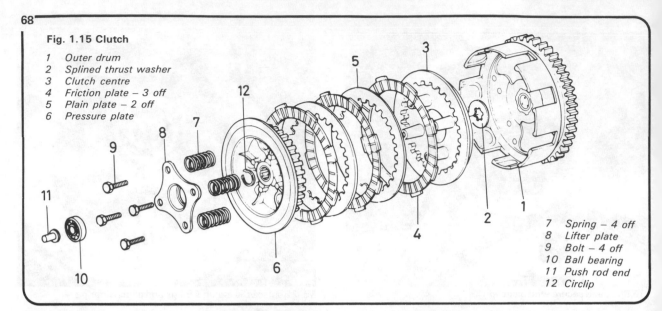

Fig. 1.15 Clutch

1 Outer drum
2 Splined thrust washer
3 Clutch centre
4 Friction plate – 3 off
5 Plain plate – 2 off
6 Pressure plate

7 Spring – 4 off
8 Lifter plate
9 Bolt – 4 off
10 Ball bearing
11 Push rod end
12 Circlip

36.1a Check that the clutch pushrod is in place

36.1b Refitting right-hand outer cover; note position of two dowels (arrowed)

36.2 Note correct position of clutch cable bracket

37.1 Piston ring gaps must be aligned with the locating pegs

37.2a Oil the small-end bearing before fitting. Note clean rag in crankcase mouth

37.2b Marking on the piston crown should face to the rear (inlet side) of the engine

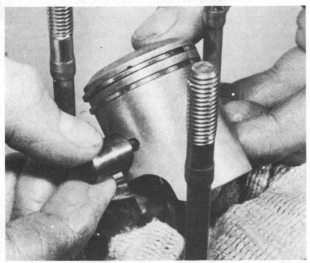

37.2c Place the piston in position and push the gudgeon pin through

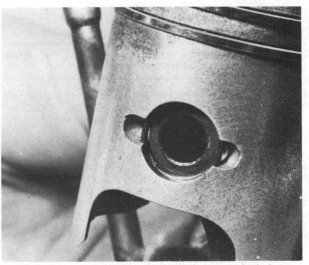

37.2d Ensure that the circlips are securely located in their grooves

37.4 Carefully replace the cylinder barrel

37.5a Note correct position of head gasket

37.5b Replace cylinder head

38 Engine and gearbox reassembly: installing the rebuilt unit in the frame – final adjustment

1   Lift the engine/gearbox unit up until the top mounting on the cylinder head lines up with the bracket on the frame. Push the top mounting bolt through from left to right. Replace the nut but only tighten it by hand for the moment.

2   Swing the bottom half of the engine gently backwards into position, guiding the carburettor on to the inlet stub studs with the other hand. Ensure that the carburettor drain tube and battery breather pipe are located in the tube clamps on the crankcase rear and are not trapped against the frame. Slide the middle and bottom mounting bolts through from left to right and hand tighten their respective nuts.

3   Check finally that the engine is seated correctly in its mountings and that nothing is trapped. Using a torque wrench, tighten the three mounting bolts to the specified torque setting. Carefully replace and tighten down the two nuts securing the carburettor to the intake manifold.

4   Lightly grease a fresh exhaust gasket and place it in the exhaust port. Manoeuvre the exhaust pipe into position and hand tighten the two front flange securing nuts. Hand tighten the single mounting bolt on the frame (MB50) or the earth strap securing bolt under the seat (MT50). Once the pipe is properly mounted, fully tighten the two nuts and single bolt. Replace the seat and tighten its mounting bolts (MT50). If the rear brake adjustment was slackened off (MB50) during engine removal, do not forget to adjust it correctly before running the machine.

5   Replace the tachometer cable (MB50). Fit the clutch cable end into the clutch operating arm and adjust the cable to give 10 – 20 mm ($\frac{3}{8}$ to $\frac{3}{4}$ in) free play at the clutch lever tip. Replace the kickstart lever using the marks made on stripping the machine as an aid to correct positioning.

6   Moving round to the left-hand side of the machine, unplug the oil tank/pump feed pipe and push it over the stub on the oil pump. Secure with the spring clip. Fit the oil pump cable end into the pump operating arm and adjust the cable. This is described in Section 20 of Chapter 2.

7   Replace the footrest bar and tighten the two mounting bolts (MB50). Engage the gearbox sprocket on the chain and slide it over the end of the output shaft. Slide the sprocket retaining plate down to the sprocket and turn it until the holes for the retaining bolts are lined up. Fit and tighten down the two bolts, using the back brake to lock the rear wheel if necessary. Adjust the drive chain and back brake if required.

8   Check that the neutral indicator switch cover is in place and fit the left-hand outer cover. Tighten the four securing bolts. Replace the gearchange lever using the marks made on stripping the machine as an aid to correct positioning. Replace the sparking plug cap.

9   Plug the generator lead wires back into the connector box on the main loom and secure the lead using cable ties around the frame lower tube. Replace the battery and connect its lead wires. Replace the left-hand side panel.

10   If this has not already been done, fill the gearbox with the recommended amount of oil.

39 Starting and running the rebuilt engine

1   Turn on the fuel tap, close the choke, and attempt to start the engine by means of the kickstart pedal. Do not be disillusioned if there is no sign of life initially. A certain amount of perseverance may prove necessary to coax the engine into activity even if new parts have not been fitted. Should the engine persist in not starting, check that the sparking plug has not become fouled by the oil used during re-assembly. Failing this go through the fault finding charts and work out what the problem is methodically.

2   When the engine does start, keep it running as slowly as possible to allow the oil to circulate. Open the choke as soon as the engine will run without it. During the initial running, a certain amount of smoke may be in evidence due to the oil used in the reassembly sequence being burnt away. The resulting smoke should gradually subside.

3   Once the engine has been warmed up enough to tick over smoothly, stop it and check the lubrication system. First check the gearbox oil level as described in Chapter 2, Section 22, but remember that some time must be allowed for the level to settle as the oil is being distributed around the freshly rebuilt engine and transmission components. The next operation is to bleed any air from the oil pump and lines. It is absolutely essential that this is done before the engine is run further. The full procedure is covered in Chapter 2, Section 21.

4   The final task is to check the ignition timing to ensure that the alternator stator (if disturbed) was refitted in the correct place. This is covered in Chapter 3, Section 8.

5   Check the engine for blowing gaskets and oil leaks. Before using the machine on the road, check that all the gears select properly, and that the controls function correctly.

38.4 Always use a new exhaust gasket

38.5 Replace clutch cable and check adjustment

38.7a Replace engine sprocket (chain omitted for clarity) ...

38.7b ... slide lock washer over splines and turn to align bolt holes

38.7c Securely tighten the two retaining bolts

38.8 Check that the neutral light switch cover is in place before replacing the left-hand outer cover

40 Taking the rebuilt machine on the road

1   Any rebuilt machine will need time to settle down, even if parts have been replaced in their original order. For this reason it is highly advisable to treat the machine gently for the first few miles to ensure oil has circulated throughout the lubrication system and that new parts fitted have begun to bed down.

2   Even greater care is necessary if the engine has been rebored or if the new crankshaft has been fitted. In the case of a rebore, the engine will have to be run again, as if the machine were new. This means greater use of the gearbox and a restraining hand on the throttle until at least 500 miles have been covered. There is no point in keeping to any set speed limit; the main requirement is to keep a light loading on the engine and to gradually work up performance until the 500 mile mark is reached. These recommendations can be lessened to an extent when only a new crankshaft is fitted. Experience is the best guide since it is easy to tell when an engine is running freely.

3   Remember that a good seal between the piston and the cylinder barrel is essential for the correct functioning of the engine. A rebored two-stroke engine will require more careful

running-in, over a long period, than its four-stroke counterpart. There is a far greater risk of engine seizure during the first hundred miles if the engine is permitted to work hard.

4   If at any time a lubrication failure is suspected, stop the engine immediately and investigate the cause. If an engine is run without oil, even for a short period, irreparable engine damage is inevitable.

5   Do not on any account add oil to the petrol under the mistaken belief that a little extra oil will improve the engine lubrication. Apart from creating excess smoke, the addition of oil will make the mixture much weaker, with the consequent risk of overheating and engine seizure. The oil pump alone should provide full engine lubrication.

6   Do not tamper with the exhaust system or run the engine without the baffle fitted to the silencer. Unwarranted changes in the exhaust system will have a marked effect on engine performance, invariably for the worse. The same advice applies to dispensing with the air cleaner or the air cleaner element.

7   When the initial run has been completed allow the engine unit to cool and check all the fittings and fasteners for security. Re-adjust any controls which may have settled down during initial use.

Chapter 2 Fuel system and lubrication

For modifications and information relating to later models, see Chapter 7

Contents

Specifications

Fuel tank capacity

	MB	MT
Overall	9.0 lit (2.0 Imp gal, 2.4 US gal)	6.8 lit (1.5 Imp gal)
Reserve	2.0 lit (0.4 Imp gal, 0.5 US gal)	1.0 lit (0.21 Imp gal)

Fuel grade

Manufacturer's recommendation ...... Unleaded or leaded (minimum 91 octane RON)

Carburettor

	MB (US)	MB (UK)	MT
Make	Keihin	Keihin	Keihin
ID No	PF15A-C	PF05C-A	PF05B-A
Venturi diameter	16 mm (0.63 in)	13 mm (0.51 in)	13 mm (0.51 in)
Main jet	105	65	65
Needle	37B	N/A	N/A
Needle position	2nd groove	2nd groove	2nd groove
Float level	13.5 mm (0.53 in)	13.5 mm (0.53 in)	13.5 mm (0.53 in)
Pilot air screw	1⅜ turns	1¾ turns	2 turns
Idle speed	1400 rpm	1300 rpm	1300 rpm

Engine lubrication

Type	Honda 2-stroke oil injection system
Filter	Gauze strainer
Oil tank capacity:	
MB	1.1 lit (2.0 Imp pint, 2.4 US pint)
MT	1.5 lit (2.6 Imp pint)

Gearbox lubrication

Capacity:	
At oil change	0.9 lit (1.58 Imp pint, 1.9 US pint)
At engine rebuild	1.0 lit (1.76 Imp pint, 2.2 US pint)

1 General description

The fuel system comprises a petrol tank from which fuel is fed via a tap and pipe, and a throttle valve type Keihin carburettor. A plunger type choke is fitted to aid cold starting. To prevent the ingress of abrasive dust and other foreign matter an air filter is fitted. The air filter box is connected to the carburettor and houses a foam filter element.

Engine lubrication is provided by an oil pump driven from the engine. The pump is supplied with oil by a tank forward of the petrol tank on the MB models or beneath the seat on the MT model. The pump delivers oil to the inlet stub where the oil is injected into the flow of incoming fuel/air mixture. The oil is carried into the crankcase where it lubricates the left-hand main bearing, connecting rod bearings and the cylinder bore. The clutch, transmission components, and kickstart mechanism are contained in a separate housing which forms part of the main crankcase and provides a suitable reservoir for the separate lubrication of these components. Oil from this reservoir lubricates the right-hand main bearing.

2 Petrol tank: removal and replacement

MB model
1 Unscrew the retaining knob on the petrol tank front cover and lift the cover away from its rear mounting grommets. Using a suitable pair of pliers, compress the ears of the wire petrol pipe retaining clip and slide it down the pipe until it is clear of the petrol tap spigot. Turn the petrol tap to the 'Off' position and disconnect the petrol pipe by pulling it off the petrol tap spigot. Remove the seat which is secured by two nuts underneath the rear mudguard to the rear of the frame and by a hook at its front which engages a bracket on the fuel tank. Disconnect the tail lamp and rear indicator lamp wires at their snap connectors immediately in front of the tail lamp assembly and pull the wires leading to the main loom down through the retaining rubber grommet and clear of the clamps underneath the petrol tank.
2 Slacken and remove the four petrol tank fastening bolts. Two are at the extreme rear of the tank, and two at the front, on each side of the oil tank. Carefully lift the tank clear.
3 Refitting is a straightforward reversal of the removal

process. Check for fuel leaks after the petrol pipe has been refitted and its clip secured.

MT model
4 Using a suitable pair of pliers, compress the ears of the wire petrol pipe retaining clip and slide the clip down until it is clear of the petrol tap spigot. Turn the petrol tap to the 'Off' position and disconnect the petrol pipe by pulling it off the petrol tap spigot. The two side panels are then removed by pulling them free of their bottom mounting grommets and then disengaging the two upper locating tabs on each panel. Remove the seat which is secured by two bolts at the rear and by a hook at its front which engages underneath the petrol tank.
5 Slacken and remove the two bolts at the rear of the tank. Lift the tank at the rear and disengage it from its front mounting. Lift the tank clear.
6 Refitting is a straightforward reversal of the removal sequence. Check for fuel leaks after the petrol pipe has been refitted and its clip secured.

3 Petrol tank: examination and renovation

1 Inspect the tank for signs of petrol leakage or rusting, both of which will be immediately apparent, and will require immediate attention.
2 If traces of dirt have been appearing continually in the fuel lines and carburettor, the tank must be very carefully washed out, rinsed in clean petrol and checked for serious internal rusting.
3 If the tank is to be stored it should be placed in a safe place away from any area where fire is a hazard or where the paint finish may become damaged.
4 Any signs of fuel leakage should be dealt with promptly in view of the risk of fire or explosion should fuel drip onto the hot exhaust system. It is not recommended that the tank is repaired using welding or brazing techniques, because even a small amount of residual fuel vapour can result in a dangerous explosion. A more satisfactory alternative is to use one of the resin-based tank sealing compounds. These are designed to line the tank with a tough fuel-proof skin, sealing small holes or splits in the process. The suppliers of these products advertise regularly in the motorcycle press.

2.1a Slacken and remove the two seat mounting bolts — one is shown arrowed

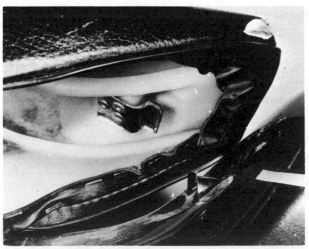

2.1b Unhook the seat from its front mounting on the fuel tank

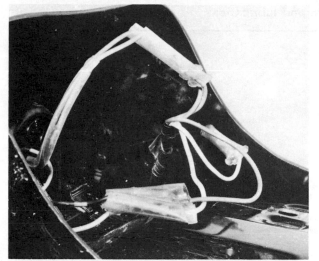

2.1c Disconnect the tail lamp and rear indicator lamp wires

2.2a The fuel tank rear mounting bolts must be removed ...

2.2b ... and then the two front mounting bolts (flasher relay removed for clarity)

2.4 The seat mounting bolts must be removed – MT50 ...

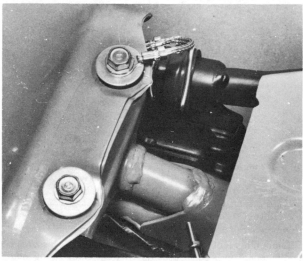

2.5a ... to expose the fuel tank rear mounting bolts

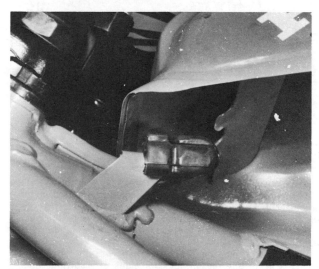

2.5b Unhook the fuel tank from its front mounting

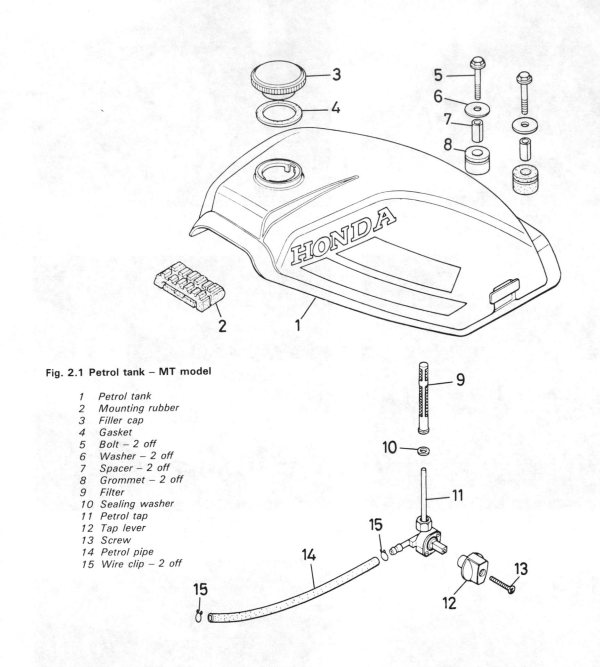

Fig. 2.1 Petrol tank – MT model

 1   *Petrol tank*
 2   *Mounting rubber*
 3   *Filler cap*
 4   *Gasket*
 5   *Bolt – 2 off*
 6   *Washer – 2 off*
 7   *Spacer – 2 off*
 8   *Grommet – 2 off*
 9   *Filter*
10   *Sealing washer*
11   *Petrol tap*
12   *Tap lever*
13   *Screw*
14   *Petrol pipe*
15   *Wire clip – 2 off*

4   Petrol feed pipe: examination

1   The petrol feed pipe is made from thin walled synthetic rubber and is of the push-on type. It is necessary to replace the pipe only if it becomes hard or splits. It is unlikely that the retaining clips will need replacing due to fatigue as the main seal between the pipe and union is effected by an interference fit.

2   If the petrol pipe has been replaced with the transparent plastic type for any reason, look for signs of yellowing which indicate that the pipe is becoming brittle due to the plasticiser being leached out by the petrol. It is a sound precaution to renew a pipe when this occurs, as any subsequent breakage whilst in use will be almost impossible to repair. **Note**: On no account should natural rubber tubing be used to carry petrol, even as a temporary measure. The petrol will dissolve the inner wall, causing blockages in the carburettor jets which will prove very difficult to remove.

5   Petrol tap: removal, examination and replacement

1   Before the petrol tap can be removed, it is first necessary to drain the tank. This is easily accomplished by removing the feed pipe from the carburettor foat chamber and allowing the contents of the tank to drain into a clean receptacle, with the tap turned to the 'Reserve' position. Alternatively, the tank can

be removed and placed on one side, so that the fuel level is below the tap outlet. Take care not to damage the paintwork.

2   The tap unit is retained by a gland nut to the threaded stub on the underside of the tank. It can be removed after the fuel pipe has been pulled off the tap.

3   If the tap lever leaks, it will be necessary to renew the tap as a complete unit. It is not possible to dismantle the tap for repair.

4   When reassembling the tap, reverse the procedure for dismantling.

5   Check that the feed pipe from the tap to the carburettor is in good condition and that the push-on joints are a good fit, irrespective of the retaining wire clips. If particles of rubber are found in the filter, replace the pipe, since this is an indication that the internal bore is breaking up.

6   If there have been indications of water contamination in the fuel, the removal of the tap presents a good opportunity to drain and flush the tank completely. Many irritating fuel system faults can be traced to water in the petrol. This often appears as a result of condensation inside the petrol tank. The resulting blobs of water are easily drawn into the carburettor, where they can cause intermittent blockages in the jets and drillings. Any accumulations of water should therefore be flushed from the tank before the tap is refitted. The tubular filter gauze should be removed and cleaned carefully prior to reassembly.

6   Carburettor: removal

1   Turn the petrol tap to the 'Off' position and disconnect the petrol pipe. Disconnect the float bowl drain tube and air vent tube. Slacken and remove the two nuts securing the carburettor to the inlet stub. Slacken the clamp securing the air filter hose to the carburettor.

2   Disconnect the clutch cable and tachometer cable (MB50). Push the carburettor back and clear of its mounting studs. Carefully remove it from the engine. Unscrew the black plastic carburettor top and tape it to the frame by the throttle cable to prevent damage to the throttle valve and needle.

3   Be careful not to allow any dirt into the inlet port while the carburettor is being examined. If the removal procedure as described proves difficult, it is possible to remove the carburettor still mounted on the inlet stub. To do this, slacken and remove the four stub retaining bolts and lift the two components up. This will give enough room to separate the two and remove them from the engine.

7   Carburettor: dismantling and reassembly

1   First drain the remaining petrol from the float chamber by unscrewing the drain plug at its base. Slacken and remove the two retaining screws and remove the float bowl. It may need a very gentle tap at the front area to free it.

2   Slide out the float pivot pin and withdraw the float and float needle. The main jet is located at the centre of the carburettor and is identified by its slotted cheese head. It can be unscrewed on its own or together with the hexagon headed needle jet holder to which it is attached. Both must be removed before the needle jet can be reached. Press the needle jet out from above.

3   The projection adjacent to the main jet is the pilot (slow) jet. This is pressed into the carburettor body and cannot be removed. Carefully screw the pilot air screw inwards counting the number of turns necessary to seat it lightly in the body. Note the exact number of turns and then remove the screw. Remove the choke (starter) assembly. This is only available as one piece and there is therefore no point in stripping it further.

4   Turning back to the throttle valve assembly, disconnect the end of the cable from the valve by sliding it down the slot cut in the side of the valve. Remove the throttle valve, throttle return spring and mixing chamber cap. If the cable is to be renewed, remove the rubber sealing cap as well.

5   With the throttle valve components set out on a clean sheet of paper on the working surface, remove the needle retaining clip from inside the throttle cable and slide out the needle. Do not disturb the small needle clip unless absolutely necessary as it is easily lost or damaged.

6   Reassembly is a straightforward reversal of the dismantling procedure. Each part must be scrupulously clean and new O-rings must be used as required. Screw the pilot air screw gently in until it just seats and unscrew it the original number of turns. This will serve as a basis for tuning the cleaned and rebuilt carburettor. While working on the carburettor, care must be taken to avoid overtightening any of the components. All of these are delicate and easily damaged.

7   When the carburettor is fitted once more in the engine, the tachometer cable must be replaced (MB50), the clutch cable must be replaced and adjusted, and the oil pump cable adjustment must be checked and altered if necessary whenever the throttle cable adjustment is altered. Do not forget to connect the float bowl drain tube and air vent tube.

8   The tuning procedure for re-setting a carburettor is given in Section 10 of this Chapter.

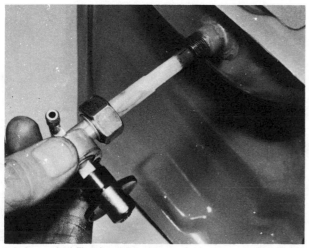

5.2 Gauze fuel filter is attached to the fuel tap

6.2 Unscrew carburettor top to release throttle valve assembly

7.1 Remove float bowl which is secured by two screws

7.2a Slide out float pivot pin to remove float assembly

7.2b Main jet and needle jet holder can be removed together

7.2c Needle jet must be pushed out of its seating

7.3 The choke plunger assembly must be renewed if badly worn or damaged

7.4 Remove throttle valve assembly from the cable

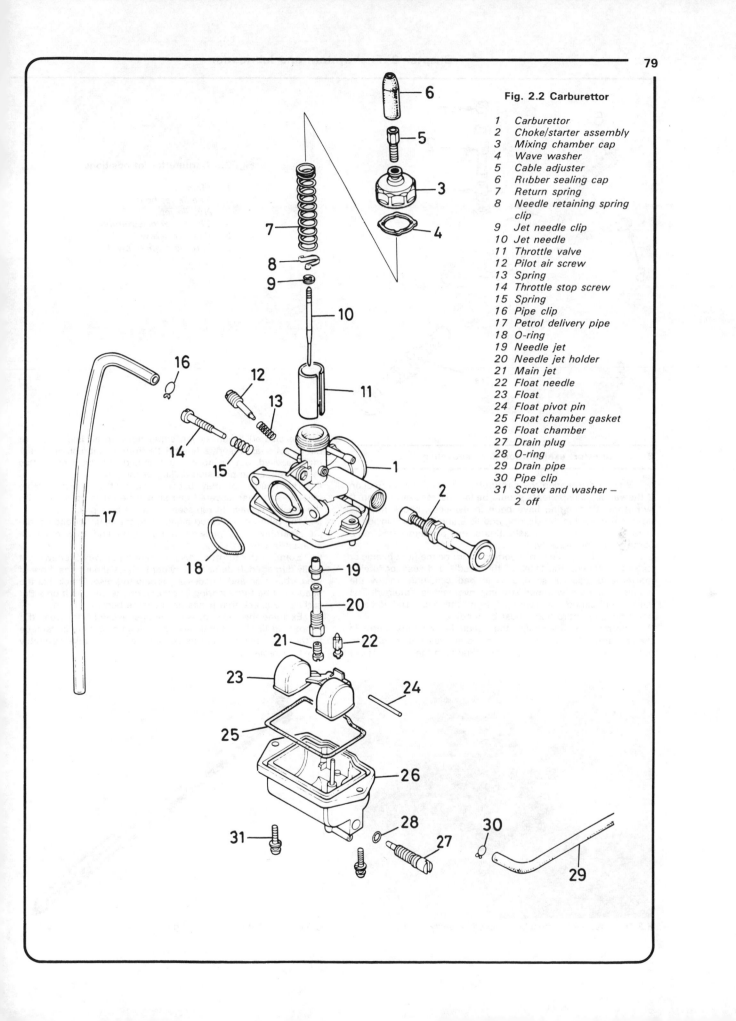

Fig. 2.2 Carburettor

1 Carburettor
2 Choke/starter assembly
3 Mixing chamber cap
4 Wave washer
5 Cable adjuster
6 Rubber sealing cap
7 Return spring
8 Needle retaining spring clip
9 Jet needle clip
10 Jet needle
11 Throttle valve
12 Pilot air screw
13 Spring
14 Throttle stop screw
15 Spring
16 Pipe clip
17 Petrol delivery pipe
18 O-ring
19 Needle jet
20 Needle jet holder
21 Main jet
22 Float needle
23 Float
24 Float pivot pin
25 Float chamber gasket
26 Float chamber
27 Drain plug
28 O-ring
29 Drain pipe
30 Pipe clip
31 Screw and washer – 2 off

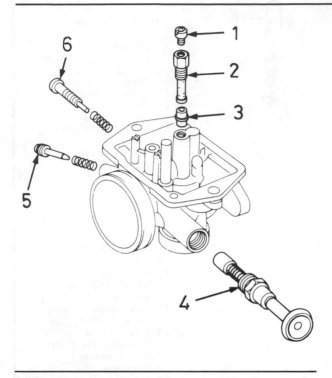

Fig. 2.3 Carburettor jet positions

1   *Main jet*
2   *Needle jet holder*
3   *Needle jet*
4   *Choke/starter assembly*
5   *Pilot air screw*
6   *Throttle stop screw*

8   Carburettor: examination and renovation

1   Having dismantled the carburettor as described in Section 7 the various components should be laid out for examination. If symptoms of flooding have been in evidence, check that the float is not leaking, by shaking and listening for petrol inside. It is rare to find leaks in plastic floats, this problem being more common in the brass type.

2   A more likely cause of flooding is dirt on the float needle or its seat. Examine the faces of the needle and seat for foreign matter and also for scoring. If in bad condition, renew the needle and note whether any improvement is obtained. The valve seat cannot be removed from the body and if badly damaged the entire body must be renewed.

3   The main jet screws into the needle jet, which is central in the carburettor body. It is not prone to any real degree of wear, but can become blocked by contaminants in the petrol. These can be cleared by an air jet, either from an air line or a foot pump. As a last resort, a fine bristle from a nailbrush or similar may be used, but on no account should wire be used as this may damage the precision drilling of the jet.

4   The needle jet may become worn after a considerable mileage has been covered and should be renewed along with the needle. Always fit replacement parts as a pair.

5   The pilot jet is located adjacent to the main jet and needle jet assembly. It is pressed into position and thus must be cleaned in situ.

6   Examine the throttle valve for scoring or wear, renewing if badly damaged. If damage is evident, check the internal bore of the carburettor, and if necessary renew this also. Check that the needle is free from scoring or other damage and roll it on a flat surface to check that it has not become bent.

7   Examine the choke passage plunger assembly for wear. If it is not held firmly in the extended position or if there is damage to the brass plunger and its seating face, the whole assembly must be replaced.

8.2 The float needle must be checked carefully for dirt or wear

8.6a Examine the needle for signs of wear

8.6b Examine the throttle valve for wear or scoring. Note correct position of spring clip inside throttle valve

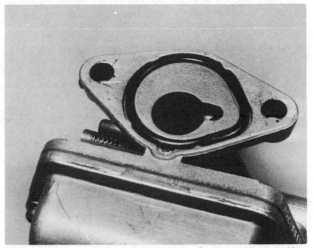

8.6c Carefully check the condition of the O-rings and renew if necessary

9 Carburettor: checking the float height

1   It is important that the level of fuel in the float bowl is maintained at the prescribed height to avoid adverse affects on the mixture strength. It is worth noting that unless the correct float height is set, it will be impossible to set the remaining adjustments to obtain efficient running.

2   The float height is measured between the gasket face of the carburettor body and the bottom of the float. This should be done with the carburettor turned 90° to its normal position so that the weight of the float is not applied to the valve needle. The latter should just bear upon the valve seat when the measurement is made.

3   The correct float height is given in the specifications Section of this Chapter. If the setting is faulty the float and float needle must be very carefully examined for wear and the relevant part or parts replaced. No adjustment is possible.

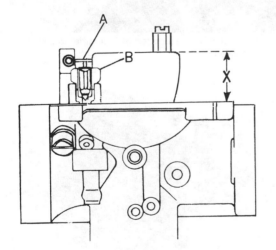

Fig. 2.4 Checking the float level

A   Float tongue
B   Float valve
X   13.5 mm (0.53 in)

10 Carburettor: adjustments and settings

1   The various jet sizes, throttle valve cutaway and needle position are predetermined by the manufacturer and should not require modification. Check with the Specifications list at the beginning of this Chapter if there is any doubt about the types fitted.

2   Before any attempt at adjustment is made, it is important to understand which parts of the instrument control which part of its operating range. A carburettor must be capable of delivering the correct fuel/air ratio for any given engine speed and load. To this end, the throttle valve, or slide as it is often known, controls the volume of air passing through the choke or bore of the instrument. The fuel, on the other hand, is regulated by the pilot and main jets, by the jet needle, and to some extent, by the amount of cutaway on the throttle valve.

3   As a rough guide, up to $\frac{1}{8}$ throttle is controlled by the pilot jet, $\frac{1}{8}$ to $\frac{1}{4}$ by the throttle valve cutaway, $\frac{1}{4}$ to $\frac{3}{4}$ throttle by the needle position and from $\frac{3}{4}$ to full throttle by the size of the main jet. These are only approximate divisions, which are by no means clear cut. There is a certain amount of overlap between the various stages.

4   If any particular carburation fault has been noted, it is a good idea to try to establish the most likely cause before dismantling or adjusting takes place. If, for example, the engine runs normally at road speeds, but refuses to tick over evenly, the fault probably lies with the pilot mixture system, and will most likely prove to be an obstructed jet. Whatever the problem may appear to be, it is worth checking that the jets are clear and that all the components are of the correct type. Having checked these points, refit the carburettor and check the settings as follows.

5   Start the engine, and allow it to attain its normal working temperature. This is best done by riding the machine for a few miles. Set the pilot air screw to the position given in the specifications Section. Set the throttle stop screw to give a normal idling speed. Try turning the pilot air screw inwards by about $\frac{1}{4}$ turn at a time, noting its effect on the idling speed, then repeat the process, this time turning the screw outwards. The pilot air screw should be set in the position which gives the fastest consistent tickover. If desired, the tickover speed may be reduced further by lowering the throttle stop screw, but care should be taken that this does not cause the engine to falter and stop after the throttle twistgrip has been opened and closed a few times.

6   Throttle cable adjustment should be checked at regular intervals and after any work is done to the carburettor, oil pump, or to the cable itself. Slacken the locknut of the adjuster on the

twistgrip, and screw the adjuster in to get maximum free play in the cable. Specified throttle cable free play is 2-6 mm ($\frac{1}{8}-\frac{1}{4}$ in) measured at the inner flange of the twistgrip rubber. To measure this, use a piece of chalk or some paint to mark both the twistgrip rubber, at its inner flange, and the twistgrip drum. These two marks will provide a convenient reference point for future adjustment. Carefully open the throttle by rotating the twistgrip rubber in the usual way until all the free play in the cable has been taken up. Measure the distance around the circumference of the drum between the static mark on the drum and the mark that has moved with the twistgrip rubber. If this distance is more or less that the specified amount, use the adjuster on the carburettor top to adjust the cable as necessary. The adjuster on the twistgrip can be used if necessary to complete the operation, but note that it is normally only used for minor adjustments. Tighten the adjuster locknuts, slide the rubber sealing sleeve back down over the adjuster on the carburettor top, and fully open and close the throttle several times. Check that the adjustment has remained the same.

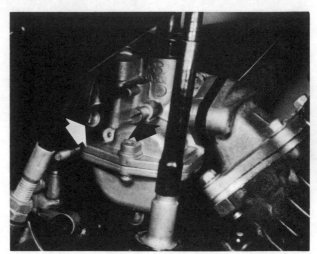

10.5 Position of throttle stop screw and pilor air screw

11 Reed valve assembly: removal, examination and refitting

1   Remove the oil feed pipe from the inlet stub union and plug it to prevent the loss of oil or the entry of air or dirt. Remove the carburettor as described in Section 6 of this Chapter. Slacken and remove the four inlet stub retaining bolts and displace the stub. It may need a gentle tap using a soft-faced mallet to free it. Remove the reed valve assembly.

2   The reed valve assembly provides a supplementary method of controlling the intake timing which functions in addition to the normal piston porting arrangement. The normal piston-ported intake tract is designed to open earlier and close later than is usual in engines of this type, thus producing much better high-speed performance at the expense of the low to medium speed ranges. The reed valve operates automatically as a result of the combination of atmospheric pressure and piston position, which in practice makes the engine more efficient at the low to medium speed ranges. Piston position and reed valve therefore combine to give the engine more power at all engine speeds than can be available to a conventionally-ported unit. However, for the UK market, the reed opening is restricted by two projecting ribs cast in the barrel and by the stopper plate on the valve itself, to assist in producing the reduced power output required by law. In this case the reed serves little purpose other than to reduce petrol consumption by eliminating the blow-back of air/fuel mixture through the carburettor which is an inevitable product of a piston-ported engine.

3   As far as maintenance is concerned, the reed valve requires none as it is extremely simple in construction and is automatic in operation. The assembly, however, is also extremely delicate and must be kept clean at all times and handled very carefully. Check the whole assembly for cracks or other signs of wear and make sure that the reed petals seat firmly on the rubber valve seat. Any sign of damage at all will mean the whole assembly will have to be renewed. No repairs are possible, and it is not advisable to attempt to strip the assembly further as no individual parts are available. Furthermore do not attempt to modify the assembly by bending the stopper plate or by any other means as this will at least adversely affect the engine performance. More probably the stress induced in the petals by making them operate beyond their designed limits will cause them to crack, allowing the pieces to drop straight into the engine with disastrous consequences.

4   Reassembly is a straightforward reversal of the removal procedure. Always fit new gaskets to prevent induction leaks and be careful not to overtighten the inlet stub bolts. When connecting the oil feed pipe, if the end of the pipe is full of oil when it is unplugged, bleeding the system will not be necessary. If however, no oil is visible, the feed pipe will have to be bled as described in Section 21 of this Chapter.

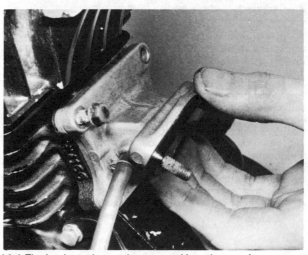

11.1 The intake stub must be removed in order to gain access to the reed valve

11.3 The reed valve assembly is extremely delicate and requires very careful handling. Do not dismantle it further

11.4 The reed valve must be installed with the stopper plate uppermost

12.2a Slacken and remove the three screws, withdraw the air filter cover and ...

12 Air filter: removal, examination and replacement

1   The air used in combustion is drawn into the carburettor via an air filter element. This performs the vital job of removing dust and any other airborne impurities which would otherwise enter the engine, causing premature wear. It follows that the element must be kept clean and renewed if damaged, as it will have an adverse effect on performance if neglected. Apart from the obvious problem of increased wear caused by a damaged element, a clogged or broken filter will upset the mixture setting, allowing it to become too rich or too weak.

2   Remove the right-hand side panel (MT50). Slacken and remove the three retaining screws and remove the air filter cover. Remove the metal frame which supports the element and withdraw the element itself.

3   The element should be cleaned by washing it in a high flash point solvent such as white spirit. Squeeze the element dry, but do not wring it out as this will damage the foam. Soak the cleaned dry element in clean gear oil (SAE 80 or 90) and squeeze the surplus out. The element should be wet but not dripping. The air cleaner assembly can now be refitted.

12.2b ... displace the element which is supported by a metal frame

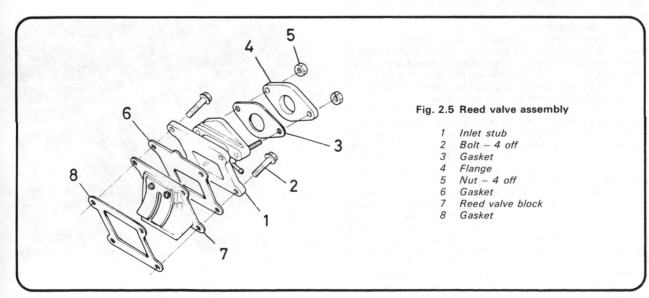

Fig. 2.5 Reed valve assembly

1   Inlet stub
2   Bolt – 4 off
3   Gasket
4   Flange
5   Nut – 4 off
6   Gasket
7   Reed valve block
8   Gasket

Fig. 2.6 Air filter

1   *Air filter case*
2   *Induction duct*
3   *Washer*
4   *Bolt*
5   *Element frame*
6   *Element*
7   *Element frame*
8   *Air filter cover*

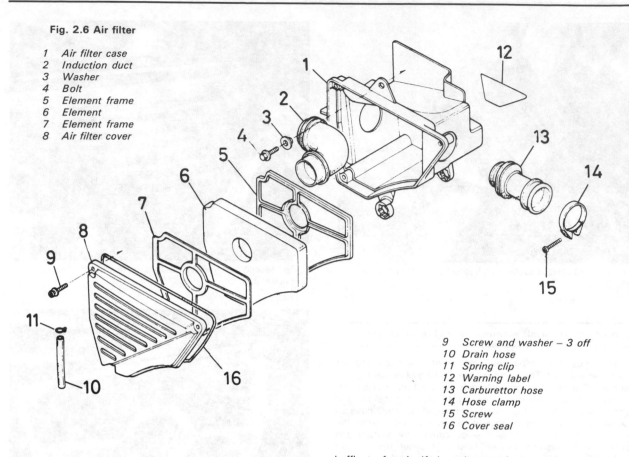

9   *Screw and washer – 3 off*
10 *Drain hose*
11 *Spring clip*
12 *Warning label*
13 *Carburettor hose*
14 *Hose clamp*
15 *Screw*
16 *Cover seal*

13 Exhaust system: general description, removal and replacement

1   The exhaust system on the MB50 models consists of a one-piece welded unit comprising exhaust pipe and silencer together. There is a removable baffle tube at the rear for cleaning purposes. The MT50 exhaust is broadly similar but is routed upwards and over the engine unit to exit at a much higher level. This is purely for styling purposes. It consists of a front pipe and a separate silencer unit joined at the rear of the petrol tank by a rubber seal. The silencer unit has a removable baffle for cleaning purposes.

2   To remove the exhaust system on the MB50 models the two nuts which secure the front flange of the exhaust system to the cylinder barrel must be slackened and removed, and also the single bolt which holds the rear exhaust mounting bracket to the frame. Slacken and remove the single screw which retains the baffle tube and withdraw the baffle tube.

3   On MT50 models the seat must first be removed. This is held by two bolts at the rear and by a hook which engages under the petrol tank at the front. This exposes the two petrol tank rear mounting bolts, the right-hand one of which also secures an earth strap which must be released before removal of the exhaust pipe. To complete removal of the pipe, slacken and remove the two nuts which secure the front flange of the exhaust pipe to the cylinder barrel and very carefully manoeuvre the pipe forward and clear of the frame. The silencer unit is secured by a nut and lock washer on the right-hand top suspension unit mounting and by a bolt to the rear cowl. Slacken and remove these and lift the silencer away. Remove the single screw which secures the baffle tube and withdraw the baffle tube. Baffle tubes are well known for their tendency to stick in the silencer as carbon or rust build up around them and jam them in place. If such a case is found, try rotating the

baffle to free it. If the tube remains stuck in position some means will have to be found of removing it without causing too much damage to the tube or to the silencer. If necessary, take the assembly to a dealer for expert advice.

4   For both models refitting is a straightforward reversal of the removal procedure. Always renew the exhaust port gasket to prevent leaks, and carefully examine the rubber seal at the exhaust pipe/silencer joint on MT50 models. Renew this if cracked, perished or damaged.

13.2a The MB50 exhaust is retained by two nuts at the front ...

13.2b ... and a single bolt at the rear

13.2c The baffle tube is removable for cleaning purposes

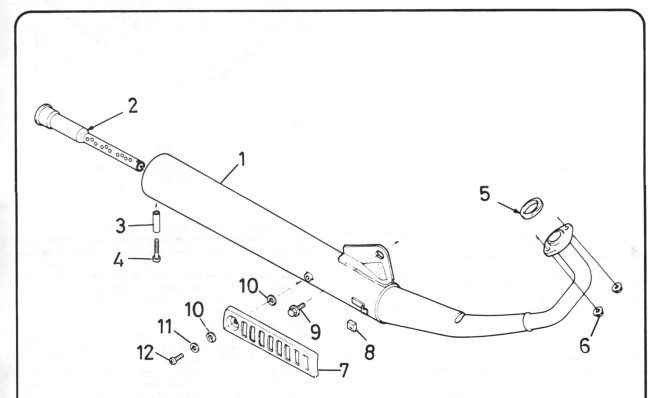

Fig. 2.7 Exhaust system – MB50

1	Exhaust system	5	Gasket	9	Bolt
2	Baffle	6	Nut – 2 off	10	Damping ring – 2 off
3	Collar	7	Heat shield	11	Washer
4	Screw	8	Rubber block	12	Screw

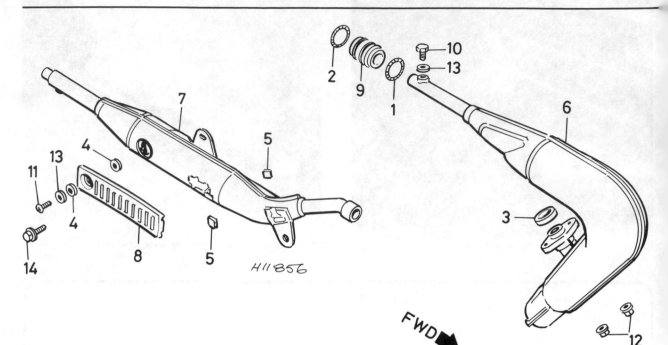

Fig. 2.8 Exhaust system – MT model

1	Front retaining ring	6	Exhaust pipe	11	Screw
2	Rear retaining ring	7	Silencer	12	Nut – 2 off
3	Gasket	8	Heat shield	13	Washer – 2 off
4	Damping ring – 2 off	9	Rubber seal	14	Bolt
5	Rubber block – 2 off	10	Bolt		

14 Exhaust system: cleaning

1   Carefully check the exhaust pipe for carbon build-up. This will occur mainly in the area of the exhaust port and in the tailpipe. Remove all traces of this with a scraper.

2   The component most likely to cause trouble and therefore require attention is the silencer baffle, which will block up with a sludge composed of carbon and oil if not cleaned out at regular intervals. A two-stroke engine is very susceptible to this fault, which is caused by the oily nature of the exhaust gases. As sludge builds up, back pressure will increase, with a resulting fall-off in performance.

3   There is no necessity to remove the exhaust system in order to gain access to the silencer baffle. It is retained by a small bolt passing through a reinforced plate which is positioned about one inch from the end of the silencer tailpipe. With this bolt removed, the baffle can be eased out of position.

4   If the build up of carbon and oil is not too great, a wash with a petrol/paraffin mix will probably suffice as a cleaning medium. Otherwise more drastic action will be necessary, such as the application of a blow lamp flame to burn away the accumulated deposits. Before the baffle is refitted it must be completely clean with none of the holes in the baffle obstructed. Note that the glass-fibre packing used by the manufacturer can be removed quite easily by cutting the retaining wire and unwrapping the glassfibre. This should be done as soon as possible as the packing acts as an effective trap for the carbon/oil sludge and therefore promotes rapid build-up of carbon deposits. In the author's opinion this packing should not be replaced on the baffle tube as it has no apparent effect on noise level, assuming that the baffle tube and silencer are in good condition, and

merely ensures that decarbonising intervals are far more frequent than necessary. The manufacturer's recommendation is that it should be replaced when necessary and this may be done if required.

5   When replacing the baffle, make sure that the retaining bolt is located correctly and fully tightened. If the baffle bolt falls out, the baffle will work loose, creating excessive exhaust noise accompanied by a marked fall-off in performance.

6   Do not run the machine without the baffle in the silencer or modify the baffle in any way. Although the changed exhaust note may give the illusion of increased power, the chances are that the performance will be reduced, accompanied by a noticeable lack of acceleration. There is also a risk of prosecution by causing an excessive noise. The carburettor is jetted to take into account the fitting of a silencer of a certain design and if this balance is disturbed the carburation will suffer accordingly.

15 Oil injection system: description

1   The oil injection system employed by Honda on these machines is a simple one, designed to avoid the inconvenience of having to mix petrol and oil in the petrol tank for engine lubrication. It consists of a separate plastic oil tank from which oil is fed to a mechanical pump situated on the crankcase and driven from the engine by reduction gear. The pump delivers oil at a predetermined rate via a synthetic rubber feed pipe to an oilway in the inlet stub. In consequence the oil is carried into the engine by the incoming charge of air/fuel mixture from the carburettor. The pump's output is varied according to the throttle position by a control cable linked to the throttle cable at

a junction box, this cable operating a control box lever on the pump body.

2 In this way the engine always receives the correct amount of oil according to its needs, a much more efficient system of lubrication which shows itself in a less smoky exhaust and much longer intervals between decarbonising operations than is possible for a petroil lubricated two-stroke engine unit.

16 Oil tank: removal and replacement

MB50

1 Remove the petrol tank as described in Section 2 of this Chapter. Disconnect the oil line at the oil pump and place a finger over the end to stop temporarily the flow of oil. The pipe can then be plugged using a screw or bolt of suitable size. Slacken and remove the two oil tank retaining bolts and lift the oil tank clear.

MT50

2 Remove the seat and exhaust silencer as described in Section 13 of this Chapter. Remove the forward section of the rear mudguard which is a black plastic mudguard secured by two nuts at its rear and by clips at the front. Slacken and remove the two nuts and disengage the mudguard section from its front mountings. Prise out the rubber grommet which is found underneath the rear mudguard and disconnect the tail lamp and rear indicator lamp wires at their respective snap connectors. Remove the rear indicator lamps, which are each retained by two bolts. Remove the rear section of the rear mudguard complete with the tail lamp assembly. Slacken and remove the two retaining bolts on the top surface of the rear cowl and remove the rear mudguard stay from underneath it.

3 Disengage the wiring loom from its clamps underneath the rear cowl, then slacken and remove the four bolts securing the rear cowl to the frame. Disconnect the oil feed pipe at the oil pump and place a finger over the end to stop temporarily the flow of oil. The pipe can then be plugged using a screw or bolt of suitable size. Lift the rear cowl and oil tank clear of the frame and remove the oil filler cap to disengage the tank from the cowl.

All models

4 Refitting the oil tank is a reversal of the removal sequence. Care must be taken to ensure the correct assembly of the various items and that all nuts and bolts are properly tightened.

Ensure that the oil line and wiring loom are routed correctly and clamped in position securely where clamps or cable ties are provided for this purpose. It is essential that all traces of air are bled from the oil tank/oil pump feed line and from the pump itself as the presence of air in the system will interrupt oil delivery, resulting in engine damage. See Section 21 of this Chapter for full details. The task of bleeding will be eased by allowing oil to flow through the oil tank/oil pump feed line before it is connected to the pump again, thus expelling air from the feed line and leaving only the air in the pump itself to be removed.

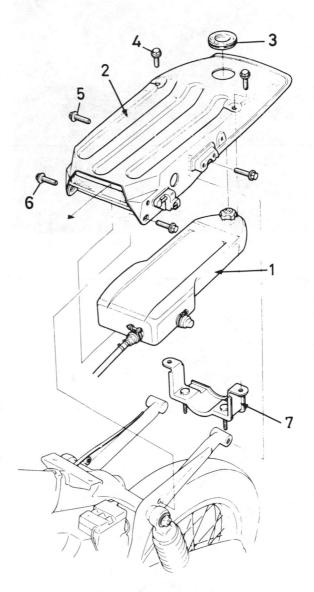

Fig. 2.9 Oil tank – MT models

1 Oil tank
2 Rear mudguard
3 Grommet
4 Bolt – 2 off
5 Bolt – 2 off
6 Bolt – 2 off
7 Mudguard stay

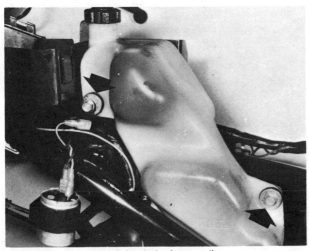

16.1 MB50 oil tank retaining bolts (arrowed)

17 Oil tank and filter: examination and cleaning

1   The oil tank must be removed as described in Section 16 of this Chapter for cleaning and examination of both the tank and filter whenever the presence of dirt is suspected in either. Drain the oil into a clean container by unplugging the end of the oil supply line and leaving the tank to drain.
2   Slacken the clip at the base of the oil tank and withdraw the

oil filter assembly. The filter gauze itself can then be detached and cleaned by blowing from the inside with compressed air, or flushing in clean petrol (gasoline).
3   Carefully check the oil tank for leaks or other damage and replace it if necessary. Ensure that it is completely clean inside before refilling with oil. Bleed the oil system of air as described in Section 21. See also the last paragraph of the preceding Section.

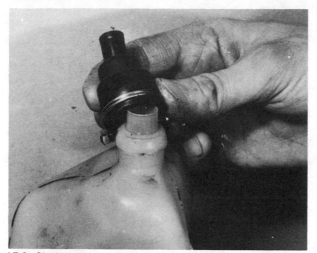

17.2a Slacken the metal clip and remove the sealing rubber to expose ...

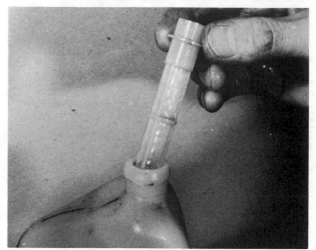

17.2b ... the oil tank filter gauze

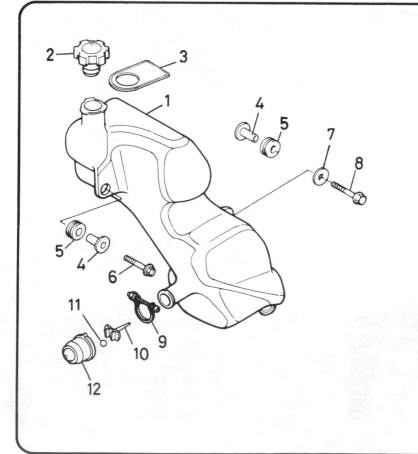

Fig. 2.10 Oil tank – MB model

1   Oil tank
2   Filler cap
3   Oil level advice label
4   Collar – 2 off
5   Grommet – 2 off
6   Bolt
7   Washer
8   Bolt
9   Clamp
10 Level indicator
11 Ball bearing
12 Oil level sight glass

18 Oil pump: removal and refitting

1   To remove the oil pump, disconnect the oil tank/oil pump feed line, placing a finger over the end to stop temporarily the flow of oil. The pipe can then be plugged using a screw or bolt of suitable size, taking care not to damage the end of the pipe. Disconnect the oil pump cable by slackening the two nuts at the adjuster bracket and sliding the cable clear of the bracket. The cable end nipple can then be disengaged from the oil pump control lever. Disconnect the oil pump/inlet stub feed pipe at the stub union. Slacken and remove the two oil pump retaining bolts and withdraw the pump.

2   Refitting is a straightforward reversal of the removal procedure. Apply a little grease to the pump mounting spigot and align the drive blade on the pump with the slot in the drive gear shaft. Ensure that the pump mounting bolts are tightened securely and connect the oil tank/oil pump feed line to the pump again after unplugging it; similarly connect the oil pump/inlet stub feed pipe to the oil pump and route it through its retaining bracket mounted on the crankcase. Leave the end free at the inlet stub union to enable bleeding to be carried out. Refit the oil pump cable and adjust it as described in Section 20 of this Chapter. The system must now be cleared of air by bleeding as described in Section 21.

18.2 Grease the oil pump mounting spigot before replacing

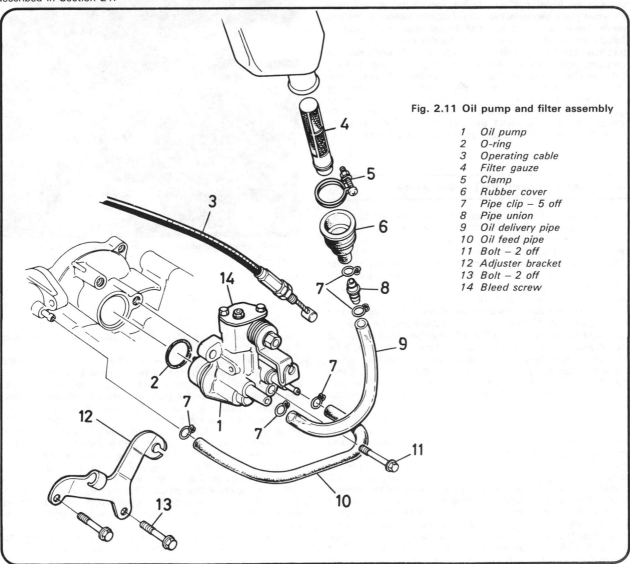

Fig. 2.11 Oil pump and filter assembly

1   Oil pump
2   O-ring
3   Operating cable
4   Filter gauze
5   Clamp
6   Rubber cover
7   Pipe clip – 5 off
8   Pipe union
9   Oil delivery pipe
10 Oil feed pipe
11 Bolt – 2 off
12 Adjuster bracket
13 Bolt – 2 off
14 Bleed screw

19 Oil pump: examination

1 When the oil pump has been removed as described in Section 18 of this Chapter, carefully examine it for damage to the main body casting and for correct operation of the control lever. Check that the O-ring around its fitting spigot is in good condition and replace it if necessary.

2 If there are any signs of damage, or if you have good reason to suspect that the pump is not working properly, discard it and fit a new one. Stripping the pump for repair is not a practical proposition as there are no parts available at all to recondition it.

20 Oil pump: cable adjustment

1 Oil pump cable adjustment must be checked at the specified service intervals and whenever the carburettor, oil pump or throttle cable are disturbed. First the throttle cable must be adjusted correctly as decribed in Section 10 of this Chapter. Open the throttle fully and check that the reference mark on the pump control lever lines up exactly with the index mark on the pump body. Note that the double line of the control lever reference mark allows some tolerance when aligning the two marks. Always align the upper of the two lines, if in doubt, so that the pump delivery rate errs on the side of too much, rather than too little. There is another single line, reference mark on the pump control lever which is to be ignored on this machine. If the two marks are not aligned as described with the throttle fully open, slacken the cable adjuster locknut and turn the adjusting nut as required. Once the cable is adjusted correctly, tighten the adjuster locknut and fully open and close the throttle two or three times to check the lever operation and settle the cable. Check that the adjustment has remained the same.

21 Oil injection system: the bleeding procedure

1 Bleeding must be carried out whenever any part of the oil injection system is disturbed, if the oil in the tank has been allowed to drain completely or run dangerously low, or if you have any reason to suspect the presence of air in the system. Air in the system will rapidly produce an airlock which will interrupt the constant supply of oil, resulting in severe engine damage due to the consequent loss of lubrication. The oil tank must be kept full of oil at all times during this operation.

2 The bleeding operation consists of two parts, removing air from the oil tank, oil tank/oil pump feed line and the oil pump itself, and removing air from the delivery side of the pump and the oil pump/inlet stub feed line. To complete the first part, thoroughly clean the oil pump and the area of crankcase around it and pack clean rag around the base of the pump. Check that the oil tank is full of oil, topping it up to the base of the filler neck if necessary. Slacken and remove the hexagon-headed bleed screw which is situated on the flat plate on the top of the pump. Oil will flow from the orifice thus exposed. Watch carefully until you can see no more air bubbles in the oil, and then replace and tighten down the hexagon-headed bleed screw. If the oil tank/oil pump feed line has been completely emptied for any reason, this stage of the bleeding procedure can be speeded up by disconnecting the feed line at the pump and, in effect, draining the oil tank into a clean container which must be placed to catch the oil. This will fill the oil tank/oil pump feed line much faster and expel all the air in the base of the tank, the filter, and the feed line as it does so. Once the feed line is full of oil, reconnect it to the pump and proceed as described above to clear any air from the pump. If this method is used check to ensure that no hidden air bubbles subsequently emerge in the

20.1a Ensure that reference marks on the pump control lever line up with index mark on pump body

20.1b Slacken locknut and turn adjuster nut of oil pump cable to adjust

feed line. The surplus oil, if totally clean, can be poured back into the oil tank.

3 Once any air in the oil tank, feed line and oil pump has been eliminated, the second stage of bleeding can be carried out, but as it involves running the engine, it must be done in a well-ventilated area. Check the oil level in the oil tank and top up as necessary. Disconnect the petrol pipe at the tap and drain any petrol remaining in the petrol tank into a clean container. Mix about a pint of 25/50 : 1 petroil mixture and pour this into the tank. Connect the petrol pipe up again and switch the petrol tap to the 'Res' position. This procedure is essential as the only way to expel air from the delivery side of the pump and the oil pump/inlet stub feed line is to pump oil through it, running the engine to operate the pump. The engine will therefore be running for a while with its normal oil supply disconnected and the petroil mixture is necessary to provide temporary lubrication.

4 Disconnect the oil feed line at the inlet sub union if this has not already been done. Start the engine and slowly warm it up until it will tick over smoothly. Using one finger, move the oil

pump control lever around to the fully open position and keep it there. Do not run the engine any faster than is absolutely necessary during this operation, and if possible keep it at a constant idling speed. Once again watch the end of the feed line very carefully. If the line has been completely emptied it may take as long as 10 minutes for the oil to appear. When it does appear, watch the air bubbles in it and only stop the procedure when you are certain that no more air bubbles are appearing. Due to the slow rate of delivery of the oil pump (0.20 cc/min at idle speed), this operation is time-consuming and dull. It must, however, be done very carefully if the engine is not to suffer severe and premature damage. As soon as the oil is free of air bubbles reconnect the oil feed line to the inlet stub union and stop the engine.

5   Once the full bleeding operation has been carried out, top up the oil tank to just below the filler neck, replace the filler cap and ensure that all the feed pipe unions are plugged firmly into place and that they are all secured by the wire retaining clips. Ensure that the oil lines are correctly routed and that they are held in place by such clamps or cable ties as are provided for this purpose. Wash off any surplus oil and check that the rag has been removed from the base of the oil pump. Drain the petroil mixture from the petrol tank and replace it with the clean petrol originally taken out. Connect the petrol pipe up and secure it with the wire retaining clip. Check the oil pump control lever has returned to the fully closed position and then fully open and close the throttle several times to settle the cable and to check that the pump control lever is operating correctly. Recheck the oil pump cable adjustment as described in Section 20.

6   When taking the machine out on the road after bleeding the oil injection system, remember that the exhaust will be excessively smoky until the surplus oil has been used or burnt up. Remember also to check for oil leaks in the system, these being readily apparent if the surplus oil was washed off as described. Any such leaks should be corrected immediately, before the machine is used further.

22 Gearbox lubrication: description and maintenance

1   The gearbox oil is contained inside the crankcases and lubricates the right-hand crankshaft main bearing, the clutch and primary drive, and the gearbox and ancillary components.
2   The crankcase reservoir is reached through a screwed plug in the right-hand outer cover and drained through a single drain plug situated in the underside of the crankcase. The level is checked by removing a small level plug in the right-hand outer cover immediately in front of the kickstart shaft.

3   The oil should be drained with the machine standing upright on level ground. The engine should be fully warmed up first, as this thins the oil to ensure more rapid draining, and ensures that any particles of dirt are held in suspension in the oil, and are more likely to be removed with it. Once the oil is fully drained, refit the drain plug and tighten it to 2.0-2.5kgf m (14-18lbf ft). Check the condition of the sealing washer and fit a new one first, if necessary. On refilling the gearbox, use 1 litre (1.76/2.2 Imp/US pint) after a full rebuild and 0.9 litre (1.58/1.9 Imp/US pint) at routine oil changes. The difference is the amount of residual oil left in the crankcase after routine draining. With the machine standing upright on level ground with its engine fully warmed up, remove the level plug to check the level. Oil should trickle gently from the level plug orifice. After checking that all plugs are securely tightened, ensure that there are no oil leaks.

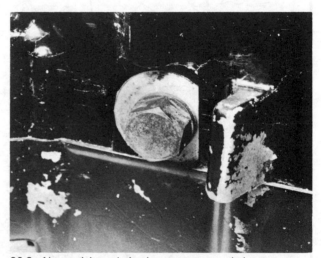

22.3a Always tighten drain plug to recommended torque setting

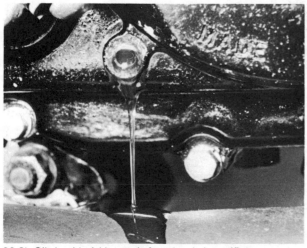

22.3b Oil should trickle gently from level plug orifice

22.3c Add engine oil via filler hole if necessary

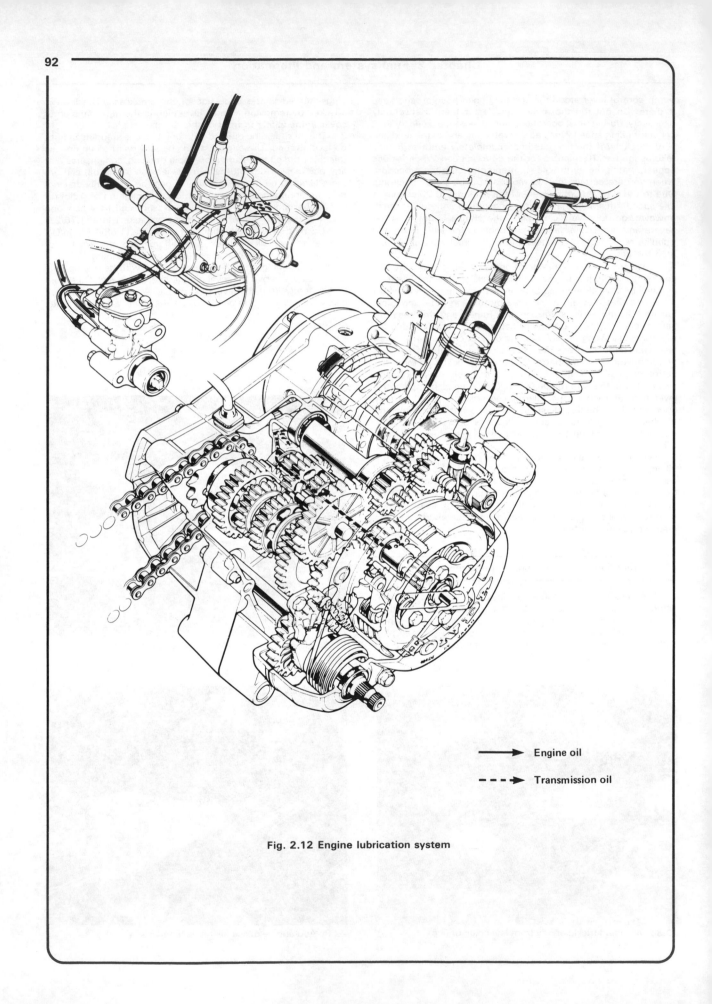

Engine oil

Transmission oil

Fig. 2.12 Engine lubrication system

Chapter 3 Ignition system

For modifications and information relating to later models, see Chapter 7

Contents

Specifications

Ignition system
Type .... Capacitor discharge ignition (CDI)

Ignition timing
Initial .... 19° ± 3° BTDC @ 3000 rpm
Initial retard speed (UK) .... 5000 – 7000 rpm
Initial retard speed (US) .... 3000 – 5000 rpm
Full retard (UK) .... 10° ± 5° BTDC @ 9000 rpm
Full retard (US) .... 10° ± 5° BTDC @ 7000 rpm

Sparking plug
Make .... NGK or ND
Type:
  UK hot .... BR6HS or W20FSR
  UK standard .... BR7HS or W22FSR
  UK cold .... BR8HS or W24FSR
  US hot .... BR7HS or W22FSR
  US standard .... BR8HS or W24FSR
  US cold .... BR9HS or W27FSR
Gap .... 0.6 – 0.7 mm (0.024 – 0.028 in)

Ignition HT coil resistance
Primary .... 0.2 – 0.3 ohm
Secondary .... 3.4 – 4.2 K ohm

1 General description

The Honda MB/MT50 is equipped with a CDI (capacitor discharge ignition) system. The system is powered by a source coil built into the generator stator. Power from this coil is fed directly to the CDI unit mounted beneath the frame, where it passes through a diode which converts it to direct current (dc). The charge is stored in a capacitor at this stage.

The spark is triggered by the pulser coil which is built into the stator. As the magnetic rotor passes the pulser coil a small alternating current (ac) pulse is induced. This enters the CDI unit where it is rectified by a second diode. The heart of the CDI unit is a component known as a thyristor. It acts as an electronic switch which remains off until a small current is applied to its gate terminal. This causes the thyristor to become conductive, and it will remain in this state until any stored charge has discharged through the primary windings of the coil.

The sudden discharge of the low-tension energy through the coil's primary windings in turn induces a high tension charge in the secondary coil. It is this which is applied to the centre electrode of the sparking plug, where it jumps the air gap to earth, igniting the fuel/air mixture.

As engine speed rises, it becomes necessary for the timing of the ignition spark to change in relation to the crankshaft to allow combustion of the fuel/air mixture to take place at the optimum position. Contrary to normal practice, where the ignition is advanced as engine speed rises, on this machine the ignition retards progressively as engine speed is increased. This unusual condition should be borne in mind when checking the ignition timing. The ignition timing change is controlled by the voltage build-up time in the pulser, which varies with the speed of the engine, acting on the thyristor gate circuit.

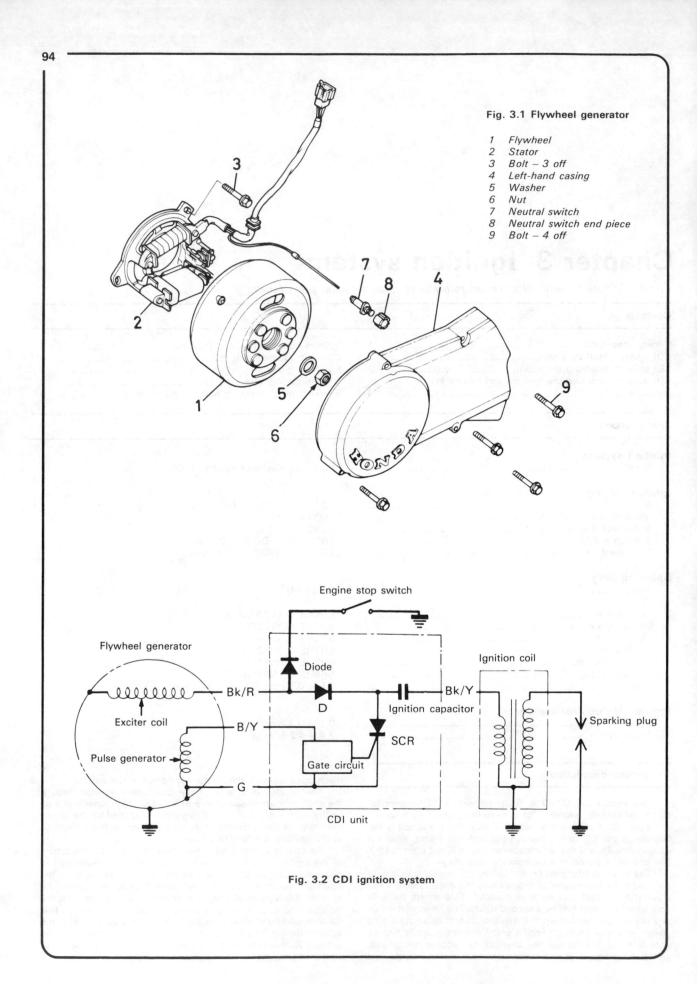

Fig. 3.1 Flywheel generator

1 Flywheel
2 Stator
3 Bolt – 3 off
4 Left-hand casing
5 Washer
6 Nut
7 Neutral switch
8 Neutral switch end piece
9 Bolt – 4 off

Fig. 3.2 CDI ignition system

2 CDI system: fault diagnosis

1 As no means of adjustment is available, any failure of the system can be traced to the failure of a system component or a simple wiring fault. Of the two possibilities, the latter is by far the most likely. In the event of failure, check the system in a logical fashion, as described below.

2 Remove the sparking plug, giving it a quick visual check, noting any obvious signs of flooding or oiling. Fit the plug into the plug cap and rest it on the cylinder head so that the metal body of the plug is in good contact with the cylinder head metal. The electrode end of the plug should be positioned so that sparking can be checked as the engine is spun over using the kickstart.

3 *Important note.* The energy levels in electronic systems can be very high. On no account should the ignition be switched on whilst the plug or plug cap are being held. Shocks from the HT circuit can be most unpleasant. Secondly, it is vital that the plug is in position and soundly earthed when the system is checked for sparking. The CDI unit can be seriously damaged if the HT circuit becomes isolated.

4 Having observed the above precautions, turn the ignition switch, and where fitted, the engine kill switch to 'On' and kick the engine over. If the system is in good condition a regular, fat blue spark should be evident at the plug electrodes. If the spark appears thin or yellowish, or is non-existent, further investigation will be necessary. Before proceeding further, turn the ignition off and remove the key as a safety measure.

5 Ignition faults can be divided into two categories, namely those where the ignition system has failed completely, and those which are due to a partial failure. The likely faults are listed below, starting with the most probable sources of failure. Work through the list systematically, referring to the subsequent sections for full details of the necessary checks and tests.

Total or partial ignition system failure

a) Loose, corroded or damaged wiring connections, broken or shorted wiring between any of the component parts of the ignition system
b) Faulty main switch or engine kill switch (where fitted)
c) Faulty ignition coil
d) Faulty CDI unit
e) Faulty generator

3 CDI system: checking the wiring

1 The wiring should be checked visually, noting any signs of corrosion around the various terminals and connectors. If the fault has developed in wet conditions it follows that water may have entered any of the connectors or switches, causing a short circuit. A temporary cure can be effected by spraying the relevant area with one of the proprietary de-watering aerosols, such as WD40 or a similar de-watering agent. A more permanent solution is to dismantle the switch or connector and coat the exposed parts with silicone grease to prevent the ingress of water. The exposed backs of connectors can be sealed off using a silicone rubber sealant.

2 Light corrosion can normally be cured by scraping or sanding the affected area, though in serious cases it may prove necessary to renew the switch or connector affected. Check the wiring for chafing or breakage, particularly where it passes close to part of the frame or its fittings. As a temporary measure, damaged insulation can be repaired with PVC tape, but the wire concerned should be renewed at the earliest opportunity.

3 Using the wiring diagram at the end of the manual, check each wire for breakage or short circuits using a multimeter set on the resistance scale or a dry battery and bulb wired as shown in the accompanying illustration. In each case, there should be continuity between the ends of each wire.

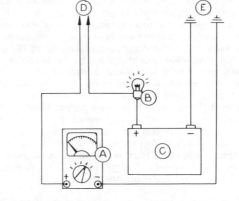

Fig. 3.3 Method of checking the wiring using a battery and bulb or a multimeter

A Multimeter
B Bulb
C Battery
D Positive probe
E Negative probe

4 CDI system: checking the ignition and engine kill switches

1 The ignition system is controlled by the ignition switch or main switch, which is housed at the centre of the instrument console, and additionally, on US models, by the engine kill switch incorporated in the right-hand handlebar switch cluster. The ignition switch has four terminals and leads, of which two are involved in controlling the ignition system. These are the IG terminal (black/white lead) and the E terminal (green lead). The two terminals are connected when the switch is in the 'OFf' position and prevent the ignition system from functioning by shorting the CDI unit to earth. On US models a duplicate set of terminals with identical wiring colours forms the kill switch, thus when either switch is set to 'Off' the ignition switch is rendered inoperative. When both switches are set to the 'On' position, the CDI to earth connection is broken, and the system is allowed to function.

2 If the operation of either switch is suspect reference should be made to the wiring diagram at the end of this book. The switch connections are shown in diagrammatic form and indicate which terminals are connected in the various switch positions. The wiring from the switches can be traced back to their respective connectors where test connections can be made most conveniently.

3 The purpose of the test is to check whether the switch connections are being made and broken as indicated by the diagrams. In the interests of safety the test is made with the machine's battery disconnected, thus avoiding accidental damage to the CDI system or the owner. The test can be made with a multimeter set on the resistance scale, or with a simple dry battery and bulb arrangement, as shown in the accompanying line drawing. Connect one probe lead to each terminal and note the reading or bulb indication in each switch position.

4 If the test indicates that the black/white lead is earthed irrespective of the switch position, check that the engine kill switch is set at the 'Run' position. If this fails to affect the result, trace and disconnect the ignition (black/white) and earth (green) leads from the ignition switch. Repeat the test with the switch isolated. If no change is apparent, the switch should be considered faulty and renewed.

5 If the ignition switch works normally when isolated, the fault must lie in the black/white lead between the CDI unit and the ignition and kill switches or in the kill switch itself. As already mentioned, the ignition and kill switches perform the same function, each earthing the ignition circuit when set on the 'Off' position, thus unless both are disconnected from earth, the ignition circuit will remain inoperative.

6   The kill switch is checked in the same manner as described above. If a fault is discovered in either switch, try cleaning it with a water dispersant aerosol spray, such as WD40, Contect or similar. If this fails to effect a cure, it may prove necessary to renew the switch, a decision not to be taken lightly in view of the cost. One solution would be to try to obtain a good secondhand switch from a motorcycle breaker.

7   The ignition switch is mounted on the underside of the instrument console, and may be removed after the latter has been detached. The console is retained by two bolts, as is the switch itself. The kill switch is housed in the right-hand handlebar switch cluster and is removed by separating the two halves of the switch. Although repair should be considered impracticable, it may prove to be worthwhile attempting it if the switch is otherwise useless. The ignition switch, however, is a sealed unit and cannot be dismantled.

5   Ignition coil: location and testing

1   The ignition coil is a sealed unit, and will normally give long service without need for attention. It is mounted beneath the frame gusseting to the rear of the steering head and is covered in use by the fuel tank. If follows that it will be necessary to remove the tank in order to gain access to the coil.

2   If a weak spark and difficult starting cause the performance of the coil to be suspect, it should, in general, be tested by a Honda service agent or an auto-electrical expert. They will have the necessary appropriate test equipment. It is, however, possible to perform a number of basic tests, using a multimeter with ohms and kilo ohms scales. The primary winding resistance should be checked by connecting one of the meter probe leads to the Lucar terminal and the other earthed against the coil mounting lug. The secondary windings are checked by connecting the probe leads to the high tension lead, having removed the plug cap, and to the coil mounting lug. Check the readings obtained against the figures given in the specifications Section of this Chapter.

3   Should any of these checks not produce the expected result, the coil should then be taken to a Honda service agent or auto-electrician for a more thorough check. If the coil is found to be faulty, it must be replaced; it is not possible to effect a satisfactory repair.

5.1a Location of ignition HT coil – MB50

5.1b Location of ignition HT coil – MT50

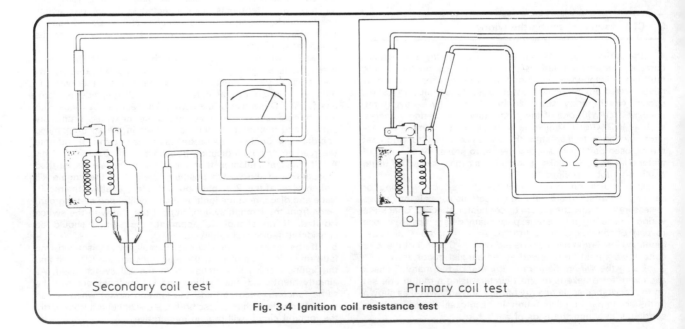

Secondary coil test

Primary coil test

Fig. 3.4 Ignition coil resistance test

Spark plug maintenance: Checking plug gap with feeler gauges

Altering the plug gap. Note use of correct tool

Spark plug conditions: A brown, tan or grey firing end is indicative of correct engine running conditions and the selection of the appropriate heat rating plug

White deposits have accumulated from excessive amounts of oil in the combustion chamber or through the use of low quality oil. Remove deposits or a hot spot may form

Black sooty deposits indicate an over-rich fuel/air mixture, or a malfunctioning ignition system. If no improvement is obtained, try one grade hotter plug

Wet, oily carbon deposits form an electrical leakage path along the insulator nose, resulting in a misfire. The cause may be a badly worn engine or a malfunctioning ignition system

A blistered white insulator or melted electrode indicates over-advanced ignition timing or a malfunctioning cooling system. If correction does not prove effective, try a colder grade plug

A worn spark plug not only wastes fuel but also overloads the whole ignition system because the increased gap requires higher voltage to initiate the spark. This condition can also affect air pollution

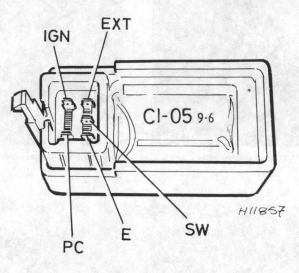

CDI unit test connections

Unit: kΩ

Tester positive (+) probe / Tester negative (−) probe	SW	EXT	PC	E	IGN
SW		∞	∞	∞	∞
EXT	0.1–20		∞	∞	Needle swings, then returns
PC	0.5–200	0.5–100		0.5–30	∞
E	0.2–60	0.1–20	∞		∞
IGN	∞	∞	∞	∞	

Multimeter reading table – US model

Unit: k Ω

Tester (+) / Tester (−)	SW	EXT	PC	E	IGN
SW		∞	∞	∞	∞
EXT	0.1–5		∞	∞	Needle swings, then returns
PC	0.5–200	0.5–50		0.5–10	∞
E	0.2–10	0.1–5	∞		∞
IGN	∞	∞	∞	∞	

Multimeter reading table – UK models

Fig. 3.5 CDI unit testing

6 CDI unit: location and testing

1   The CDI unit takes the form of a sealed metal box mounted beneath the fuel tank. In the event of malfunction the unit may be tested in situ after the fuel tank has been removed and the wiring connectors traced and separated. Honda advise against the use of any test meter other than the Sanwa Electric Tester (Honda part number 07308-0020000) or the Kowa Electric Tester (TH-5H), because they feel that the use of other devices may result in inaccurate readings.

2   Most owners will find that they either do not possess a multimeter, in which case they will probably prefer to have the unit checked by a Honda Service Agent, or own a meter which is not of the specified make or model. In the latter case, a good indication of the unit's condition can be gleaned in spite of inaccuracies in the readings. If necessary, the CDI unit can be taken to a Honda Service Agent or auto-electrical specialist for confirmation of its condition.

3   The test details are given in the accompanying illustration in the form of a table of meter probe connections with the expected reading in each instance. The Sanwa tester should be set to the kilo ohms range, the Kowa tester to the x100 ohm range. If an ordinary multimeter is used the resistance range may be determined by trial and error. The diagram illustrates the CDI unit connections referred to in the table. For owners not possessing a test meter the unit or the complete machine can be taken to a Honda Service Agent for testing.

7 Flywheel generator: testing

1   The ignition system is powered by a source coil and triggered by a pulser coil, both of which are built into the generator stator. It follows that if the generator malfunctions it will affect the operation of the ignition system, possibly without affecting the remainder of the electrical system. Six leads exit from the stator. Of these, identify the plain green, the black/red and the blue/yellow wires.

2   Disconnect the wires at their connectors. Using a multimeter set on the ohms scale measure the resistance between the terminals of those wires. The values should be as shown below:

    Black/red to green lead (source coil) 50 – 300 ohms
    Blue/yellow to green lead (pulser coil) 10 – 100 ohms

If the readings obtained fall outside the limits given the generator stator is faulty. Unfortunately this means that the complete flywheel generator must be renewed; individual generator components are not available as spare parts. A check should be made to ensure that the fault is not due to a broken or damaged wire which could be repaired easily. If no apparent fault is found, it must be assumed that the coil or coils which gave the wrong reading have indeed malfunctioned. In such a case it is advised that the generator assembly be taken to an authorised Honda dealer for confirmation of this before a new assembly is purchased as this is likely to be very expensive.

8 Ignition timing: checking

1   Checking the ignition timing should only be necessary if the stator plate has been disturbed. See Section 31 of Chapter 1 and accompanying photographs for details of correct fitting of the stator. It should be regarded purely as a check that all is in order, as no adjustment is possible if a malfunction occurs.

2   The ignition timing can be checked only whilst the engine is running using a stroboscopic lamp and thus a suitable timing lamp will be required. The inexpensive neon lamps should be adequate in theory, but in practice may produce a pulse of such low intensity that the timing mark remains indistinct. If possible,

6.1a Location of CDI unit – MB50 (rectifier arrowed)

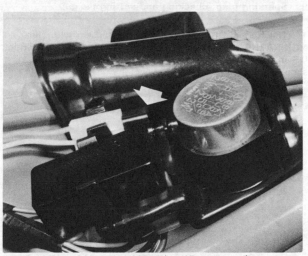

6.1b Location of CDI unit – MT50 (rectifier arrowed)

7.2 If any fault should occur, the complete stator assembly must be renewed with the rotor

one of the more precise zenon tube lamps should be employed powered by an **external** source of the appropriate voltage.

3 Remove the left-hand outer cover. Connect the timing lamp to the machine as directed by the lamp's manufacturer. Start the engine and aim the lamp at the generator rotor. Increase engine speed to 3000 rpm, at which point the fixed index mark on the crankcase wall should align with the 'F' mark on the rotor. Raise the engine speed to 8500 – 9500 rpm (6500 – 7500 rpm US models) and check that the fixed index mark aligns with the two parallel lines between the 'F' and 'T' marks. These parallel lines form the full retard reference marks. The transition from 'F' (initial retard) reference mark to the full retard marks should be made smoothly and easily. Please note that the engine should only be held at the higher speed for the bare minimum of time necessary to check the marks.

4 If there is any doubt about the ignition timing as a result of this check, take the machine to an authorised Honda dealer for an expert opinion. As already stated, there is no means of adjustment of the ignition timing on these machines, and replacement of the alternator stator and rotor is the only solution. This is likely to prove rather expensive and an expert opinion would be a good idea to avoid wasting money.

9 Sparking plug: checking and setting the gap

1 The Honda MB/MT50 is fitted as standard with either an NGK BR7HS or ND W22FSR (NGK BR8HS or NDW24FSR for US models). In most operating conditions the standard plug should prove satisfactory. However alternatives are listed to allow for varying altitudes, climatic conditions, and the varying uses to which the machine is put. Consult a local authorised Honda dealer for advice before alternating the plug specification from standard.

2 The correct electrode gap is 0.6 – 0.7 mm (0.024 – 0.028 in). The gap can be assessed using feeler gauges. If necessary, alter the gap by removing the outer electrode, preferably using a proper electrode tool. **Never** bend the centre electrode, otherwise the porcelain insulator will crack, and may cause damage to the engine if particles break away whilst the engine is running.

3 After some experience the sparking plug electrodes can be used as a reliable guide to engine operating conditions. See accompanying photographs.

4 It is advisable to carry a new spare sparking plug on the machine, having first set the electrodes to the correct gap. Whilst sparking plugs do not fail often, a new replacement is well worth having if a breakdown does occur.

5 Never overtighten a sparking plug otherwise there is risk of stripping the threads from the cylinder head, especially as it is cast in light alloy. A stripped thread can be repaired without having to scrap the cylinder head by using a 'Helicoil' thread insert. This is a low-cost service, operated by a number of dealers.

6 Before replacing a sparking plug into the cylinder head coat the threads sparingly with a graphited grease to aid future removal. Use the correct size spanner when tightening the plug otherwise the spanner may slip and damage the ceramic insulator. The plug should be tightened sufficiently to seat firmly on the sealing washer, and no more.

Chapter 4 Frame and forks

For modifications and information relating to later models, see Chapter 7

Contents

Specifications

Frame	Welded tubular steel	

Front forks

Type	Oil damped telescopic	
	MB	**MT**
Oil capacity (per leg)	72.5 – 77.5 cc	83 – 88 cc
	(2.0 – 2.2/2.5 – 2.6 Imp/	(2.3 – 2.5 Imp oz)
	US oz)	
Oil grade	Fork oil or ATF	
Fork spring free length	475 mm (18.70 in)	534.20 mm (21.03 in)
Wear limit	465 mm (18.31 in)	523.50 mm (20.61 in)
Fork stanchion bend (max)	0.2 mm (0.008 in)	0.2 mm (0.008 in)

Rear suspension

Type	Two hydraulically damped, coil spring units on pivoted forks	
Spring free length	179.7 mm (7.07 in)	206.5 mm (8.13 in)
Wear limit	176.1 mm (6.93 in)	202.4 mm (7.97 in)

Torque wrench settings

	kgf m	lbf ft
Fork crown nut	6.0 – 9.0	43 – 65
Handlebar clamp bolts	0.8 – 1.2	6 – 9
Top yoke pinch bolts	0.9 – 1.3	7 – 9
Fork top bolt:		
MB, MT (UK) models	3.5 – 4.0	25 – 29
MB (US) model	6.0 – 7.0	43 – 51
Bottom yoke pinch bolts	2.0 – 3.0	14 – 22
Front wheel spindle MT	5.5 – 6.5	40 – 47
Front wheel spindle nut:		
MB (UK) model	3.5 – 5.0	25 – 36
MB (US) model and MT	5.5 – 6.5	40 – 47
Rear wheel spindle nut	5.5 – 6.5	40 – 47
Swinging arm pivot bolt	5.5 – 6.5	40 – 47
Rear suspension mountings	3.0 – 4.0	22 – 29

1 General description

The frame of the Honda MB/MT50 consists of a pressed steel centre spine braced by triangulated steel tubes which support the pivoted rear fork mounting and seat rails. The engine hangs below the frame and does not form a part of it, which makes access for servicing work and for engine removal very easy. The front suspension employs oil-damped telescopic forks and at the rear conventional coil sprung and oil damped suspension units act on a pivoted fork.

2 Front fork removal: general

1   It is unlikely that the forks will require removal from the frame unless the fork seals are leaking or accident damage has been sustained. In the event that the latter has occurred, it should be noted that the frame may also have become bent, and whilst this may not be obvious when checked visually, could prove to be potentially dangerous.

2   If attention to the fork legs only is required, it is unnecessary to detach the complete assembly, the legs being easily removed individually.

3   If attention to the steering head assembly is required it is possible to remove the lower yoke with the fork legs still in place, if desired. It should be noted, however, that this procedure is hampered by the unwieldy nature of the assembly, and it is recommended that the fork legs be removed prior to dismantling the steering head and fork yokes.

4   Before dismantling work can begin it will be necessary to arrange the machine so that the front wheel is raised clear of the ground. This is best done by lashing the rear of the machine down, either to a fixed object in the workshop or to a suitable weight. On MT models support the machine on blocks placed beneath the engine.

5   Front wheel removal is fully described in Section 3 of Chapter 5. If removal of the steering head assembly is required it is best to completely remove the speedo cable and brake cable or brake hose at this stage. If fork leg removal only is contemplated, it will suffice to tape these items to the frame to keep them out of harm's way. For MB50 models the mudguard and brake caliper must be removed. Slacken and remove the two bolts securing the caliper mounting bracket to the front fork lower leg and tape the caliper to the frame as previously described. On no account should the hydraulic hose unions be unnecessarily disturbed, or the hose twisted, as it is easily damaged. Place a wooden wedge firmly between the pads to prevent ejection of the caliper piston if the front brake lever is accidentally applied. Remove the mudguard by slackening and removing the four retaining bolts. Note that it is not necessary to remove the front mudguard of the MT50 unless bottom yoke replacement is required. In all other circumstances it is better to leave it in place.

6   At this stage, if removal of the handlebars or the steering head assembly is required, removal of the petrol tank is recommended. See the relevant section in Chapter 2 for details. This is to prevent damage to the paintwork of the tank, and to allow easier access to the front fork components. At the very least, the tank should be covered with an old blanket or similar padding.

3 Front forks: removing the fork legs

MB50 (UK) model

1   Once the front wheel and mudguard have been removed, fork leg removal is straightforward, but first of all the fairing must be removed. To do this, slacken and remove the two dome-headed nuts which secure the fairing stays to their clamps on the fork stanchion. Withdraw the fairing and put it to one side where it will not be damaged.

2   Slacken and remove the two fork top bolts which project vertically through the handlebar/top yoke assembly. Slacken but do not remove the two bottom yoke pinch bolts. Slide the fork legs down through the bottom yoke and remove them. A tap may be needed below the top of each leg, using a hammer and wooden drift to free the leg. If the leg jams in the bottom yoke, tap a screwdriver blade into the slot in the bottom yoke clamps to open up the clamp slightly and free the leg. Care should be taken when doing this to prevent overstressing the clamps. Remove the fairing clamps and keep them with the fairing.

MB50 (US) model and MT50

3   Once the front wheel, with brake caliper and front mudguard where applicable, has been removed, the procedure is straightforward. Slacken but do not remove the two pinch bolts on both top and bottom fork yokes. Note that, on MT50 models, it may be necessary to remove the headlamp casing mounting bolts and ease the casing forward far enough to gain access to the bottom yoke pinch bolts.

4   Slide the fork legs down through the yokes and remove them. A tap may be needed on the top of each leg, using a hammer and wooden drift to free the leg. If the leg jams in the yoke tap a screwdriver blade into the slot in the yoke clamps to open the clamps up enough to free the leg. Care should be taken when doing this to prevent overstressing the clamps.

2.5a Slacken and remove retaining bolts ...

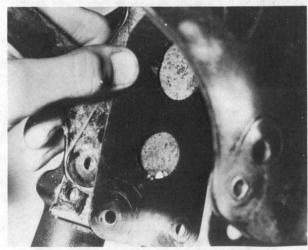

2.5b ... and withdraw front fork brace and front mudguard together – MB50

2.5c Removal of the MT50 front mudguard is not necessary

3.2a The fork top bolts must first be removed ...

3.2b ... and the bottom yoke pinch bolts slackened ...

3.2c ... before the fork legs can be withdrawn

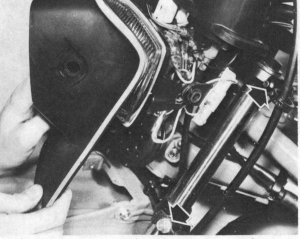
3.3 Headlamp casing removal may be necessary to gain access to the pinch bolts (arrowed) – MT50

4 Steering head: removal and refitting

1   It is assumed that the instructions in Sections 2 and 3 of this Chapter have been followed in full, especially with regard to the petrol tank. Stripping the steering head, as with any other work on the cycle parts, is quite straightforward assuming certain precautions are observed. Make a careful note of the order in which parts are removed, return all nuts, bolts, and washers to their original positions for safekeeping, and do not disturb any part unless absolutely necessary, eg hydraulic brake hose connections. Prior to disconnecting any electrical components the battery positive lead should be disconnected from the terminal to prevent accidental short circuits.

MB50 (UK) model
2   Slacken and remove the two headlamp mounting bolts, disconnect the headlamp and parking lamp wires and remove the headlamp assembly. Similarly remove the front winker assemblies. Slacken the knurled rings on the speedometer and tachometer cables and withdraw these clear of the steering head area. Disconnect all wires leading to the instrument panel,

slacken and remove the three screws securing the bottom cover and remove the cover. Slacken the two dome-headed nuts securing the instrument panel to the headlamp bracket and remove the instrument panel. Free the hydraulic brake hose from its clamp on the bottom yoke, slacken and remove the two bolts securing the handlebar master cylinder split clamp to the handlebar, and remove the whole hydraulic system. Store this upright to prevent any chance of brake fluid loss.

3　Remove the horn from the bottom yoke. The official method of removing the handlebars is to disconnect all the cables and wiring, remove the switches, twistgrip assembly and mirrors before touching the handlebars themselves. However it is possible simply to slacken and remove the fork crown nut, then to lift the handlebars off the steering head and back clear of the working area. If of course the handlebars are to be replaced or examined, the first course must be taken; however if this is not so, the second course is a great deal simpler.

MB50 (US) model

4　Slacken and remove the two headlamp securing screws, withdraw the headlamp assembly, disconnect the wires and put the assembly on one side. Slacken and remove the two bolts which secure the headlamp shell and remove this. Disconnect the wires leading to the instrument panel, slacken the knurled rings retaining the speedometer and tachometer cables and withdraw the cables clear of the steering head area. Remove the three screws securing the instrument panel bottom cover, withdraw this, slacken and remove the two dome-headed nuts retaining the instrument panel and remove the instrument panel.

5　Remove the horn by slackening its single retaining bolt. Free the hydraulic brake hose from its clamp on the bottom yoke. Slacken and remove the two bolts securing the handlebar master cylinder split clamp to the handlebar, and remove the whole hydraulic system. Store the reservoir upright to prevent any chance of brake fluid loss. The recommended method of removing the handlebar is to strip all the controls from them first. However unless handlebar replacement is required, this is not necessary. Slacken and remove the four handlebar retaining bolts, withdraw the two upper clamps and lift the handlebar assembly off the top yoke and back clear of the steering head area. It will be immediately obvious why removal or protection of the petrol tank was recommended in Section 2. Slacken and remove the fork crown nut, and withdraw the top yoke. This may need a careful tap with a soft-faced mallet to free it. Removal from the top yoke of the headlamp bracket and indicators is not necessary.

MT50 model

6　Slacken and remove the two headlamp retaining bolts, disengage the headlamp casing from its bottom mounting, disconnect the headlamp and parking lamp wires and withdraw the headlamp assembly far enough for access to be gained to the speedometer cable and ignition switch wires. Disconnect the speedometer cable at its knurled ring, unplug the ignition switch block connector and disconnect the warning lamp wires. Put the headlight and speedometer to one side. Remove the horn.

7　If the handlebars are to be replaced the controls and switches must first be removed by disconnecting all the control cables and wiring. If this is not required however, slacken and remove the four handlebar retaining bolts, withdraw the two upper clamps and lift the handlebar assembly off the top yoke and back clear of the steering head area. Slacken and remove the fork crown nut, and withdraw the top yoke. This may need a careful tap with a soft-faced mallet to free it.

All models

8　Using a pin spanner or C-spanner, slacken and remove the steering head adjusting nut and then withdraw the top cone. Support the bottom yoke with the other hand while doing this. Some means of catching the steel balls must be devised such as a large piece of rag wrapped around the bottom yoke, or a large plastic tray or container placed to catch the balls as they fall. If care is used, the balls in the top race will stay in place and enable you to watch the lower ones. There is a total of 42 steel balls of $\frac{3}{16}$ in diameter, 21 being used in each race. Withdraw the bottom yoke and place all the balls in a separate container to await examination and reassembly.

9　On reassembly, the bottom yoke must be installed first, as described in Section 5 of this Chapter, whereupon the rebuilding process is a straightforward reversal of the removal procedure described in this Section and in Sections 2 and 3 of this Chapter. Where such settings are given, use a torque wrench to tighten the relevant nuts and bolts. Note that the handlebar mounting clamps and the master cylinder mounting clamp have markings on them to show the correct method of installation. On the handlebar split clamps this consists of a punch mark in one end and a punch mark in the handlebar itself. The punch-marked end of the split clamp must always be at the front, and the punch mark in the handlebar must be aligned with the top face of the lower clamp. The master cylinder mounting clamp has an arrow or the word 'Up' cast in it to show which way up it must be fitted and the joint between the two clamp halves should be aligned with a punch mark in the handlebars. This will ensure that the master cylinder is mounted exactly level to facilitate checking the brake fluid level.

10　Pay careful attention to giving the control cables easy and smooth runs and note that the handlebar switch halves and the lever split clamps all have their respective reference marks punched in the handlebars to ensure that they are replaced in their correct positions. Refer to the colour-coding of the electrical wiring shown in the diagram at the back of this book when connecting the wiring. Do not forget to connect the battery again and to test all the circuits before using the machine on the road. Ensure that the punch marks on the headlamp shell are correctly aligned with the reference marks on the headlamp brackets to give correct headlamp beam setting.

11　Do not forget, before refitting the front wheel, to check the adjustment of the steering head bearings as described in Section 5.

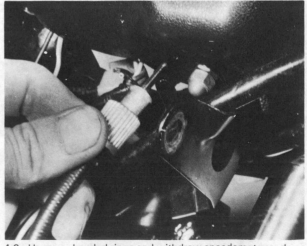

4.2a Unscrew knurled rings and withdraw speedometer and tachometer cables

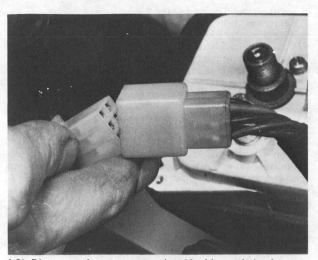

4.2b Disconnect instrument panel and ignition switch wires

4.2c Remove bottom cover ...

4.2d ... which exposes two dome-headed nuts. These must both be removed before the panel can be withdrawn

4.10 Note reference marks which must be used to ensure correct headlamp beam alignment

5 Steering head bearings: examination, refitting, and adjustment

1 Before commencing reassembly of the forks examine the steering head races. They are unlikely to wear out under normal circumstances until a high mileage has been covered. If, however, the steering gear bearings have been maladjusted, wear will be accelerated. If, before dismantling, the forks had had a pronounced tendency to stick in one position when turned, often in the straight ahead position, the cups and cones are probably indented and need to be renewed.

2 Examine the cups and cones carefully; it is not necessary to remove the cups for this. The bearing tracks should be polished and free from indentations, cracks or pitting. If signs of wear are evident, the cups and cones must be renewed. In order for the straight line steering on any motorcycle to be consistently good, the steering head bearings must be absolutely perfect. Even the smallest amount of wear on the cups and cones may cause steering wobble at high speeds and judder during heavy front wheel braking. The cups are an interference fit on their respective seatings and can be tapped from position using a

suitable long drift. The top cone, as already mentioned, is lifted away in the course of dismantling and is as easily replaced when rebuilding. The bottom cone, however, is a tight fit on the steering stem. Clamp the bottom yoke in a soft-jawed vice to hold it securely without damaging the painted finish and, using two screwdrivers or tyre levers, carefully lever the bottom cone away from its seating. Take great care not to damage the rubber dust seal and the washer which are situated underneath the bottom cone. Once the bottom cone is removed from its seating, it can be pulled easily off the steering stem. Carefully examine the rubber dust seal and replace it if worn to prevent the entry of road dirt into the steering head bearings.

3 Replace the metal washer, rubber dust seal and the bottom cone on the steering stem in that order. Position them carefully and use a hammer and a long tubular drift to tap the bottom cone on to its seating. Great care must be taken not to damage the bearing track of the bottom cone. Use a drift which will bear only on the inside shoulder of the cone to avoid the risk of such damage occurring. Tap the cups firmly into their respective seatings in the frame using a suitably-sized socket as a drift. Again take great care not to damage the bearing track surfaces.

4 The ball bearings themselves should be cleaned using

paraffin (kerosene) or petrol (gasoline) taking suitable precautions against the risk of fire. If found to be marked, chipped or discoloured in any way they should be replaced as a complete set.

5   On reassembly, pack the bottom cone and top cup liberally with grease, and place the bearings in position using the grease to hold them in place. Both races use twenty-one, $\frac{3}{16}$ inch (No 6) steel balls. Note that this number will leave a gap for one more ball which is intended, as some clearance is needed to prevent the balls skidding against one another and accelerating the rate of wear.

6   With the balls held in place as described, very carefully pack the bottom cup with grease and fit the bottom yoke. Support the yoke with one hand and pack the area around the upper bearing with grease. Replace the top cone ensuring that the balls do not become displaced in the process, and then thread the adjusting nut, with its integral dust seal, down into position. Using a pin spanner or C-spanner tighten down the nut until it seats lightly. Do not overtighten it. Turn the nut back through $\frac{1}{8}$ turn from its lightly tightened position. This will serve as the basis for correct adjustment of the steering head bearings. Bearing adjustment can be carried out correctly only when the complete front assembly is fitted and should not be forgotten during the rebuilding procedure.

7   All traces of free play must be removed from the steering head bearings without putting any preload on them. To check this, place the machine on its centre stand with a block under the engine to raise the front wheel clear of the ground. With the forks in the straight ahead position, grasp the fork lower legs in the area of the wheel spindle and attempt to push and pull the fork backwards and forwards. Any free play will immediately be felt by the fingers of the other hand between the bottom yoke and the frame around the lower steering head bearing. Free play must be eliminated by slackening the fork crown nut above the top yoke and then using a C-spanner to tighten the adjusting nut immediately under the top yoke. To check for overtightened bearings, position the machine as above, and push lightly on one handlebar end. The front forks should smoothly and easily fall away to the opposite lock. Any signs of stiffness or notchiness will be immediately apparent and should be removed by adjustment or, if necessary, replacement of the damaged parts. After adjusting the steering head bearings, tighten the fork crown nut to 6.0 – 9.0 kgf m (43 – 65 lbf ft) and recheck the bearing adjustment as described to ensure that it has remained the same.

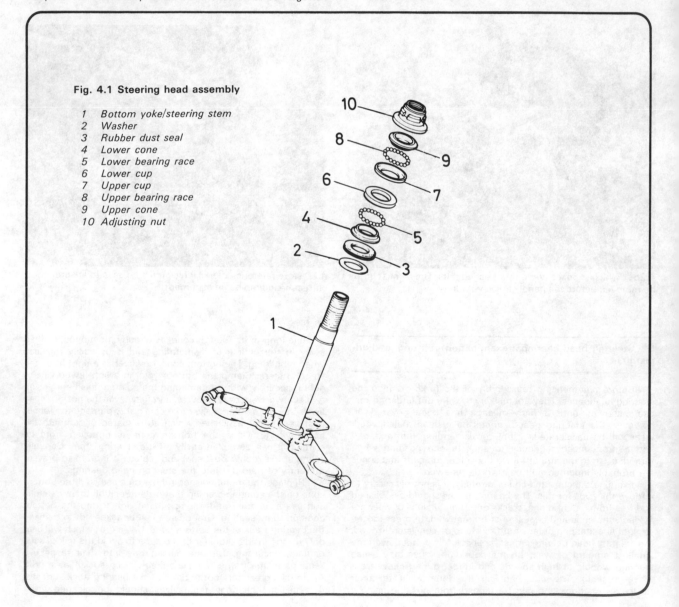

Fig. 4.1 Steering head assembly

1   Bottom yoke/steering stem
2   Washer
3   Rubber dust seal
4   Lower cone
5   Lower bearing race
6   Lower cup
7   Upper cup
8   Upper bearing race
9   Upper cone
10 Adjusting nut

6 Fork yokes: examination and renovation

1 To check the top yoke for accident damage, push the fork stanchions through the bottom yoke and fit the top yoke. If it lines up, it can be assumed the yokes are not bent. Both must also be checked for cracks. If they are damaged or cracked, fit new replacements.

7 Front forks: dismantling the fork legs

1 Slacken and remove the top bolt, noting that it will be necessary to hold the stanchion whilst this is done. The easiest method is to clamp the leg in one of the fork yokes, or failing this, to use a strap wrench. It is not advisable to clamp the stanchion in a vice, because of the risk of damage due to scoring or distorting. Use of this method is permissible if soft jaws are used. Be very careful when unscrewing the top bolt. The fork spring is under tension and will push the bolt clear with some force. It follows that pressure should be applied to the bolt to counter this, firm hand pressure being adequate.
2 It should be noted that the above applies to the MT model but only in general terms to the MB models. These latter models have a top bolt which is reinforced by a secondary threaded plug which actually pressurises the fork spring. It must be removed using a suitably-sized Allen key, and taking note of the warnings concerning fork spring pressure given above.
3 When the top bolt has been removed, invert the leg over a drain tray and leave it until the damping oil has drained. Repeat the above procedure on the remaining leg, but note that each leg should be dismantled and reassembled separately to avoid interchanging components.
4 Wrap some rag around the lower leg and clamp the assembly in a vice, taking care not to overtighten and thus distort the lower leg. Using an Allen key, slacken and remove the damper bolt from the recessed hole in the bottom of the lower leg. This will often cause some difficulty because the bolt threads are coated in a locking compound and once slightly

loose there is a tendency for the damper rod to turn in its seat. To overcome this problem a length of wooden dowel can be employed to hold the damper rod. Grind a coarse taper on one end of the dowel and insert it down the bore of the stanchion so that it engages in the recessed head of the damper rod.
5 It will now be necessary to push on the dowel to obtain grip on the damper. The dowel must not be allowed to turn, and to this end it is recommended that a self-locking wrench is clamped across its end to provide a handle. With an assistant restraining the damper rod, the bolt should now unscrew. If working alone, cut the dowel so that it lies about $\frac{1}{2}$ in lower than the top of the fully extended stanchion. The top bolt can be temporarily refitted to apply pressure to the dowel whilst the bolt is removed.
6 Disengage and slide off the dust seal which is fitted around the top of the lower leg. The stanchion can now be withdrawn, taking care not to damage the seal lip. The damper rod and rebound spring can be tipped out of the stanchion.

7.4 Use an Allen key to unscrew the damper bolt

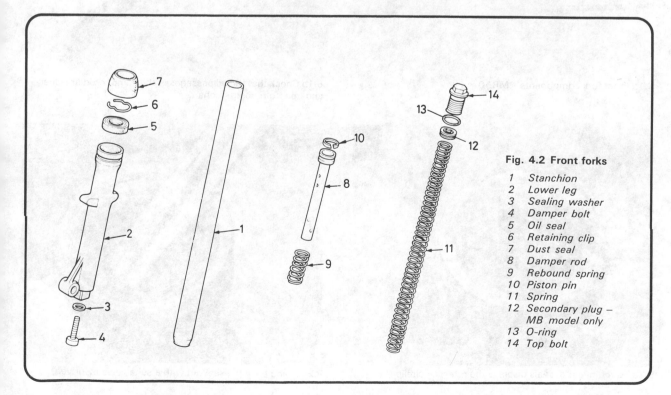

Fig. 4.2 Front forks

1 Stanchion
2 Lower leg
3 Sealing washer
4 Damper bolt
5 Oil seal
6 Retaining clip
7 Dust seal
8 Damper rod
9 Rebound spring
10 Piston pin
11 Spring
12 Secondary plug – MB model only
13 O-ring
14 Top bolt

8 Front forks: examination and renovation

1   The parts most likely to wear over an extended period of service are the internal surfaces of the lower leg and the outer surfaces of the fork stanchion or tube. If there is excessive play between these two parts they must be replaced as a complete unit. Check the fork tube for scoring over the length which enters the oil seal. Bad scoring here will damage the oil seal and lead to fluid leakage.

2   It is advisable to renew the oil seals when the forks are dismantled even if they appear to be in good condition. This will save a strip-down of the forks at a later date if oil leakage occurs. The oil seal in the top of each lower leg is retained by an internal C-ring which can be prised out of position with a small screwdriver. Check that the dust excluder rubbers are not split or worn where they bear on the fork tube. A worn excluder will allow the ingress of dust and water which will damage the oil seal and eventually cause wear of the fork tube.

3   It is not generally possible to straighten forks which have been badly damaged in an accident, particularly when the correct jigs are not available. It is always best to err on the side of safety and fit new ones, especially since there is no easy means to detect whether the forks have been over stressed or metal fatigued. Fork stanchions (tubes) can be checked, after removal from the lower legs, by rolling them on a dead flat surface. Any misalignment will be immediately obvious.

4   The fork springs will take a permanent set after considerable usage and will need renewal if the fork action becomes spongy. The length of the fork springs should be checked against the figures given in the Specifications Section.

5   The damping action of the forks is governed by the viscosity of the oil in the fork legs, and the recommended types and capacities are given in the Specifications at the beginning of this Chapter. Note that when the fork is being topped up or the damping oil changed, slightly less oil will be needed. It is recommended that a piece of wire is used as a dipstick in these cases, and the oil level measured from the top of the fork stanchion. Given that the initial oil capacity is correct it will be possible to translate this to a known oil level, and subsequent refills and experiments in oil level changes can be made on this basis.

6   It is possible to increase or reduce the damping effect by using a different oil grade, and some owners may wish to experiment a little to find a grade which suits their particular application. It is advisable to consult a Honda Service Agent who will be able to suggest which oils may be used.

7   It should be remembered that in the UK machines with leaking fork seals or fork stanchions pitted badly enough to cause damage to fork seals in the future, and thereby cause a reduction in damping efficiency will be failed as unroadworthy when submitted for the annual MOT certificate.

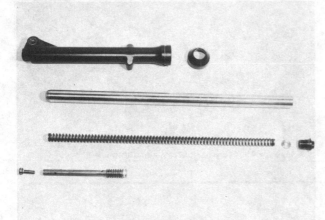

8.1a Front fork components – MB50

8.1b Check that the oil passages in the damper rod are clean and free from obstructions

8.2a To remove fork seals displace the retaining circlip ...

8.2b ... and prise the seal out with a suitable screwdriver

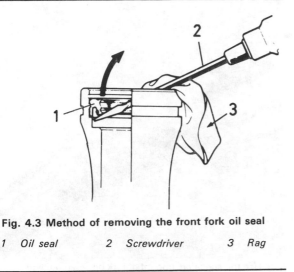

Fig. 4.3 Method of removing the front fork oil seal

1   Oil seal   2   Screwdriver   3   Rag

9   Front forks: reassembly of the fork legs

1   All of the fork leg components should be completely clean and free from dust or oil prior to reassembly. Remember that the forks are in constant motion in use, and any abrasive particles will quickly wear away the surface against which they are trapped. If new seals are required they should be fitted at this stage. A large diameter socket can be used to drive the new seal into position. Lubricate the seal lip with grease.

2   Fit the damper assembly and rebound spring into the stanchion. Feed the stanchion into the lower leg, taking care not to damage the seal. Check that the damper bolt threads are clean and dry, then coat them with Loctite. Fit the damper bolt and tighten it to 0.8 – 1.2 kgf m (6.0 – 9.0 lbf ft).

3   Slide the dust seal into position, ensuring that it locates correctly. It is worthwhile wiping some grease around the outside of the oil seal before the dust seal is fitted. This will ensure that corrosion and scoring are prevented. Fit the fork spring with the closer-spaced coils upwards. Carefully fill the fork leg with the specified amount of oil. On MB50 models fit and tighten the threaded top plug to retain the spring. On MT50 and MB50 (US) models the top bolt can now be fitted and tightened to the specified torque setting. On the MB50 (UK) model the bolt should be left until the fork legs are replaced in the yokes.

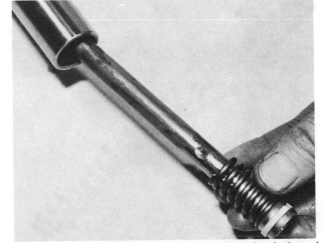

9.2a Front fork reassembly – insert the damper rod and rebound spring into the stanchion ...

9.2b ... carefully slide the stanchion into the lower leg ...

9.2c ... and replace the damper bolt. Tighen securely

9.3a Replace the dust seal

9.3b Ensure that the fork spring is fitted with the closer spaced coils to the top

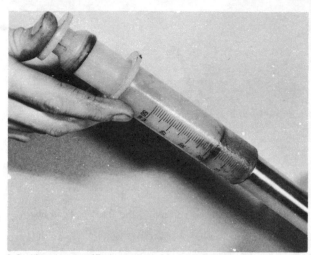

9.3c Use the specified amount of fork oil when refilling

9.3d Replace the threaded top plug – MB50

9.3e ... or the top bolt – MT50

10 Front forks: refitting the fork legs

1   Replace the front forks by following in reverse the dismantling procedures described in Section 3 of this Chapter. Before fully tightening the front wheel spindle clamps and the fork yoke pinch bolts, bounce the forks several times to ensure they work freely and are clamped in their original settings. Complete the final tightening from the wheel spindle clamp upwards.

2   Do not forget to add the recommended quantity of fork damping oil to each leg before the bolts in the top of each fork leg are replaced.

3   If the fork stanchions prove difficult to re-locate through the fork yokes, make sure their outer surfaces are clean and polished so that they will slide more easily. It is often advantageous to use a screwdriver blade to open up the clamps as the stanchions are pushed upward into position.

4   As the fork legs are fed through the yokes they will correct any slight misalignment between them should the steering head have been dismantled. Where appropriate, tighten the steering stem top nut and complete the fitting of the various ancillary components. The top of the stanchion should be flush with the top surface of the yoke.

5   Before taking the machine out on the road, make a thorough test of the brakes and suspension action, and ensure that all nuts and bolts are securely fastened. Check the adjustment of handlebar controls and that all electrical equipment functions properly.

11 Frame assembly: examination and renovation

1   If the machine is stripped for a complete overhaul, this affords a good opportunity to inspect the frame for cracks or other damage which may have occurred in service. Check the top of the front downtube and the front of the top tube where it joins the steering head, the two points where fractures are most likely to occur. The straightness of the tubes concerned can show whether the machine has been involved in a previous accident.

2   Check carefully areas where corrosion has occurred on the frame. Corrosion can cause a reduction in the material thickness and should be removed by use of a wire brush and derusting agents. Finish off by very carefully repainting the area concerned.

3   If the frame is broken or bent, professional attention is required. Repairs of this nature should be entrusted to a competent repair specialist, who will have available all the necessary jigs and mandrels to preserve correct alignment. Repair work of this nature can prove expensive and it is always worthwhile checking whether a good replacement frame of identical type can be obtained at a reasonable cost.

4   Remember that a frame which is in any way damaged or out of alignment will cause, at the very least, handling problems. Complete failure of a main frame component could well lead to a serious accident.

12 Rear suspension units: removal, examination and reassembly

1   The models featured in this manual are equipped with coil spring suspension units being oil-filled damper assemblies. The units are mounted at a steep angle to provide maximum rear wheel travel.

2   It is best to remove and attend to one unit at a time, because this will allow the machine to be supported by the remaining unit. Alternatively, place the machine on its centre stand or place blocks underneath the frame, so that the rear wheel is raised clear of the ground and the weight taken from the suspension units.

3   The units are retained by a nut at the top and a bolt at the bottom. Slacken and remove these and withdraw the unit.

4   Set the spring adjuster ring to the softest position. Clamp the unit's bottom mounting eye in a vice and enlist the aid of an assistant. With the assistant pulling the spring down, slip an open ended spanner over the slim locknut which secures the top mounting eye. Push a close fitting metal bar through the top mounting eye and use it to unscrew the top mounting from the damper shaft. Note that the assistant must keep the pressure firmly on the spring the whole time, and only release it gradually when the top mounting is removed. With the spring removed, withdraw the locknut and rebound rubber from the damper shaft, and the adjuster ring from the damper body. The parts should then be cleaned before examination.

5   Measure the free length of the spring, and renew it if it is below the service limit specified. The damper unit is sealed and cannot be dismantled. Its operation can be checked to some extent by compressing it and then extending it. The unit should show significant damping effect on rebound (extension) but much less under compression. Any signs of leakage will necessitate renewal of the damper units as a pair.

6   If the suspension units appear to be in need of renewal, thought should be given to fitting an improved proprietary replacement type. These may prove to be more expensive, but usually provide better control and durability. Most accessory shops will be able to advise and recommend the best make and type to use for any given application.

7   Reassembly of the units is a straightforward reversal of the dismantling sequence. When fitting the spring adjuster, set it at its safest position to ease spring compression. When the units have been refitted set the spring adjusters at the required setting, ensuring that the position of each adjuster matches the other.

8   Note that the top mountings have a slot in them which must face to the inside of the machine. Using a torque wrench carefully tighten the mounting nuts and bolts to the specified torque setting.

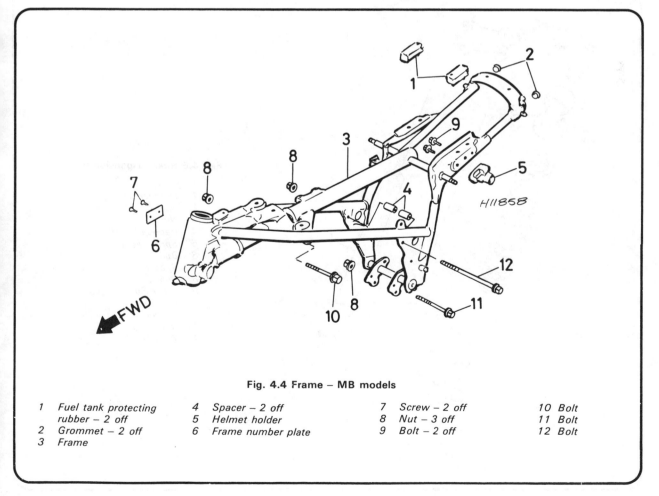

Fig. 4.4 Frame – MB models

1 Fuel tank protecting rubber – 2 off	4 Spacer – 2 off	7 Screw – 2 off	10 Bolt
2 Grommet – 2 off	5 Helmet holder	8 Nut – 3 off	11 Bolt
3 Frame	6 Frame number plate	9 Bolt – 2 off	12 Bolt

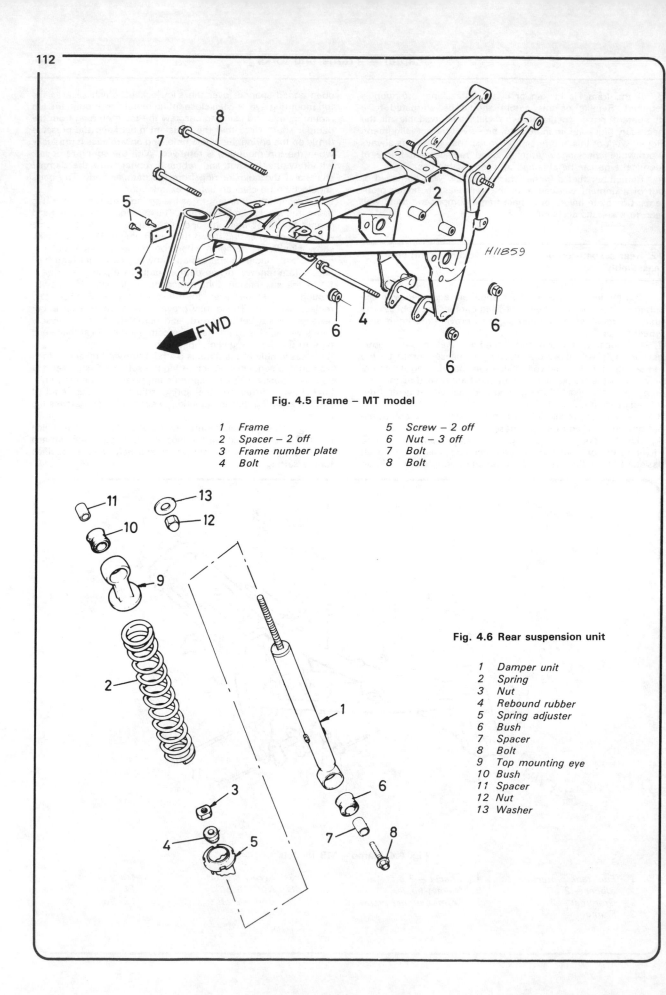

H11859

FWD

Fig. 4.5 Frame — MT model

1	Frame	5	Screw — 2 off
2	Spacer — 2 off	6	Nut — 3 off
3	Frame number plate	7	Bolt
4	Bolt	8	Bolt

Fig. 4.6 Rear suspension unit

1 Damper unit
2 Spring
3 Nut
4 Rebound rubber
5 Spring adjuster
6 Bush
7 Spacer
8 Bolt
9 Top mounting eye
10 Bush
11 Spacer
12 Nut
13 Washer

13 Swinging arm: removal, examination, renovation and refitting

1   Any wear in the swinging arm pivot bushes will cause imprecise handling of the machine, with a tendency for the rear end of the machine to twitch or hop. To check this, place the machine with the rear wheel clear of the ground, either using the centre stand or a strong wooden box under the engine. Grasp the frame firmly with one hand and the fork end of the swinging arm with the other. Try to move the swinging arm from side-to-side in a horizontal direction. Any play in the bushes should be immediately apparent at the swinging arms pivot. If there is any movement at all, the swinging arm must be removed and the bushes replaced.

2   To remove the swinging arm, the rear wheel must first be removed. See Section 13 of Chapter 5. Slacken and remove the bolts securing the bottom mountings of the suspension units, and tie the units to the frame with a length of string so that they are held clear of the swinging arm. Slacken and remove the two bolts securing the chain guard and withdraw this. Slacken and remove the swinging arm pivot bolt nut. Withdraw the pivot bolt. It may be necessary to use a hammer and long metal drift to tap the bolt out. Remove the swinging arm.

3   Carefully clean the swinging arm, pivot bolt and the area of frame around the pivot. Check very closely for signs of cracking or bending and for any corrosion. See Section 11 of this Chapter for details of remedial action. If the bushes are known to be worn, they must now be renewed. The bonded rubber bushes, as used on the MB/MT50, are notoriously difficult to remove, and two possible methods of removal are suggested.

4   The first method is shown in the accompanying photograph: it consists of a two-legged hydraulic puller adapted to suit this operation. Place against the one bush a thick steel washer with an outside diameter the same as that of the bush outer sleeve. This will ensure that the pressure is applied in the correct place, against the sleeve, and not against the rubber which would only distort and eventually shear. Position the tool as shown in the photograph and press out the two bushes and central spacer, treating them as a complete unit, far enough for the central spacer to be displaced. The tool can then be positioned on each swinging arm lug in turn, and the separate bushes pressed out individually.

5   As it is not likely that an hydraulic puller will be available an alternative method is suggested which uses much less expensive equipment. For this alternative method, it is necessary to fabricate a tool with which to press the bushes out of their housings. It is suggested that a tool similar to the one shown in the accompanying diagram is made, utilising a short length of thick-walled tube, the inside diameter of which is slightly larger than the outside diameter of the bush, a high tensile bolt and

nut, and two thick plate washers, one of which has an outer diameter slightly smaller than that of the bush. It would be best if two bolts were employed, one long enough to pass through the full width of the swinging arm and one shorter one which can be used to remove each bush from its lug as a separate unit. Assemble the tool as shown in the illustration with the long bolt passing through both bushes and the central spacer. Tighten the nut down and press out the two bushes and central spacer, treating them as a complete unit, far enough for the central spacer to be displaced. The tool should then be dismantled, the spacer removed and the tool assembled again, using the short bolt, on each of the swinging arm lugs in turn. Once a bush has been freed, it should be comparatively easy to carry on and remove it completely.

6   If, due to corrosion between the mating faces of the bush and swinging arm lug, the bushes are reluctant to move, even using this method, it is recommended that the unit be returned to a Honda Service Agent whose expertise can be brought to bear on the problem. Note that, as a means of removal, attempting to drive the bushes out will probably prove unsuccessful, because the rubber will effectively damp out the driving force, and damage to the lugs may occur.

7   New bushes may be driven in using a tubular drift against the outer sleeve, or by reversing the removal operation, using the fabricated puller. Whichever method is adopted, the outer sleeve should be lubricated sparingly, and care must be taken to ensure that the bush remains square with the housing bore. The swinging arm must be properly supported whilst doing this. Ensure that the central spacer is located correctly before the bushes are in their final positions otherwise fitting the spacer will be impossible.

8   On reassembly liberally grease the pivot bolt and the inside diameter of the bushes and central spacer. This will minimise wear on the pivot bolt and also prevent corrosion. Replace the swinging arm in the frame, push the pivot bolt through from left to right and hand tighten the pivot bolt nut. Untie the rear suspension units and lower them into place, fit the mounting bolts and tighten them. Using a torque wrench, tighten the swinging arm pivot bolt nut and suspension unit bottom mounting bolts to the respective torque settings given in the specifications Section of this Chapter. It is important that the pivot bolt is not tightened until the swinging arm is in its normal working position. This minimises the distortion of the rubber bushes which might otherwise occur, thus producing premature wear.

9   The remainder of the reassembly procedure is a straightforward reversal of the removal sequence. Before taking the machine out on the road, check the rear brake, suspension action and chain adjustment, and that all nuts and bolts are secure.

13.2a Remove the chainguard front mounting bolt ...

13.2b ... and the rear mounting bolt

13.2c Remove the suspension unit bottom mounting bolts ...

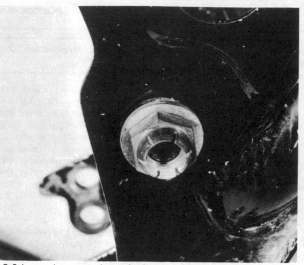

13.2d ... and remove the swinging arm pivot bolt nut

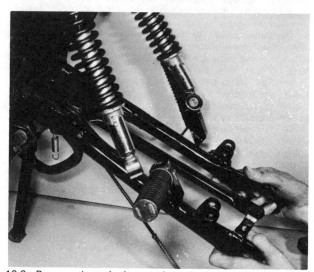

13.2e Remove the swinging arm from the frame

13.3 Carefully examine the swinging arm and bushes for wear or damage

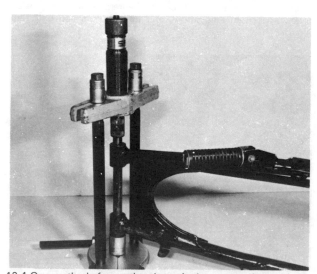

13.4 One method of removing the swinging arm bushes

13.9 Ensure that the inner edge of the chainguard is correctly located in its clip

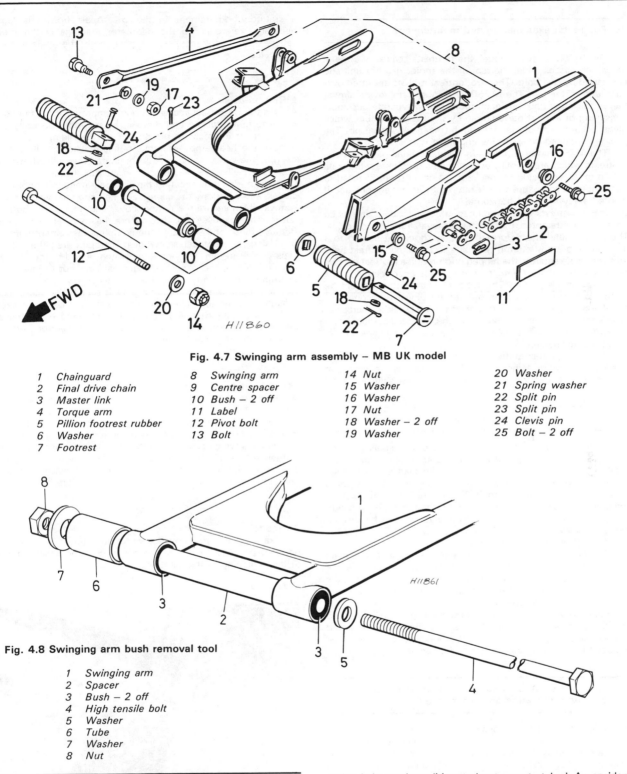

Fig. 4.7 Swinging arm assembly – MB UK model

1	Chainguard	8	Swinging arm	14	Nut
2	Final drive chain	9	Centre spacer	15	Washer
3	Master link	10	Bush – 2 off	16	Washer
4	Torque arm	11	Label	17	Nut
5	Pillion footrest rubber	12	Pivot bolt	18	Washer – 2 off
6	Washer	13	Bolt	19	Washer
7	Footrest				

20	Washer
21	Spring washer
22	Split pin
23	Split pin
24	Clevis pin
25	Bolt – 2 off

Fig. 4.8 Swinging arm bush removal tool

1 Swinging arm
2 Spacer
3 Bush – 2 off
4 High tensile bolt
5 Washer
6 Tube
7 Washer
8 Nut

14 Stands: examination and maintenance

1 The prop stand, or side stand, consists of a steel leg attached to the left-hand side of the frame by means of a pivot bolt which passes through a frame lug. An extension spring holds the stand in a horizontal, retracted position when not in use.

2 Check that the pivot bolt Is secured and that the extension spring is in good condition and not overstretched. An accident is almost certain if the stand extends whilst the machine is on the move.

3 The centre stand is secured by a tubular, headed pivot shaft which is retained in turn by a split pin. The stand should be removed occasionally, and the pivot shaft cleaned and regreased. Check that the return spring is in good condition and not likely to fall whilst the machine is in use. If stretched, cracked or badly rusted, the spring should be renewed.

15 Footrests: examination and maintenance

1   On the MB50 (UK) model, the footrests consist of a metal bar which passes under the rear of the engine/gearbox unit and is secured by two bolts. The two footrest rubbers are fitted over each end of the bar. The MB50 (US) model employs a similar bar as the mounting, but each footrest is a separate assembly consisting of a short bar covered by the footrest rubber which pivots on each end of the main bar by means of a clevis pin. The pins are retained by split-pins and plain washers.

2   The MT50 model employs individual cleated-pattern metal footrests which are pivoted by clevis pins on separate brackets bolted on to each side of the frame. A small spring is fitted to each footrest to ensure that it returns to its correct position if pivoted away from the horizontal.

3   If the footrests become damaged in an accident, it may be possible to straighten them after removal from the machine. The area around the deformed portion should be heated to a dull red before any attempt is made to bend the footrest back into shape. If required, the hinged portion of the footrest may be separated from the frame or bar bracket after removing the split-pin and clevis pin. The rubber, where fitted, should be removed prior to application of heat, for obvious reasons.

4   If there is evidence of failure of the metal either before or after straightening, it is advised that the damaged component is renewed. If a footrest breaks in service, loss of machine control is almost inevitable.

5   Refitting of the footrest assemblies is a reversal of the removal procedure. When refitting the clevis pin, ensure that the return spring is correctly located and a new split-pin fitted.

16 Rear brake pedal: examination and maintenance

1   On all models the rear brake pedal pivots on a plain shaft on the lower right-hand side of the frame and is secured by a plain washer and split-pin. On MB50 models the shaft is an extension of the centre stand pivot and so a certain amount of work is necessary to gain access to it. The exhaust system must be removed as described in Section 15 of Chapter 2. The stoplight switch spring and pedal return spring must then be disconnected followed by the brake rod itself. On MT50 models the brake pedal is much more exposed.

2   On all models withdraw the split pin, remove the plain washer and withdraw the brake pedal. Replacement is the reversal of the above procedure, but it is recommended that the shaft is well greased to prevent wear and corrosion, and that the retaining split pin is renewed.

3   Repair of the brake pedal is the same as given in Section 15 of this Chapter. Note that the warning that is given about footrest failure applies equally to the brake pedal, It should be replaced if there is any doubt as to its condition.

17 Speedometer and tachometer heads: removal, examination, renovation and reassembly

1   Before operations are described in detail, there are a few general observations to be made about these instruments. They must be carefully handled at all times and must never be dropped or held upside down. Dirt, oil, grease and water all have an equally adverse effect on them, and so a clean working area must be provided if they are to be removed.

2   The instrument heads are very delicate and should not be dismantled at home. In the event of a fault developing, the instrument should be entrusted to a specialist repairer or a new unit fitted. If a replacement unit is required it is well worth trying to obtain a good secondhand item from a motorcycle breaker in view of the high cost of a new instrument.

3   Remember that a speedometer in correct working order is

a statutory requirement in the UK. Apart from this legal necessity, reference to the odometer readings is the most satisfactory means of keeping pace with the maintenance schedules.

MB50 models

4   On the UK model access is greatly improved if the fairing is removed first. Slacken and remove the two bolts securing the headlamp. It is safest to disconnect the headlamp wires and remove the headlamp assembly, but is quicker to allow it to hang by the wires while work is completed on the instruments. Disconnect all wires leading to the instrument panel, slacken the two knurled nuts securing the speedometer and tachometer cables, and withdraw the cables. Slacken and remove the three screws which secure the bottom cover and remove the bottom cover. This exposes the two dome headed retaining nuts. Remove these and withdraw the complete instrument panel.

5   Using an electrical screwdriver, carefully free the plastic clips which retain the ignition switch and lift the switch upwards out of the panel. Taking great care not to invert the instrument panel any more than is necessary, free the four plastic clips, one at each corner, which secure the instrument mounting to the top cover and remove the top cover. Slacken and remove the two retaining screws to remove whichever instrument is required. Replacement is a straightforward reversal of the removal sequence.

MT50 models

6   Removal is covered in the relevant part of Section 4 of this Chapter. Remove the speedometer from the headlamp assembly by removing the three retaining screws. Remove the ignition switch by using an electrical screwdriver to free the plastic clips which secure it to the speedometer assembly. No further stripping is possible as the speedometer is supplied complete with its housing for this model. Replacement is a straightforward reversal of the removal procedure.

All models

7   Examination and renovation of the instrument heads is not normally possible for the private owner. See the general notes at the beginning of this Section.

17.5a Use a suitable screwdriver to free the four plastic clips ...

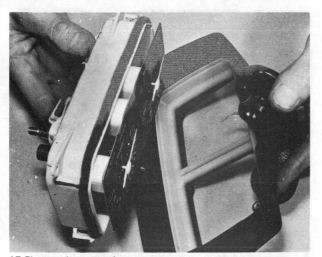

17.5b ... and remove the top cover

17.5c Remove the two retaining screws ...

17.5d ... and withdraw the instrument

18 Speedometer and tachometer drive cables: examination and maintenance

1   If the operation of the speedometer or tachometer becomes sluggish or jerky it can often be attributed to a damaged or kinked drive cable. Remove the cable from the machine by releasing the locating screw at the lower end and the knurled ring at the instrument head. Turn the inner cable to check for any tight spots. If the cable tends to snatch as it is rotated it is likely that the inner has become kinked and will require renewal.
2   Check that the outer cable is in sound condition with no obvious damage. The inner and outer cables are available separately where necessary. When fitting a new cable or refitting an old one, remove the inner and grease all but the upper six inches or so. This will ensure that the cable is adequately lubricated without incurring the risk of grease working up into the instrument head. Ensure that the cable is routed in a smooth path between the drive gearbox and instrument panel, avoiding any tight bends which would result in the cable becoming kinked.

19 Speedometer and tachometer drives: location and examination

MB50
1   The speedometer drive gearbox is situated on the left-hand side of the front wheel hub. It is a single component which cannot be stripped easily. Note that there are no parts available to recondition it and any damage or malfunction can only be corrected by renewing the gearbox. The only maintenance required is that a small quantity of grease be packed into it whenever the front wheel is removed for wheel bearing examination or replacement.
2   The tachometer drive consists of a worm mechanism driven by the crankshaft through the balancer idler gear and a driven gear mounted vertically in the right-hand outer cover. This mechanism is lubricated by the gearbox oil and is fully enclosed, therefore requiring no maintenance at all. Again any damage or malfunction can only be corrected by renewing the parts concerned. Inspect the mechanism whenever the right-hand outer cover is removed.

MT50
3   The speedometer drive assembly is contained within the front wheel brake backplate and should be examined and repacked with grease whenever work is carried out on the wheel bearings or brake assembly.
4   To remove the main drive gear from its housing, place the brake backplate assembly, inner side uppermost, on a work surface. Remove the brake shoes and springs, as described in Section 11 of Chapter 5, and inspect the large dust seal for signs of damage or deterioration. To renew this seal, carefully lever it out of position using the flat of a screwdriver; great care must be taken not to damage the surrounding alloy casting. The new seal may be fitted after removal, examination and fitting of the drive gear assembly.
5   The main drive gear may now be withdrawn from the brake backplate housing; some difficulty may be experienced in withdrawal due to the gear being engaged with the worm drive gear and to the retentive qualities of the grease around the base of the gear. Note the position of the two thrust washers below the gear and remove them from the housing.
6   Remove all old grease from the drive gear, thrust washers, brake backplate housing and worm gear by wiping the components with a clean rag. Inspect the gears for broken teeth and signs of excessive wear due to lack of lubrication. If it is considered necessary to renew the worm drive gear, then the brake backplate assembly should be returned to an official

Honda Service Agent who will be able to remove and insert a new gear assembly.

7   Refit the two thrust washers into the brake backplate housing, followed by the main drive gear. Pack the housing with the recommended grease as these components are fitted. Fit a new dust seal, if required, into its recess in the brake backplate by pressing it into position evenly and squarely. The brake shoes and springs may now be refitted and the brake backplate assembly re-inserted into the wheel hub. Ensure that the speedometer drive tabs are aligned with the corresponding slots in the wheel hub boss.

8   There is, of course, no tachometer fitted to the MT50 model.

20 Fairing: MB50-UK model

1   The fairing fitted by Honda to these machines is a simple plastic moulding retained by two tubular brackets mounted on clamps to the upper fork stanchions. It has a transparent windscreen which is secured by seven rivets and is available separately if required.

2   Care and maintenance is restricted to ensuring that the mounting brackets are securely tightened and that the fairing is kept clean. See Section 22 for details of recommended cleaning.

21 Cleaning the machine

1   After removing all surface dirt with a rag or sponge which is washed frequently in clean water, the machine should be allowed to dry thoroughly. Application of car polish or wax to the cycle parts will give a good finish, particularly if the machine receives this attention at regular intervals.

2   The plated parts should require only a wipe with a damp rag, but if they are badly corroded, as may occur during the winter when the roads are salted, it is permissible to use one of the proprietary chrome cleaners. These often have an oily base which will help to prevent corrosion from recurring.

3   If the engine parts are particularly oily, use a cleaning compound such as Gunk or Jizer. Apply the compound whilst the parts are dry and work it in with a brush so that it has an opportunity to penetrate and soak into the film of oil and grease. Finish off by washing down liberally, taking care that water does not enter the carburettor, air cleaner or any of the electrical connectors.

4   If possible, the machine should be wiped down immediately after it has been used in the wet, so that it is not garaged under damp conditions which will promote rusting. Make sure that the chain is wiped and re-oiled, to prevent water from entering the rollers and causing harshness with an accompanying rapid rate of wear. Remember there is less chance of water entering the control cables and causing stiffness if they are lubricated regularly as described in the Routine Maintenance Section.

5   The matt black finish on the engine casings will tend to wear through or chip over a period of time. It can be restored with one of the proprietary aerosol paints, but care must be taken to ensure that a heat resistant paint is chosen.

22 Cleaning the plastic mouldings

1   The moulded plastic cycle parts, which include the front and rear mudguards, the sidepanels and number plate assemblies,

19.7 Ensure the speedometer drive is packed with fresh grease and that the seal is in good condition

20.1 Slacken and remove the two dome-headed nuts to remove the fairing

need treating in a different manner than normal metal cycle parts.

2   These plastic parts will not respond to cleaning in the same way as painted metal parts; their construction may be adversely affected by traditional cleaning and polishing techniques, and lead as a result, to the surface finish deteriorating. It is best to wash these parts with a household detergent solution, which will remove oil and grease in a most effective manner.

3   Avoid the use of scouring powder or other abrasive cleaning agent because this will score the surface of the mouldings making them more receptive to dirt, and permanently damaging the surface finish.

Chapter 5 Wheels, brakes and tyres

For modifications and information relating to later models, see Chapter 7

Contents

Specifications

Wheels

	MB models	MT models
Type	3-spoke Comstar	Wire spoked, steel rims

Brakes

Type:	MB models	MT models
Front	Hydraulic disc	Single leading shoe
Rear	Single leading shoe	Single leading shoe

	All models	
Disc thickness	3.8 – 4.2 mm (0.150 – 0.165 in)	
Wear limit	3.0 mm (0.118 in)	
Disc runout	0.0 – 0.15 mm (0.0 – 0.006 in)	
Wear limit	0.3 mm (0.012 in)	
Drum ID	110.0 mm (4.33 in)	
Wear limit	111.0 mm (4.37 in)	
Lining thickness	4.0 mm (0.16 in)	
Wear limit	2.0 mm (0.08 in)	

Tyres

	MB models	MT models
Front	2.50 – 18 4PR	2.50 – 19 4PR
Rear	2.50 – 18 6PR	3.00 – 16 6PR

Tyre pressures

Solo:	MB models	MT models
Front	25 psi (1.75 kg/cm^2)	21 psi (1.5 kg/cm^2)
Rear	32 psi (2.25 kg/cm^2)	21 psi (1.5 kg/cm^2)
Pillion:		
Front	25 psi (1.75 kg/cm^2)	21 psi (1.5 kg/cm^2)
Rear	40 psi (2.8 kg/cm^2)	40 psi (2.8 kg/cm^2)

Torque wrench settings

	kgf m	lbf ft
Brake disc bolts	2.7 – 3.3	20 – 24
Sprocket nuts	5.5 – 6.5	40 – 47
Brake hose bolts	2.5 – 3.5	18 – 25

Brake caliper/bracket top mounting bolt	2.0 – 2.5	14 – 18
Brake caliper bracket/fork leg bolts	2.4 – 3.0	17 – 22
Brake pad pin bolts	1.5 – 2.0	11 – 14
Rear brake torque arm mounting bolts	1.8 – 2.5	13 – 18

1 General description

The wheels fitted to the Honda MB50 models are of Comstar type. Each wheel consists of three pairs of aluminium alloy spokes bolted to a light alloy hub at the centre, and riveted to a chromed steel rim on the outside. The rims carry 2.50-18 tyres both at the front and at the rear. The front brake disc is bolted to the front hub and is acted on by a hydraulically operated caliper. The rear drum brake is rod operated.

The Honda MT50 model employs conventional wire spoked wheels with a full-width brake drum at front and rear and chromed steel rims, the front being of 19 inch diameter and the rear 16 inch. The tyres are 2.50 section front and 3.00 rear, and employ the current semi-knobbly trail pattern. The brakes are cable operated at the front and rod operated at the rear.

2 Front wheel: examination and renovation

1 Place the machine on its centre stand so that the front wheel is clear of the ground. Spin the wheel by hand and check the rim for alignment, noting that the service limit is 2.0 mm (0.08 in). Small irregularities can be corrected by tightening the spokes in the affected area. Any flats in the wheel rim will be evident at the same time. In this latter case it will be necessary to have the wheel rebuilt with a new rim. The machine should not be run with a deformed wheel since this will have a very adverse effect on handling.

2 Check for loose or broken spokes. Tapping the spokes is a good guide to the correct tension; a loose spoke will always produce a different sound and should be tightened by turning the nipple in an anti-clockwise direction. Always check for runout by spinning the wheel again. If the spokes have to be tightened by an excessive amount, it is advisable to remove the tyre and tube as soon as detailed in Section 18 of this Chapter. This will enable the protruding ends of the spokes to be ground off, thus preventing them from chafing the inner tube and causing punctures.

3 The Comstar wheels differ in that they are built up with pressed spokes riveted to the hub and rim. As such, the wheel must be considered a single unit, as Honda do not offer any form of rebuilding facility. A number of private engineering shops offer this service, but it must be noted that Honda do not approve of this course of action.

4 Spin the wheel and check for rim alignment by placing a pointer close to the rim edge. If the total radial or axial alignment variation is greater than 2.00 mm (0.08 in) the manufacturers recommend that the wheel is renewed. This policy is, however, a counsel of perfection and in practice a larger runout may not affect the handling properties excessively. As remarked upon earlier, repair of a damaged wheel is not possible; the wheel must be renewed.

5 Check the rim for localised damage in the form of dents or cracks. The existence of even a small crack renders the wheel unfit for further use unless it is found that a permanent repair is possible using arc-welding. This method of repair is highly specialised and therefore the advice of a wheel specialist should be sought.

6 Inspect the spoke blades for cracking and security. Check carefully the area immediately around the rivets which pass through the spokes and into the rim. In certain circumstances where steel spokes are fitted electrolytic corrosion may occur between the spokes, rivets and rim due to the use of different metals.

3 Front wheel: removal and refitting

MB50

1 Place the machine on its centre stand and support the front wheel clear of the ground with a wooden block under the engine. Slacken and remove the screw retaining the speedometer cable and withdraw the cable. Remove the split pin from the wheel spindle nut and unscrew the nut. Remove the wheel spindle. It may be necessary to use a hammer and soft metal drift gently to tap out the spindle. Withdraw the front wheel. Wedge a piece of wood between the brake pads to prevent ejection of the caliper piston should the front brake lever be inadvertently applied while the wheel is removed.

2 Refitting is a straightforward reversal of the removal procedure. Guide the brake disc carefully between the brake pads to avoid damage. Make sure that the wheel spindle is clean and completely free of corrosion, then grease it lightly before fitting to ease dismantling in the future. Ensure that the speedometer drive gearbox is correctly located on the driving piece in the hub, and ensure that the cable mounting boss is located correctly against the lug on the fork lower leg. Tighten the wheel spindle nut to the appropriate torque setting given in the Specifications Section of Chapter 4. Replace the split pin with a new one and spread its ends correctly. Lastly apply the front brake lever repeatedly until the pads are moved back against the disc and full lever pressure is restored, check for free front wheel rotation, for correct speedometer operation, and that the front brake works properly.

MT50

3 Place the machine on a strong wooden box or similar support to hold the front wheel clear of the ground. Slacken and remove the screw retaining the speedometer cable and withdraw the cable. Disconnect the front brake cable by slackening the adjuster locknut, whereupon the cable can gently be pulled clear of the adjuster bracket and the cable end nipple can be disengaged from the operating arm. Slacken and remove the wheel spindle nut and, using a spanner on the right-hand end of the spindle, unscrew the spindle. Once the threaded part of the spindle is clear of the left-hand lower leg it may be necessary gently to tap out the spindle by using a hammer and soft metal drift. Withdraw the front wheel.

4 Refitting is a straightforward reversal of the removal procedure. Ensure that the speedometer drive tabs in the brake backplate are aligned with the corresponding slots in the wheel hub boss and align the groove in the brake backplate with the lug on the left-hand lower fork leg when replacing the wheel. Make sure that the wheel spindle is clean and completely free from corrosion, then grease it lightly before fitting to ease dismantling in the future. Push it through the right-hand lower fork leg and the wheel hub and tighten it by hand only, at first, in the left-hand lower fork leg. Connect the front brake cable again and apply the brake lever hard to centralise the brake shoes and backplate with the brake drum. While keeping firm pressure on the brake lever, tighten the wheel spindle by the hexagon on its right-hand end to 5.5 – 6.5 kgf m (40 – 47 lbf ft). Replace the wheel spindle nut and tighten this also to 5.5 – 6.5 kgf m (40 – 47 lbf ft). Replace the speedometer cable and tighten its retaining screw. Adjust the front brake as described in Section 11 of this Chapter. Finally check for free wheel rotation, for correct speedometer operation, and that the front brake works properly.

3.1a Slacken and remove the speedometer cable retaining screw ...

3.1b ... in order to remove the speedometer cable

3.2a Ensure that the speedometer drive butts against the lug on the lower fork leg ...

3.2b ... before tightening the spindle nut. Note the use of a new split pin

3.3a Slacken and remove the speedometer cable retaining screw – MT50

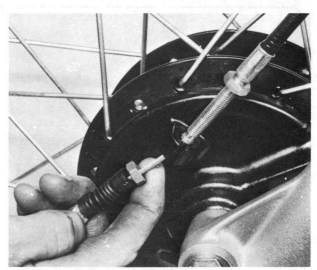

3.3b Remove the front brake cable

3.4a Align speedometer drive tabs with the slots on the wheel hub boss

3.4b Lug on lower fork leg must engage in the groove in the brake backplate

3.4c Push spindle through the hub and screw it into the left-hand fork lower leg

3.4d Centralise brake shoes before tightening wheel spindle and spindle nut

Fig. 5.1 Front wheel – MB models

1   Wheel
2   Tyre
3   Inner tube
4   Rim tape
5   Brake disc
6   Bolt – 3 off
7   Right-hand spacer
8   Oil seal
9   Right-hand bearing
10 Centre spacer
11 Left-hand bearing
12 Speedometer drive plate
13 Dust seal
14 Speedometer gearbox

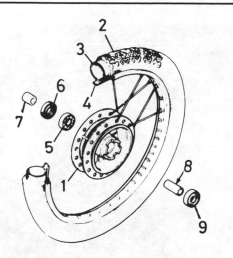

4 Front wheel bearings: removal, examination and refitting

1   Before the front wheel bearings can be examined, the front wheel must be removed as described in Section 3 of this Chapter. On the MB50 models, the speedometer drive gearbox must be withdrawn, followed by the oil seal and speedometer drive ring. Heat the end of an old flat-bladed screwdriver and bend the tip into a slightly curved shape with no sharp edges. This will give a useful tool for levering out the oil seal without damaging the sealing lip or the spring beneath it. The spacer and dust seal on the disc side of the hub can then be withdrawn, if desired, in a similar manner, or they can be driven out with the bearings. For MT50 models the brake backplate must be withdrawn. The dust seal and spacer on the opposite side of the hub can be removed as described above or driven out with the bearings as desired.

2   Although the two types of hub are vastly dissimilar in external appearance, they are essentially the same in design. Bearing removal procedure is the same in both cases. Support the wheel firmly on two wooden blocks as close to the hub centre as possible to prevent distortion, ensuring that enough space is allowed to permit bearing removal. Place the end of a small flat-ended drift against the upper face of the lower bearing and tap the bearing downwards out of the wheel hub. The spacer located between the two bearings may be moved sideways slightly in order to allow the drift to be positioned against the face of the bearing. Move the drift around the face of the bearing whilst drifting it out of position, so that the bearing leaves the hub squarely. The end spacer and dust seal will be driven out along with the bearing.

3   With the one bearing removed, the wheel may be lifted and the spacer withdrawn from the hub. Invert the wheel and remove the second bearing, using a similar procedure to that used for the first.

4   Wash the bearings thoroughly in clean petrol to remove all traces of the old grease. Check the bearing tracks and balls for wear or pitting or damage to the hardened surfaces. A small amount of side movement in the bearing is normal but no radial movement should be detectable. Check the bearings for play and roughness when they are spun by hand. All used bearings will emit a small amount of noise when spun but they should not chatter or sound rough. If there is any doubt about the condition of the bearings they should be renewed.

5   Carefully clean the bearing recesses in the hub and the centre space of the hub. All traces of the old grease, which may be contaminated with dirt, must be removed. Examine the oil seals which are removed and renew them if any damage or wear is found.

6   Before replacing the bearings pack them with high melting point grease. This applies equally to the original bearings, if

Fig. 5.2 Front wheel – MT model

1   Hub
2   Tyre
3   Inner tube
4   Rim tape
5   Right-hand bearing
6   Oil seal
7   Right-hand spacer
8   Centre spacer
9   Left-hand bearing

refitted, and to new ones, if the originals are to be replaced. With the wheel firmly supported on the two wooden blocks, tap a bearing into place in the hub noting that the sealed surface must face outwards. Use a hammer and a tubular metal drift or socket spanner which bears only on the outer race of the bearing to drive the bearing into position. If the inner race or sealed surface of the bearing is used to drive it into place, severe damage will be done to the bearing due to the high side loadings thus imposed.

7   Once one bearing has been installed, invert the wheel, fit the central spacer and pack the remaining space no more than $\frac{2}{3}$ full of grease. This is important as although some grease must be present, it will expand when hot and if too much grease is in the centre space, it will force its way past the seals and out onto the brake components. Once the grease is packed in, fit the second bearing in the same manner as the first. The dust-seal in the right-hand side of the hub can be pressed into position by hand. The wheel spacer can then be greased and pushed into the dust seal.

8   On MB50 models the speedometer drive ring should now be fitted, ensuring that the drive tangs are located in the slots provided for them in the hub. Use a hammer and a tubular drift or socket spanner which bears on the outside diameter of the oil seal to drive the oil seal gently into position. Install the speedometer drive gearbox and fit the front wheel assembly back into the front forks as described in the relevant paragraphs of Section 3. On MT50 models replace the brake backplate in the hub and replace the front wheel in the forks as described in Section 3.

4.1a Remove the speedometer drive gearbox ...

4.1b ... and the oil seal to expose ...

4.1c ... the speedometer drive, which can then be lifted out

4.5 Replace the hub oil seals as necessary

4.6 Ensure that bearings are packed with fresh grease and that the sealed surfaces are in good condition

5 Front disc brake: general

1   As already mentioned, the front brake is of the hydraulically-operated disc type. It should be noted that a number of precautions should be taken when dealing with this system, because brake failure can have disastrous consequences.

2   The hydraulic system must be kept free from air bubbles. Any air in the system will be compressed when the brake lever is operated instead of transmitting braking effort to the disc. It follows that efficiency will be impaired, and given sufficient air, this can render the brake inoperative. If any part of the hydraulic system is disturbed, the system must always be bled to remove any air. See Section 10 for details. It is vital that all hoses, pipes and unions are examined regularly and renewed if damage, deterioration or leakage is suspected.

3   Hydraulic fluid is specially formulated for given applcations, and must always be of the correct type. Any fluid conforming to SAE J1703 or DOT 3 may be used; other types may not be suitable. On no account should any other type of oil or fluid be used. Old or contaminated fluid must be discarded. It is dangerous to use old fluid which may have degraded to the point where it will boil in the caliper creating air bubbles in the system. Note that brake fluid will attack and discolour paintwork and plastics. Care must be taken to avoid contact and any accidental splashes washed off immediately.

4   Cleanliness is more important with hydraulic systems than in any other single area of the motorcycle. Dirt will rapidly destroy seals, allowing fluid to leak out or air to be drawn in. Water, even in the form of moist air, will be absorbed by the fluid which is hygroscopic. Fluid degraded by water has a lowered boiling point and can boil in use. The master cylinder and any cans of fluid must be kept securely closed to prevent this.

6 Front disc brake: examination, renovation, and pad removal

1   Check the front brake master cylinder, hose and caliper unit for signs of fluid leakage. Pay particular attention to the condition of the hose, which should be renewed without question if there are signs of cracking, splitting or other exterior damage.

Tyre changing sequence — tubed tyres

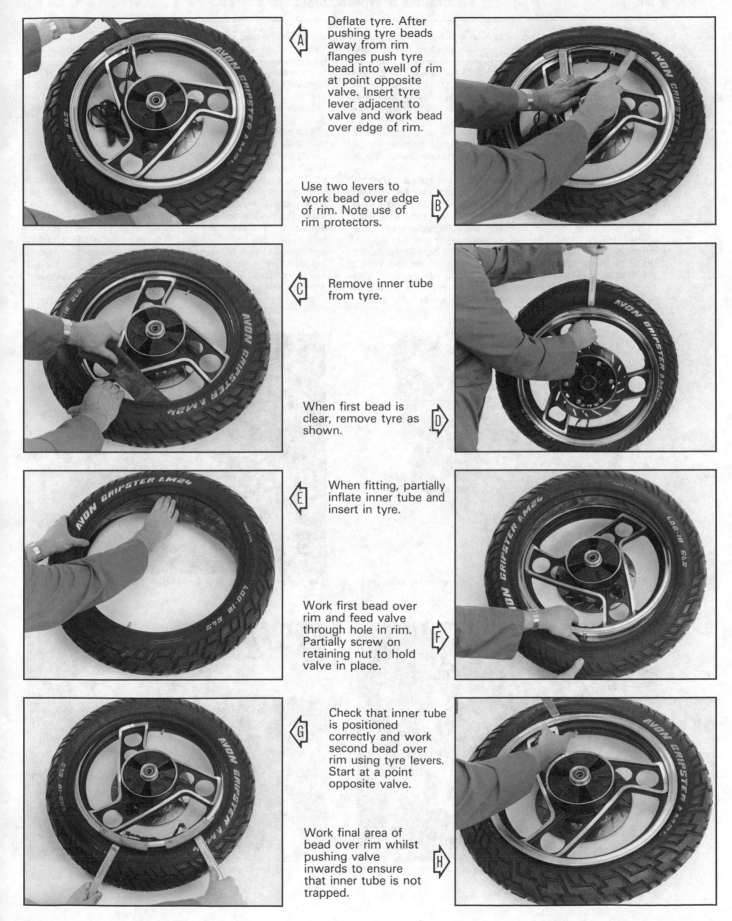

A Deflate tyre. After pushing tyre beads away from rim flanges push tyre bead into well of rim at point opposite valve. Insert tyre lever adjacent to valve and work bead over edge of rim.

B Use two levers to work bead over edge of rim. Note use of rim protectors.

C Remove inner tube from tyre.

D When first bead is clear, remove tyre as shown.

E When fitting, partially inflate inner tube and insert in tyre.

F Work first bead over rim and feed valve through hole in rim. Partially screw on retaining nut to hold valve in place.

G Check that inner tube is positioned correctly and work second bead over rim using tyre levers. Start at a point opposite valve.

H Work final area of bead over rim whilst pushing valve inwards to ensure that inner tube is not trapped.

2   Check the level of hydraulic fluid by viewing through the translucent reservoir. If the fluid is below the lower level mark, with the handlebars so placed that the reservoir is vertical, brake fluid of the correct grade should be added. The correct fluid should conform to SAE J1703 or DOT 3 (USA) specifications. **Never use engine oil** or any fluid other than that recommended. Other fluids have unsatisfactory characteristics and will rapidly destroy the seals.

3   The brake pads should be inspected for wear. Each has a red groove which marks the limit of the friction material. When this limit is reached, **both** pads must be renewed, even if only one has reached the wear mark.

4   The wear marks may be seen from above the caliper either in front or behind the fork lower leg. The pads may be removed by straightening the tabs of the lock washer and slackening the two pad retaining pin bolts. Slacken and remove the two brake caliper mounting bracket/lower fork leg bolts and withdraw the caliper. Using a broad-bladed screwdriver or small tyre lever, gently prise the pads apart to push the piston back and allow for the extra space necessary if the pads are to be renewed. Watch the fluid level in the master cylinder during this operation. If it has been overfilled, there will almost certainly be a spillage of fluid. Withdraw the two pin bolts and lock washer. Carefully withdraw the two pads, noting the position of the anti-squeal shim on the back of each, and the pad spring, noting carefully its position in the caliper.

5   Refitting the pads is a straightforward reversal of the removal procedure. Carefully locate the pad spring in the caliper with its centre projecting towards the pads, and ensure that the anit-squeal shims are fitted with their projecting tangs located over the outer edge of the pad. Refer to the accompanying photographs if in doubt. When replacing the pin bolts, ensure that their surfaces are clean and free from corrosion, and that they pass smoothly through the holes in each shim and pad. Great care is essential at this point. Do not tighten the bolts until the caliper is replaced on the fork lower leg. Tighten the pad retaining pin bolts to 1.5 – 2.0 kgf m (11 – 14 lbf ft) and bend the lock washer tabs against a convenient flat on the bolt head. Tighten the brake caliper mounting bracket/lower fork leg bolts to 2.4 – 3.0 kgf m (17 – 22 lbf ft). Apply the front brake lever repeatedly until the pads are moved back into firm contact with the disc and full lever pressure has been restored. Check the fluid level in the master cylinder and top up as necessary. If new pads have been fitted, they must be bedded in, using only light application of the lever, for approximately 100 miles.

6.3 Replace both pads when red groove (arrowed) is worn away

6.4a Flatten the tabs on the pad retaining bolt lock washer

6.4b Slacken and remove the two caliper mounting bracket/fork leg bolts ...

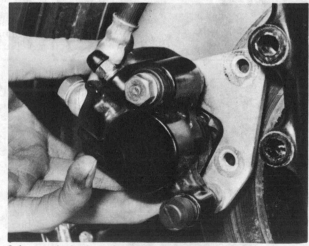

6.4c ... and withdraw the caliper assembly

6.4d Remove the two pad retaining pin bolts ...

6.4e ... and withdraw the brake pads

7 Front disc brake: removal, examination and replacement of the disc

1   It is unlikely that the disc will require attention until a considerable mileage has been covered, unless premature scoring or accidental damage has occurred. To remove the disc, detach the front wheel as described in Section 3 of this Chapter. The disc is bolted to the front wheel on the right-hand side by three bolts which pass into the hub. Replacement is a straight-forward reversal of this procedure, but the use of thread locking cement on the three mounting bolts is recommended. They must be tightened to the torque setting given in the specifications Section of this Chapter.

2   The brake disc can be checked for wear and for warpage while the front wheel is still in the machine. Using a micrometer, measure the thickness of the disc at the point of greatest wear. If the measurement is much less than the specified wear limit of 3.0 mm (0.118 in) the disc should be renewed. Check the warpage of the disc by setting up a suitable pointer close to the outer periphery of the disc and slowly spinning the front wheel. If the total warpage is more than 0.3 mm (0.012 in) the disc should be renewed. A warped disc, apart from reducing braking efficiency, is likely to cause juddering during braking and will also cause the brake to bind while it is not in use.

3   A lightly scored disc can be repaired by having it skimmed, but it should be noted that this work should only be entrusted to a reputable engineering firm who must be made aware of the specified minimum thickness if a ruined disc is not to result.

6.4f Note correct position of the pad spring before it is removed for cleaning

8 Front disc brake: overhauling the master cylinder

1   The master cylinder is unlikely to give trouble unless the machine has been stored for a long period or until a considerable mileage has been covered. The usual signs of trouble are leakage of fluid, causing a gradual fall in the fluid level and bad braking performance.

2   To gain access to the master cylinder, commence the dismantling operation by attaching a bleed tube to the caliper unit bleed valve. Open the bleed valve one complete turn, then operate the front brake lever until all the hydraulic fluid is pumped out of the reservoir. Close the bleed valve and remove the bleed tube.

3   Remove the banjo bolt and fluid hose from the end of the

7.2 The brake disc is removed by slackening the retaining bolts

master cylinder unit and remove the lever pivot bolt, the lever and the front brake switch. Detach the master cylinder from the handlebars by removing the two bolts and the securing clamp.

4   Access is now available to the piston and the cylinder and it is possible to remove the assembly, together with the relevant seals. Remove the circlip and sealing boot, followed by the next internal clip. The remainder of the components can be pushed out. Take note of the way in which the seals are fitted because they must be replaced in the same order and position. Failure to observe this necessity will result in brake failure.

5   Clean the master cylinder and piston with either hydraulic fluid or alcohol. On no account use abrasives or other solvents such as petrol. If any signs of damage or wear are evident, renewal is necessary. It is not practicable to reclaim either the piston or the cylinder bore.

6   Soak the new seals in hydraulic fluid for about 15 minutes prior to fitting, then reassemble the parts in exactly the same order, using the reversal of the dismantling procedure. Lubricate with hydraulic fluid and make sure the feathered edges of the seals are not damaged.

7   Refit the assembled master cylinder to the handlebars and reconnect the handlebar lever and hose. Refill the reservoir with hydraulic fluid and bleed the entire system by following the procedure described in Section 10 of this Chapter.

8   Check that the brake is working correctly before taking the machine on the road, to restore pressure and align the pads correctly. Use the brake gently for the first 50 miles or so to let the new components bed down correctly.

9   It should be emphasised that repairs to the master cylinder are best entrusted to a Honda Service Agent, or alternatively, that the defective parts should be replaced by a new unit. Dismantling and reassembly requires a certain amount of skill and it is imperative that the entire operation is carried out under surgically clean conditions.

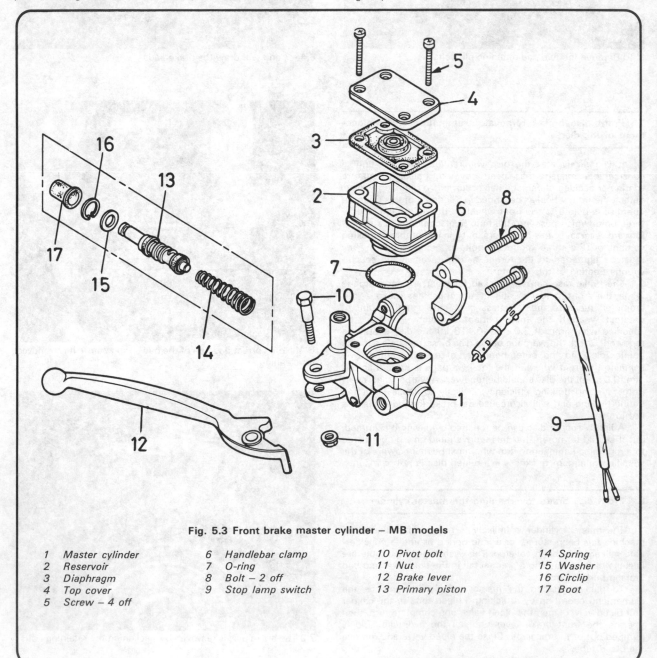

Fig. 5.3 Front brake master cylinder – MB models

1	Master cylinder	6	Handlebar clamp	10	Pivot bolt	14	Spring
2	Reservoir	7	O-ring	11	Nut	15	Washer
3	Diaphragm	8	Bolt – 2 off	12	Brake lever	16	Circlip
4	Top cover	9	Stop lamp switch	13	Primary piston	17	Boot
5	Screw – 4 off						

9 Front disc brake: overhauling the caliper unit

1   Front wheel removal is not necessary to gain access to the caliper. Straighten the tabs of the lock washer and slacken the two pad retaining pin bolts. Similarly slacken the single brake caliper/mounting bracket bolt and the two brake caliper mounting bracket/lower fork leg bolts. Very slightly slacken the brake hose banjo union bolt. Remove the two brake caliper mounting bracket/lower fork leg bolts and withdraw the caliper. Remove the pads as described in Section 6 of this Chapter. Remove the single brake caliper/mounting bracket bolt and withdraw the mounting bracket from the caliper. Apply the front brake lever gently to push the piston out of its housing in the caliper. Have a suitable container, such as a clean polythene bag, ready to catch the piston as it is pushed clear. Do not let it drop.

2   Once the piston is out of the caliper, slacken and remove the brake hose union bolt and allow the brake fluid to drain into a suitable container. Continue pumping the handlebar lever until all the fluid is drained. Remember that brake fluid is an excellent paint stripper, do not let it come into contact with any painted surface or any plastic. Remove the various seals from their bearings and prepare all the component parts of the caliper for cleaning and examination.

3   The parts removed should be cleaned thoroughly, using only brake fluid as the liquid. Petrol, oil or paraffin will cause the various seals to swell and degrade, and should not be used under any circumstances. When the various parts have been cleaned, they should be stored in polythene bags until re-assembly, so that they are kept dust free.

4   Examine the psiton for score marks or other imperfections. If it has any imperfections it must be renewed, otherwise air or hydraulic fluid leakage will occur, which will impair braking efficiency. With regard to the various seals, it is advisable to renew them all, irrespective of their appearance. It is a small price to pay against the risk of a sudden and complete front brake failure. Check the slider bolts for wear, together with the holes in the support bracket in which they slide. Wear at these points will cause brake judder and poor brake release.

5   Reassemble under clinically clean conditions, by reversing the dismantling procedure. Apply a very light smear of silicone grease to the piston seal in the caliper bore and to the dust-seal. Lubricate the caliper bore and piston with clean hydraulic fluid. Install the piston with its flat surface inwards, towards the caliper body. Before fitting the sleeve and lower bush, lubricate the mating surfaces between them and the caliper with silicone grease. Also grease the surfaces of the caliper/mounting bracket bolt and pin, to ensure smooth operation of the caliper. Check that the various external sealing rubbers are correctly fitted. Tighten the brake hose union bolt and all mounting bolts to the torque settings given in the specifications Section of this Chapter. Once reassembly is complete, bleed the system, as described in Section 10 of this Chapter and check that the brake is working properly before the machine is taken out on the road. Remember to wash away any surplus brake fluid from the area of the master cylinder or caliper, before it has a chance to do any damage to the finish.

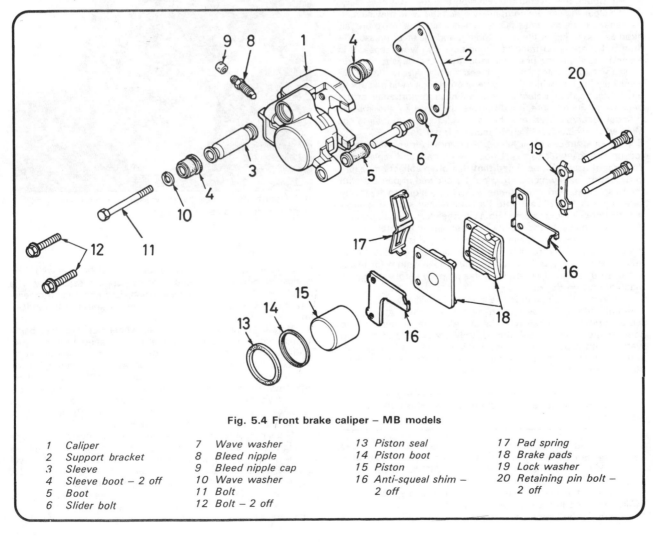

Fig. 5.4 Front brake caliper – MB models

1 Caliper	7 Wave washer	13 Piston seal	17 Pad spring
2 Support bracket	8 Bleed nipple	14 Piston boot	18 Brake pads
3 Sleeve	9 Bleed nipple cap	15 Piston	19 Lock washer
4 Sleeve boot – 2 off	10 Wave washer	16 Anti-squeal shim – 2 off	20 Retaining pin bolt – 2 off
5 Boot	11 Bolt		
6 Slider bolt	12 Bolt – 2 off		

10 Front disc brake: bleeding the hydraulic system

1   Removal of all the air from the hydraulic system is essential for the efficiency of the braking system. Air can enter the system due to leaks or when any part of the system has been dismantled for repair or overhaul. Topping up the system will not suffice, as air pockets will still remain, even small amounts causing dramatic loss of brake pressure.

2   Check the level in the reservoir, and fill almost to the top. Again, beware of spilling the fluid on to painted or plastic surfaces.

3   Place a clean jar below the brake caliper and attach a clear plastic tube from the caliper bleed screw to the container. Place some clean hydraulic fluid in the container so that the pipe is always immersed below the surface of the fluid. Ensure that the pipe is long enough to loop upwards slightly before it descends to the container. This will keep a small amount of brake fluid around the bleed nipple and make it easier to see air bubbles.

4   If the system is being refilled after a major overhaul, gently apply the front brake repeatedly until a measure of lever pressure is restored. Refill the reservoir if necessary. Keeping pressure on the brake lever, unscrew the bleed nipple far enough to release the pressure completely. This should be approximately $\frac{1}{4}$ - $\frac{1}{2}$ turn with a spanner. As soon as pressure is released, screw the bleed nipple in again. Release the lever gradually, wait a few seconds and repeat the operation again. A mixture of brake fluid and air bubbles should be seen in the clear tubing. Check the level in the reservoir and top up if necessary.

5   To clear the system completely of air, the cycle may have to be repeated many times. Only when there are no more air bubbles appearing in the clear tubing, and the lever pressure is firm and there is no trace of sponginess can work cease. It is essential to apply the brake lever gently, and always to build up pressure before releasing the bleed nipple. Always keep the lever fully applied while the nipple is open, or air will be sucked back through the nipple and work will have to start again at the beginning. Even more important is the level in the master cylinder reservoir. This must be kept well topped up if air is not allowed in which would again mean a fresh start.

6   When all traces of air have been removed from the system, top up the reservoir to the 'Upper' level mark and replace the diaphragm. It should be noted that this often collects moisture in its upper folds which should not be allowed in contact with the fresh brake fluid. It will be necessary, therefore, to dry it very carefully and fold it back into its compressed state whenever the master cylinder is topped up. With the clean, dry diaphragm correctly in place, fit the master cylinder cap and tighten its four securing screws. Check that the bleed nipple is tight, remove the clear tubing and replace the rubber bleed nipple cap. Wash off any surplus brake fluid, check the whole system for leaks, and ensure that the front brake works properly before taking the machine out on the road.

7   Brake fluid drained from the system will almost certainly be contaminated, either by foreign matter or more commonly by the absorption of water from the air. All hydraulic fluids are to some degree hygroscopic, that is, they are capable of drawing water from the atmosphere, and thereby degrading their specifications. In view of this, and the relative cheapness of the fluid, old fluid should always be discarded.

11 Front drum brake: examination, renovation and adjustment

1   The front brake assembly complete with the brake backplate can be withdrawn from the front wheel hub after removing the front wheel from the forks. With the wheel laid on a work surface, brake backplate uppermost, the brake backplate may be lifted away from the hub. It may come away quite easily, with the brake shoe assembly attached to its back.

2   Examine the condition of the brake linings. If they are thin

10.3 Equipment required for bleeding the hydraulic system

10.5 Ensure that the level in the master cylinder is kept well topped up during bleeding

or unevenly worn, the brake shoes should be renewed. The linings are bonded on and cannot be supplied separately. The linings are 4 mm (0.2 in) thick when new and should receive attention when worn to the wear limit thickness of 2 mm (0.1 in).

3   If fork oil or grease from the wheel bearings has badly contaminated the linings, the brake shoes should be renewed. There is no satisfactory way of degreasing the lining material.

4   Examine the drum surface for signs of scoring or oil contamination. Both of these conditions will impair braking efficiency. Remove all traces of dust, preferably using a brass wire brush, taking care not to inhale any of it, as it is of an asbestos nature, and consequently harmful. Remove oil or grease deposits, using a petrol soaked rag.

5   If deep scoring is evident, due to the linings having worn through to the shoe at some time, the drum must be skimmed on a lathe, or renewed. Whilst there are firms who will undertake to skim a drum whilst fitted to the wheel, it should be borne in mind that excessive skimming will change the radius of the drum in relation to the brake shoe, therefore reducing the friction area until extensive bedding in has taken place. Also full adjustment of the shoes may not be possible. If in doubt about

this, the advice of one of the specialist engineering firms who undertake this work should be sought.

6   Note that it is a false economy to try to cut corners with brake components; the whole safety of both machine and rider being dependent on their good condition.

7   Removal of the brake shoes is accomplished by folding the shoes together so that they form a 'V'. With the spring tension relaxed, both shoes and springs may be removed from the brake backplate as an assembly.

8   Before fitting the brake shoes, check that the brake operating cam is working smoothly and is not binding in its pivot. The cam can be removed by withdrawing the retaining bolt on the operating arm and pulling the arm off the shaft. Before removing the arm, it is advisable to mark its position in relation to the shaft, so that it can be relocated correctly. The shaft and arm should be already marked with a manufacturer's punch mark to indicate the correct relative positions of the two components. Lightly grease both the shaft and the faces of the operating cam and pivot prior to reassembly. Note that where a wear indicator is fitted over the splined end of the shaft, the plate should be aligned wtih the master spline on the shaft. Check the condition of the dust seal located beneath the indicator plate and renew it if considered necessary.

9   Before refitting existing shoes, roughen the lining surface sufficiently to break the glaze which will have formed in use. Glasspaper or emery cloth is ideal for this purpose but take care not to inhale any of the asbestos dust that may come from the lining surface.

10 Fitting the brake shoes and springs to the brake backplate is a reversal of the removal procedure Some patience will be needed to align the assembly with the pivot and operating cam whilst still retaining the springs in position; once they are correctly aligned though, they can be pushed back into position by pressing downwards in order to snap them into position. Do not use excessive force, or there is risk of distorting the brake shoes permanently.

11 Adjusting the front brake is best done with the front wheel free to rotate. Slacken the adjuster locknut on the brake backplate and spin the front wheel. Carefully screw the adjusting nut down until you hear the brake shoes come into contact with the brake drum. Turn the adjuster nut back by $\frac{1}{2}$–1 turn until the noise stops and tighten the locknut. Spin the wheel and apply the front brake hard once or twice to settle the brake and check that the adjustment has remained the same. This should give you 10 – 20 mm ($\frac{3}{8}$ – $\frac{3}{4}$ in) free play at the brake lever tip.

11.4 Examine brake drum for scoring or other damage

11.11 Adjust front brake by slackening locknut and turning adjusting nut as required

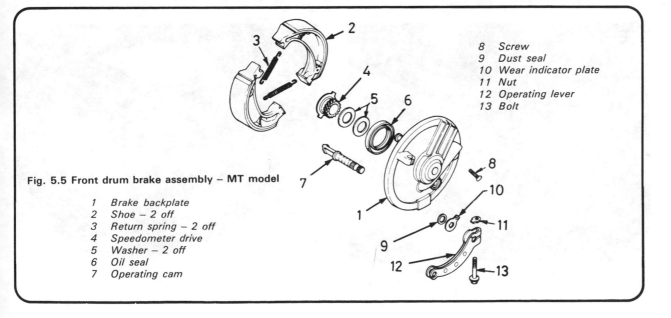

Fig. 5.5 Front drum brake assembly – MT model

1   Brake backplate
2   Shoe – 2 off
3   Return spring – 2 off
4   Speedometer drive
5   Washer – 2 off
6   Oil seal
7   Operating cam

8   Screw
9   Dust seal
10 Wear indicator plate
11 Nut
12 Operating lever
13 Bolt

12 Rear wheel: examination and renovation

1   Place the machine on its centre stand or support it with a strong wooden box under the engine (MT50) to raise the back wheel clear of the ground.
2   Check the wheel rim for truth and examine the wheel, looking for broken or loose spokes and other damage as described in Section 2 of this Chapter.

13 Rear wheel: removal and replacement

1   Place the machine on its centre stand (MB50) or support it with a strong wooden box under the engine (MT50) to raise the rear wheel clear of the ground.
2   Disconnect the rear brake rod by unscrewing the adjuster nut and removing the rod from the operating arm. Remove the split pin securing the torque arm retaining nut and slacken and remove the nut, two washers and the torque arm. Slacken and remove the rear spindle nut and withdraw the spindle. It may be necessary to use a hammer and soft metal drift gently to tap out

the spindle. Slide the rear wheel forwards and disengage the chain from the rear sprocket. Withdraw the rear wheel, tilting the machine to one side to provide clearance if necessary. Note that it is not necessary to disconnect the chain unless required. If this is the case, find the connecting link, remove its spring clip using a pair of pliers and withdraw the connecting link. Try not to let the ends of the chain pick up any dirt or debris from the floor.
3   Replacement of the wheel is a reversal of the removal procedure. Do not forget to engage the chain back on the rear sprocket before fitting the wheel spindle. Ensure that the reference marks on the chain adjuster face the correct way up, so that they can be aligned with the swinging arm index marks when chain adjustment is required. Hand tighten the spindle nut, connect the brake torque arm and brake rod again, and complete chain adjustment and rear brake adjustment before the spindle nut is tightened to the torque setting given in the Specifications Section of Chapter 4. The torque arm retaining nut should be tightened to the torque setting given in the specifications Section of this Chapter. Fit new split pins to both spindle nut and torque arm retaining nut, and spread the ends securely. Chain adjustment is described in Section 17 of this Chapter, and brake adjustment in Section 15. Check for free wheel rotation and correct brake operation.

13.2a Remove the split pin and spindle nut to allow ...

13.2b ... the spindle to be withdrawn

13.3a Carefully insert the brake backplate assembly into the hub

13.3b Replace the rear wheel in the swinging arm

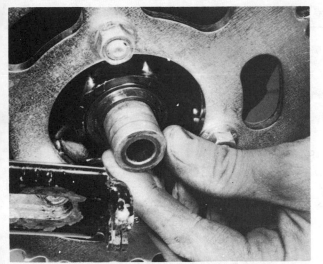

13.3c Do not omit the spacer on the sprocket side of the hub

13.3d Fully tighten all nuts and bolts, using new split pins as required

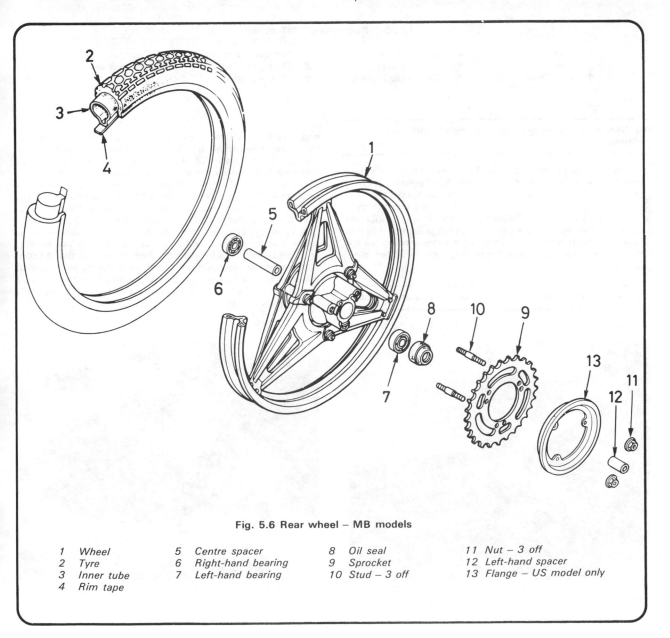

Fig. 5.6 Rear wheel – MB models

1 Wheel	5 Centre spacer	8 Oil seal	11 Nut – 3 off
2 Tyre	6 Right-hand bearing	9 Sprocket	12 Left-hand spacer
3 Inner tube	7 Left-hand bearing	10 Stud – 3 off	13 Flange – US model only
4 Rim tape			

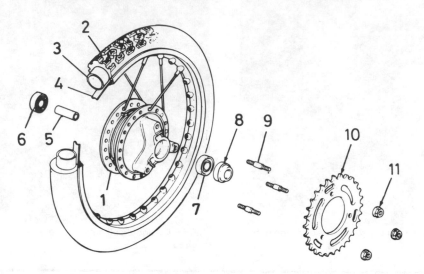

Fig. 5.7 Rear wheel – MT model

1	Hub	4	Rim tape	7	Left-hand bearing	10	Sprocket
2	Tyre	5	Centre spacer	8	Oil seal	11	Nut – 3 off
3	Inner tube	6	Right-hand bearing	9	Stud – 3 off		

14 Rear wheel bearings: removal, examination and refitting

1   The rear wheel must be first removed from the machine before work can begin on the bearings. See Section 13. Once the wheel is removed, withdraw the brake backplate.

2   Due to the uncomplicated nature of the rear hub, which is identical for MB50 and MT50 models, work is very simple and the procedures involved are described in full in Section 4 of this Chapter as the rear hub is essentially the same in design as the front. Refer to the accompanying photographs for added information.

15 Rear brake: examination, renovation, and adjustment

1   As described in Section 14, the rear brake on both MB50

and MT50 is identical to that fitted to the front of the MT50. Once the rear wheel has been removed according to the instructions in Section 13, the rear brake can be examined and attended to following the instructions given in Section 11.

2   Rear brake adjustment is made at the adjuster nut at the extreme end of the brake operating rod. Turn the nut clockwise to tighten the brake up, reducing free play at the pedal tip. Honda specify that the brake pedal should have 20 – 30 mm ($\frac{3}{4}$ – $1\frac{1}{4}$ in) of free play at the tip. Always spin the rear wheel to check that it rotates freely and that the brake is not binding once adjustment has been made. Remember also that if brake adjustment has been altered significantly the stoplight switch will have to be adjusted to suit. Turn the plastic retaining sleeve nut so that the stoplight comes on first as the brake pedal has taken up its free play and is starting to engage the brake.

14.2a Displace central spacer and tap out bearings using a hammer and a suitable drift

14.2b On reassembly do not omit the central spacer and ...

14.2c ... fit new bearings as required. Note that the sealed surface faces outwards

14.2d Tap bearings in, taking care that they are seated squarely in the hub

14.2e Renew oil seals if necessary

15.1a External wear indicator will reveal the amount of wear left in the brake linings

15.1b If replacement is necessary pull off old brake shoes ..

15.1c ... and clean and examine the brake drum ...

15.1d ... before fitting new brake shoes. Note correct position of brake shoe return springs

15.1e Align punch marks on brake cam spindle and operating arm

15.2a Turn brake adjuster nut clockwise to tighten up brake adjustment ...

15.2b ... and do not forget to check stoplight switch adjustment

16 Rear sprocket: examination and refitting

1   The rear sprocket is held on the left-hand side of the hub by three studs which are threaded directly into the hub. To remove it, slacken and remove the three retaining nuts and withdraw the sprocket.

2   Check the condition of the sprocket teeth. If they are hooked, chipped or badly worn, the sprocket must be renewed. It is bad practice to renew one sprocket on its own, however, and so if renewal of the rear sprocket is necessary, the front sprocket and chain must be renewed as well. If this is not done, the new sprocket will not accept the worn chain properly, resulting in very rapid wear of both and the need for prompt renewal of all three items.

3   On replacing the sprocket, place the chamfered inner diameter against the hub and tighten the three nuts to the torque setting given in the specifications Section of this Chapter.

16.1 Slacken and remove the three retaining nuts to withdraw the rear sprocket

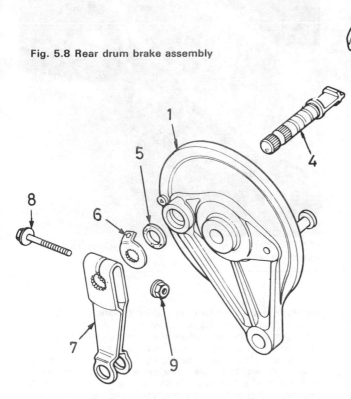

Fig. 5.8 Rear drum brake assembly

1 Brake backplate
2 Shoe – 2 off
3 Return spring – 2 off
4 Operating cam
5 Dust seal
6 Wear indicator plate
7 Operating arm
8 Bolt
9 Nut

17 Final drive chain: examination, adjustment and lubrication

1   The final drive chain is exposed for most of its travel and has only a lightweight chainguard to protect the forward part of the upper run. No provision is made for lubricating the chain.

2   Periodically the tension will need to be adjusted, to compensate for wear. This is accomplished as follows.

3   With the rear wheel raised clear of the ground and the gear lever placed in the neutral position, depress the chain at a midpoint between the sprockets, on its lower run and measure the amount of slack. If the chain tension is correct, this slack should measure 10 – 20 mm ($\frac{3}{8}$ – $\frac{3}{4}$ in).

4   The method of drive chain adjustment is the same for all the model types covered in this Manual and is as follows.

5   Remove the split-pin from the wheel spindle nut and loosen the nut just enough to allow the wheel to be drawn backwards by means of the two drawbolt adjusters. Before carrying out chain adjustment, rotate the wheel so that the chain is moved to its tightest point, as a chain rarely wears evenly during service.

6   Always adjust the drawbolts an equal amount in order to preserve wheel alignment. The fork ends are clearly marked with a series of vertical lines above or below the adjusters, to provide a simple, visual check. If desired, wheel alignment can be checked by running a plank of wood parallel to the machine, so that it touches the side of the rear tyre. If wheel alignment is correct, the plank will be equidistant from each side of the front wheel tyre, when tested on both sides of the rear wheel. It will not touch the front wheel tyre if this tyre is of smaller cross section. See the accompanying diagram.

7   On completion of chain adjustment, tighten the wheel spindle nut to the torque figure given in the Specifications Section of this Chapter and fit a new split-pin. Check that the rear wheel rotates freely and check the rear brake pedal free play.

8   Do not run the chain overtight to compensate for uneven

wear. A tight chain will place excessive stresses on the gearbox and rear wheel bearings, leading to their early failure. It will also absorb a surprising amount of power.

9   After a period of running, the chain will require lubrication. Lack of oil will accelerate the rate of wear of both chain and sprockets and will lead to harsh transmission. The application of engine oil will act as a temporary expedient, but it is preferable to remove the chain and immerse it in a molten lubricant such as Linklyfe or Chainguard after it has been cleaned in a paraffin bath. These latter lubricants achieve better penetration of the chain links and rollers and are less likely to be thrown off when the chain is in motion. A recommended alternative to using engine oil as a temporary lubricant is the aerosol type chain lubricant of which there are many makes available. This type of lubricant is very sticky and, thus, is less likely to be flung off the moving chain.

10 To check whether the chain is due for replacement, lay it lengthwise in a straight line and compress it endwise so that all the play is taken up. Anchor one end and measure the length. Now, pull the chain with one end anchored firmly, so that the chain is fully extended by the amount of play in the opposite direction. If there is a difference of more than $\frac{1}{4}$ inch per foot in the two measurements, the chains should be replaced in conjunction with the sprockets. Note that this check should be made after the chain has been washed out, but before any lubricant is applied, otherwise the lubricant may take up some of the play.

11 When replacing the chain, make sure that the spring link is seated correctly, with the closed end facing the direction of travel.

12 An equivalent British-made chain of the correct size is available from Renold Limited. When ordering a new chain always quote the size (length and width of each pitch), the number of links and the machine to which it is fitted. For example, the chain size fitted to the MB50 and MT50 in the UK is 420 (chain size) by 108 links, and for the MB50 in the US, it is 420 by 106 links. These are standard measurements; the length will vary if non-standard sprockets are fitted.

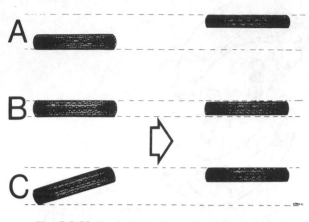

Fig. 5.9 Method of checking wheel alignment

A & C – Incorrect
B   Correct

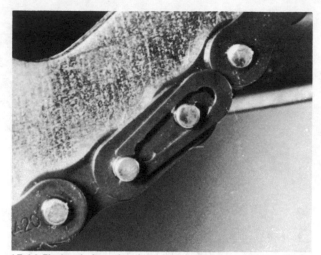

17.11 Fit the chain spring link, closed end facing direction of normal travel

18 Tyres: removal and replacement

1   At some time or other the need will arise to remove and replace the tyres, either as the result of a puncture or because a renewal is required to offset wear. To the inexperienced tyre changing represents a formidable task yet if a few simple rules are observed and the technique learned, the whole operation is surprisingly simple.

2   To remove the tyre from either wheel, first detach the wheel from the machine by following the procedure in Section 3 or 12 of this Chapter, depending on whether the front or the rear wheel is involved. Deflate the tyre by removing the valve insert and when it is fully deflated, push the bead of the tyre away from the wheel rim on both sides so that the bead enters the centre well of the rim. Remove the locking cap and push the tyre valve into the tyre itself.

3   Insert a tyre lever close to the valve and lever the edge of the tyre over the outside of the wheel rim. Very little force should be necessary; if resistance is encountered it is probably due to the fact that the tyre beads have not entered the well of the wheel rim all the way round the tyre.

4   Once the tyre has been edged over the wheel rim, it is easy to work around the wheel rim so that the tyre is completely free to one side. At this stage, the inner tube can be removed.

5   Working from the other side of the wheel, ease the other edge of the tyre over the outside of the wheel rim until the tyre is free completely from the rim.

6   If a puncture has necessitated the removal of the tyre, reinflate the inner tube and immerse it in a bowl of water to trace the source of the leak. Mark its position and deflate the tube. Dry the tube and clean the area around the puncture with a petrol soaked rag. When the surface has dried, apply the rubber solution and allow this to dry before removing the backing from the patch and applying the patch to the surface.

7   It is best to use a patch of the self-vulcanising type which will form a protective covering from the top surface of the patch, after it has sealed in position. Inner tubes made from synthetic rubber may require a special type of patch and adhesive if a satisfactory bond is to be achieved.

8   Before refitting the tyre, check the inside to make sure that the agent which caused the puncture is not trapped. Check the outside of the tyre, particularly the tread area, to make sure nothing is trapped that may cause a further puncture.

9   If the inner tube has been patched on a number of past occasions, or if there is a tear or large hole, it is preferable to discard it, and fit a new one. Sudden deflation may cause an accident, particularly if it occurs with the front wheel.

10 To replace the tyre, inflate the inner tube sufficiently for it to assume a circular shape but only just. Then push it into the tyre so that it is enclosed completely. Lay the tyre on the wheel at an angle and insert the valve through the rim tape and the hole in the wheel rim. Attach the locking cap on the first few threads, sufficient to hold the valve captive in its correct location.

11 Starting at the point furthest from the valve, push the tyre bead over the edge of the wheel rim until it is located in the central well. Continue to work around the tyre in this fashion until the whole of one side of the tyre is on the rim. It may be necessary to use a tyre lever during the final stages.

12 Make sure that there is no pull on the tyre valve and again commencing with the area furthest from the valve, ease the other bead of the tyre over the edge of the rim. Finish with the area close to the valve, pushing the valve up into the tyre until the locking cap reaches the rim. This will ensure the inner tube is not trapped when the last section of the bead is edged over the rim with a tyre lever.

13 Check that the inner tube is not trapped at any point. Reinflate the inner tube and check that the tyre is seating correctly around the wheel rim. There should be a thin line moulded around the wall of the tyre on both sides which should be equidistant from the wheel rim at all points. If the tyre is unevenly located on the rim, try boucing the wheel when the tyre is at the recommended pressure. It is probable that one of the beads has not pulled clear of the centre well.

14 Always run the tyres at the recommended pressures and never under or over-inflate. The correct pressures for solo use are given in the Specifications Section of this Chapter. If a pillion passenger is carried, increase the rear tyre pressure only to the pressure specified.

15 Tyre replacement is aided by dusting the side walls, particularly in the vicinity of the beads, with a liberal coating of French chalk. Washing up liquid can also be used to good effect but this has the disadvantage of causing the inner surfaces of the wheel rim to corrode.

16 Never replace the inner tube and tyre without the rim tape in position. If this precaution is overlooked there is a good chance that the ends of the spoke nipples chafing the inner tube and causing a crop of punctures.

17 Never fit a tyre which has a damaged tread or side walls. Apart from the legal aspects, there is a very great risk of a blow-out, which can have serious consequences.

Chapter 6 Electrical system

For modifications and information relating to later models, see Chapter 7

Contents

Specifications

Battery	UK models	US model
Make	Yuasa	Yuasa
Capacity	6V 4 Ah	12V 2.5 Ah
Earth connection	Negative (-)	Negative (-)
Fuse	10A	7A
Rectifier	Silicon	Silicon
Charging system		
Type	Alternator	Alternator
Output:		
MB	74W @ 5000 rpm	66W @ 5000 rpm
MT	66W @ 5000 rpm	N/A
Charging rate		
Charge starts at:		
Day	1200 rpm	1500 rpm
Night	1800 rpm	N/A
Charging rate:		
Day	1.3A (min)/8.7V @ 4000 rpm	5A (min)/14.5V @ 5000 rpm
	2.6A (max)/9.2V @ 8000 rpm	N/A
Night	1.0A (min)/8.7V @ 4000 rpm	N/A
	2.2A (max)/8.8V @ 8000 rpm	N/A

Bulbs

Headlamp	6V 25/25W	12V 31.5/30W
Stop/tail lamp	6V 5/21W	12V 8/27W
Indicator lamp	6V 21W	12V 23W
Pilot lamp	6V 4W	N/A
Speedometer lamp	6V 3W	12V 3.4W
Neutral warning lamp	6V 3W	12V 3.4W
Indicator warning lamp	6V 1.7W	12V 3.4W
Main beam warning lamp	N/A	12V 1.7W

1 General description

The UK market models covered by this manual are fitted with a 6 volt electrical system and the US model with a 12 volt system. The two electrical systems are essentially similar in layout and function with the exception of those components which differ according to the statutory requirements of the two countries. The source of power is a flywheel generator mounted on the crankshaft left-hand end. The alternating current (ac) provided by this is fed largely to the lights, excess power being soaked up by a resistor on the UK model which does not have its lights switched permanently on. The remainder of the generator output is converted to direct current (dc) by a silicon rectifier and is then used to charge the battery and power the ancillary electrical equipment. The generator consists of a permanent magnet rotor and a multi-coil stator, only one of the stator coils being the power source for the charging system, the other two being ignition system components.

2 Testing the electrical system

1   Simple continuity checks, for instance when testing switch units, wiring and connections, can be carried out using a battery and bulb arrangement to provide a test circuit. For most tests described in this Chapter, however, a pocket multimeter should be considered essential. A basic multimeter capable of measuring volts and ohms can be bought for a very reasonable sum and will prove an invaluable tool. Note that separate volt and ohm meters may be used in place of the multimeter, provided those with the correct operating ranges are available. In addition, if the generator output is to be checked, an ammeter of 0-5 amperes range will be required.

2   Care must be taken when performing any electrical test, because some of the electrical components can be damaged if they are incorrectly connected or inadvertently shorted to earth. This is particularly so in the case of electronic components. Instructions regarding meter probe connections are given for each test, and these should be read carefully to preclude accidental damage occurring.

3   Where test equipment is not available, or the owner feels unsure of the procedure described, it is strongly recommended that professional assistance is sought. Errors made through carelessness or lack of experience can so easily lead to damage and need for expensive replacement parts.

4   A certain amount of preliminary dismantling will be necessary to gain access to the components to be tested. Normally, removal of the seat and side panels will be required, with the possible addition of the fuel tank and headlamp unit to expose the remaining components.

3 Flywheel generator: checking the output

1   The generator output can only be checked with special equipment of the multimeter type. As it is unlikely that the average owner will have access to this equipment or the skill to use it, if the generator is suspect it should be checked by an authorised Honda dealer or an auto-electrical specialist. Before the test is carried out, the battery must be fully charged and the engine must be warmed up to normal operating temperature.

2   Remove the left-hand sidepanel to expose the battery and its leads. Connect a dc voltmeter across the battery by disconnecting the battery positive (+) lead, the red wire, and connecting one of the voltmeter leads to the positive (+) terminal lead. The other voltmeter lead is to be connected to the battery negative (-) lead, the blue wire. This should be done by pushing a metal probe inside the clear plastic insulation around the snap connector to make contact with the battery terminal lead without disconnecting the battery. An ammeter should now be connected between the battery (+) positive terminal lead and the positive (+) or red wire which forms part of the main loom.

3   For US models the headlamp must be switched on to main beam. Start the engine and note the readings taken at the engine speeds set in the specifications Section of this Chapter. Compare your readings with those given. For UK machines, where night charging rates are given, switch on the lights and switch to main beam. If the readings arrived at are correct, it may be assumed that the charging system is functioning properly. A marked reduction in output may be a result of damaged windings in the stator coil or damaged leads. These may be checked for continuity and resistance by a relatively simple test which does not require removal of the generator.

4   Disconnect the voltmeter and ammeter and connect the battery up again. Trace the generator lead from the engine to the multipin connector block. Identify the yellow, green, and white terminals. On US models this process is made much easier by the use of individual snap connectors. Connect in the multimeter and switch to the resistance mode. Check for resistance between the wires specified and compare the readings obtained with those given:

Yellow to green	0.1 – 1.0 ohm
White to green	0.3 – 1.5 ohm

5   If the readings obtained are not satisfactory, take the machine to an authorised Honda dealer for checking as the only practical solution to a fault in the stator is replacement of the stator and rotor together. This course is likely to prove very expensive, therefore an expert second opinion is advisable. If on closer inspection, a wire turns out to be broken, repair is relatively easy for the expert and it is infinitely preferable to pay a small labour charge than to pay a large sum for new parts.

6   If the readings obtained throughout these two tests are satisfactory, but a charging fault persists, the next component to be tested is the silicon rectifier unit.

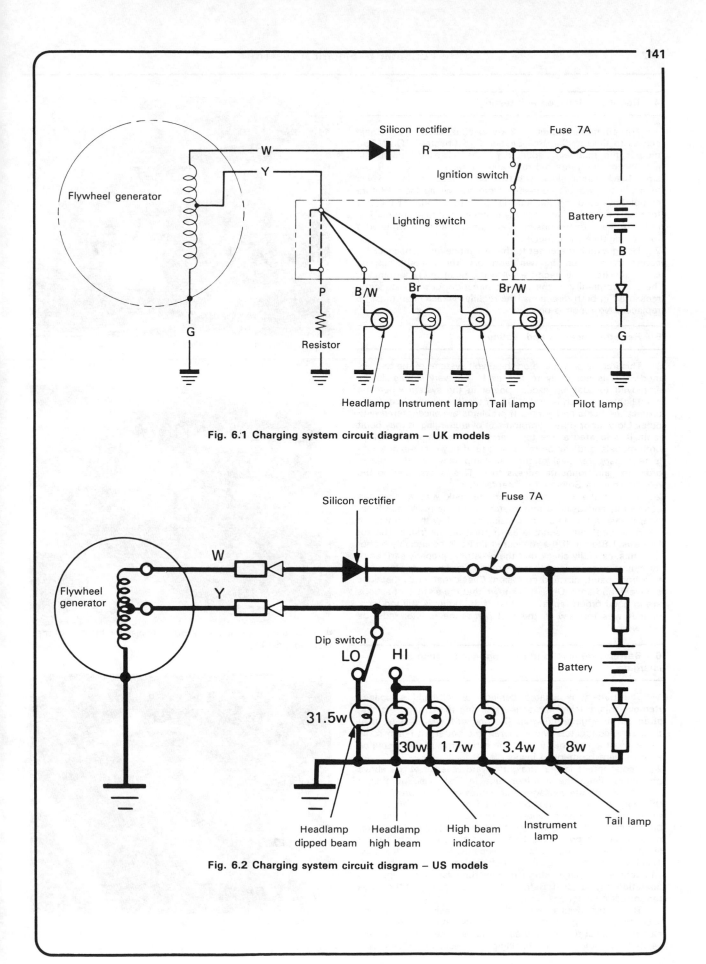

Fig. 6.1 Charging system circuit diagram – UK models

Fig. 6.2 Charging system circuit disgram – US models

4   Rectifier – location and testing

1   For all models, fuel tank removal is necessary to gain
access to the rectifier. See Section 2 of Chapter 2. On MB50
models the rectifier is located on the left-hand side at the
junction of the frame top tube and the back mudguard. It is a
small black plastic block with two male spade terminals which
fit a plastic two pin connector from the wiring loom. Before
completely removing the unit, identify the polarity of the two
terminals by the colour of the lead connected to each one. The
red wire leads to the positive (+) terminal, and the white wire
to the negative (-) terminal.
2   Using a multimeter set to the resistance function, check for
continuity between the two terminals. There should only be
continuity from the negative (-) to the positive (+) terminal. If
there is continuity in the reverse direction, or if resistance is
measured in both directions, the rectifier is faulty and must be
replaced. No repair is possible.

5   Resistor: location and testing

1   This item is only found on the 6 volt systems of the two UK
models. It is not likely to fail, as it is a very simple device
employed to soak up excess power in the system when the
main lighting switch is in the 'Off' or the 'P' position, in order to
protect the bulbs and wiring. If problems are encountered with
bulbs blowing or other symptoms of overcharging, it may be at
fault. It is located at the top rear of the headlamp bracket on
both models, and can be tested in situ. If however replacement
is necessary, removal of the headlamp may be advisable in
order to gain adequate access to it. This is described in the
relevant part of Section 17, Chapter 4.
2   To test the unit, disconnect the pink wire at its snap
connector, and using a multimeter set to the resistance function, measure the amount of resistance below the terminal of
the pink wire and a suitable earth point on the frame. The set
figure is 1.8 ohm. If the measured figure is appreciably higher
than this, carefully check that the resistor is properly earthed at
its mounting point, and that the mating surfaces are clean and
free from paint, dirt and corrosion. Check that all connections
are clean and tight. Once it is known that the earth connections
are in good order, repeat the test. If the figure is still too high,
or if it was too low in the first place, the resistor must be
renewed.

6   Battery: removal and refitting, examination and charging

1   The battery is located behind the left-hand sidepanel.
Remove this, slacken the screw securing the battery retaining
strap and disengage the strap. Disconnect the terminal leads at
their snap connectors and withdraw the battery. It is advisable
to remove the breather tube at the same time, as this would be
a convenient moment to inspect it.
2   Replacement is the straightforward reversal of the above
procedure. Feed the breather tube in first, ensuring that it
passes through the passages and clamps which are provided for
this purpose. It must not be trapped or kinked at all, as any
restriction will cause a build-up of pressure which will crack the
battery casing. It should be noted at this stage that some later
models have a two piece battery breather, in which a short
length of rubber tube vents into a separate battery holding tray.
This tray is drained by a more substantial length of tubing which
can remain in place during battery removal, simplifying this
operation a great deal. Refer to the colour coding of the wires
for correct connections.
3   The battery uses a clear or translucent casing, which can be
used to give a good guide to its condition. It permits the
electrolyte level to be easily seen and also the lead plates and
separators. Any sign of buckling in these, or of sediment

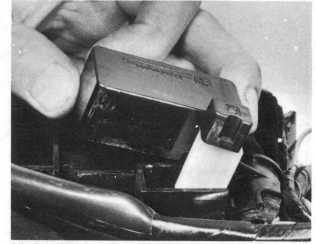

4.1a Location of rectifier – MB50

4.1b Location of rectifier – MT50 (note also the location of the
indicator relay)

5.1 Location of resistor – MT50

forming in the bottom of the casing will give some early warning of battery failure. As there are no exposed terminals, maintenance is restricted to ensuring that the electrolyte level is maintained between the upper and lower levels marked on the casing. Topping up should only be done with distilled water. Tap water should never be used, and battery acid only when severe spillage has occurred. If the addition of acid is required, use only acid with a specific gravity of 1.260 – 1.280 at 68°F/20°C. The breather tube should be free of kinks or splits. Check it for blockages, especially at the lower end. This should be done frequently if the machine is used in poor weather conditions or on dirty road surfaces. As previously mentioned it must be situated in such a way that it cannot be trapped or kinked on the machine, and must be long enough to hang clear of the frame.

4   The battery can be tested using a hydrometer. If the specific gravity falls below about 1.250, the battery must be recharged. If a hydrometer is not available take the battery to a specialist for checking.

5   If the machine is not used for a period, it is advisable to remove the battery and give it a 'refresher' charge every six weeks or so from a battery charger. If the battery is permitted to discharge completely, the plates will sulphate and render the battery useless.

6   Whilst the machine is used on the road it is unlikely that the battery will require attention other than routine maintenance because the generator will keep it fully charged. However, if the machine is used for a succession of short journeys only, mainly during the hours of darkness when the lights are in full use, it is possible that the output from the generator may fail to keep pace with the heavy electrical demand, especially if the machine is parked with the lights switched on. Under these circumstances, it will be necessary to remove the battery from time to time to have it charged independently.

7   The normal charging rate for any battery is 1/10 the rated capacity. Hence the charging rate for the UK 4Ah battery is 0.4 amp and for the US 2.5Ah battery 0.25 amp. It should be noted however that Honda recommend a charge rate of 0.2 amp for the UK 4Ah battery, which is probably due to its small size and the consequent risk of overheating. A slightly higher charge rate may be used in an emergency, but this should not exceed 1 amp (1.4 amp for US models). The higher charge rate should be avoided wherever possible as it will rapidly shorten battery life. Make sure that the battery charger connections are correct, red to positive (red lead) and black to negative (blue lead). Always remove the cell cover plugs during charging to prevent any build up of pressure, and **never** allow a naked flame or sparks near the battery. Switch off the charger if the cells become overheated.

8   Charging is complete when the specific gravity of the electrolyte rises to 1.260 – 1.280 at 68°F/20°C. A rough guide to this state is when all cells are gassing freely. At the normal (slow) rate of charge this will take between 3 – 15 hours, depending on the original condition of the battery. If the higher rate of charge must be used, **never** leave the battery charging for more than one hour, as overheating and buckling of the plates will inevitably occur.

9   A word of caution concerning batteries. Sulphuric acid is extreme corrosive and must be handled with great respect. Do not forget that the outside of the battery is likely to retain traces of acid from previous spills, and the hands should always be washed promptly after checking the battery. Remember too that battery acid will quickly destroy clothing. In the author's experience, acid seems partial to nearly new jeans in particular, and experience has shown that it is best to keep well clear of batteries unless old clothing is being worn. Note the following rules concerning battery maintenance.

Do not allow smoking or naked flames near batteries.
Do avoid acid contact with skin, eyes and clothing.
Do keep battery electrolyte level maintained.
Do avoid over-high charge rates.
Do avoid leaving the battery discharged.
Do avoid freezing.
Do use only distilled or demineralised water for topping up.

6.1 Battery location and retaining strap – MT50

7   Fuse: location and replacement

1   The electrical system is protected by a single fuse of 10 amp rating (7 amp for US models). On all models it is retained in a plastic moulding just below the battery. A spare fuse is clipped to the document compartment under the petrol tank front cover (MB models) or is held in a plastic bag near the fuse holder (MT model). Always replace the spare as soon as possible if it is used.

2   Before renewing a fuse that has blown, check that no obvious short circuit has occurred, otherwise the replacement fuse will blow immediately it is inserted. It is always wise to check the electrical circuit thoroughly, to trace the fault and eliminate it.

3   When a fuse blows while the machine is running and no spare is available, a 'get you home' remedy is to remove the blown fuse and wrap it in silver paper before replacing it in the fuse holder. The silver paper will restore the electrical continuity by bridging the broken fuse wire. This expedient should **never** be used if there is evidence of short circuit or other major electrical fault, otherwise more serious damage will be caused. Replace the 'doctored' fuse at the earliest possible opportunity, to restore full circuit protection.

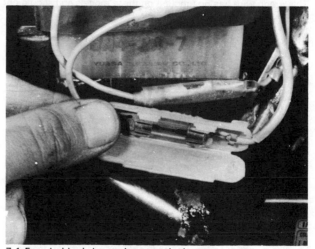

7.1 Fuse holder is located next to the battery

8 Horn: location and testing

1   The horn is mounted on the bottom yoke via a flexible mounting strip. No maintenance is required or indeed possible, other than regular cleaning to remove road dirt and occasional spraying with WD40 or similar water dispersant spray to minimise internal corrosion.

2   If the horn fails to work, first test that power is reaching the instrument by disconnecting the wires and substituting a 6 or 12 volt bulb as appropriate. Switch on the ignition and press the horn button. If the bulb fails to light, check the horn button and wiring as described in the Sections later in this Chapter. If the bulb does light, the horn circuit is proved good and the horn must be checked. Connect a fully charged 6 or 12 volt battery, as appropriate, directly to the horn. If it does not sound, a gentle tap on the outside may serve to free the internal contacts. If this fails replacement of the horn is the only alternative as repair and adjustment are not possible.

9 Flashing indicator relay: location and testing

1   The flashing indicator relay is situated underneath the petrol tank front cover on MB50 models, to the left-hand rear of the document compartment. On MT50 models it is underneath the petrol tank on the right-hand side behind the steering head. It is a small cylindrical unit secured by a rubber mounting to provide some insulation against vibration. No maintenance is necessary, and if it is found to be faulty, replacement is the only practical solution.

2   Before testing the unit, ensure that the indicator switch is working properly, that the bulbs are of the correct wattage, that the wiring is in good order, and that the indicator lamp units are earthed properly. Also check that the battery is fully charged. Faults in any one or all of these items will produce symptoms for which the indicator relay may be unfairly blamed. The only practical way of testing the unit is by substituting a known good one. If the fault is then cured, the original relay is proven faulty and must be replaced.

3   If replacement is necessary, disconnect the two wires, noting their respective terminals and remove the unit from the rubber mounting. On some new Honda parts, the two terminals are marked with blobs of correctly-coloured paint to indicate which wire goes to which terminal. If these marks are not present, replace the wires in exactly the same way as on the original unit. Note that on UK machines there is a green wire with a spade terminal in addition to the grey and black wires. This green wire has no function on these models and should not be inadvertently connected to the relay.

4   When handling indicator relays, be very careful not to let them drop or be otherwise damaged. They are very delicate.

10 Bulb replacement: headlamp

UK models

1   To replace the headlamp bulb on the MB50 model it is necessary first to remove the fairing by slackening and removing the two dome headed nuts which secure the fairing stays to their clamps on the upper fork stanchion. Withdraw the fairing. Slacken and remove the two headlamp mounting bolts and remove the headlamp assembly. Peel back the rubber cover, lift the bulb holder out against spring pressure and unhook its upper clip. Withdraw the bulb. Replacement is a straightforward reversal of the removal procedure.

2   The headlamp bulb on the MT50 model is reached by removing the two headlamp easing bolts and withdrawing the headlamp and speedometer assembly far enough for access to be gained to the bulb holder. There are two types in use on this model. The first is retained by a long coil spring fastened to the

8.1a Horn mounting – MB50 ...

8.1b ... and on the MT50

9.1 Indicator relay in situ – MB50

bulb holder and at its other end to the reflector base. This type is removed by lifting the bulb holder up against spring pressure and unhooking its upper clip. The bulb can then be withdrawn and replaced. For the second type of holder, which is a more compact type, simply twist the holder as if withdrawing a bulb and pull it away. The bulb is loosely held in the headlamp unit.

3   Both UK machines have a small pilot light bulb which is rubber mounted in the headlamp unit. It is removed in the same way as the headlamp bulb.

US model

4   This model employs a sealed beam type of unit in which replacement of the complete headlamp unit is necessary should bulb failure occur. To remove the headlamp assembly, slacken and remove the two headlamp rim retaining screws, withdraw the reflector unit, disconnect the wires at their snap connectors and remove the headlamp unit assembly. Unscrew the spring-loaded horizontal beam adjuster, slacken and remove the two headlamp unit securing screws, and remove the headlamp unit from the rim. Reassembly is a straightforward reversal of the removal procedure, but it should be noted that headlamp beam adjustment must comply with local lighting regulations.

All models

5   Vertical beam adjustment is effected by slackening the two headlamp mounting bolts and tilting the headlamp assembly as necessary. It should be noted that reference marks on the headlamp shell must be aligned with index marks stamped in the headlamp bracket. If this is done on reassembly it will serve as a basis for proper adjustment.

6   In the UK, regulations stipulate that the headlamps must be arranged so that the light will not dazzle a person standing at a distance greater than 25 feet from the lamp, whose eye level is not less than 3 feet 6 inches above that plane. It is easy to approximate this setting by placing the machine 25 feet away from a wall, on a level road, and setting the dipped beam height so that it is concentrated at the same height as the distance of the centre of the headlamp from the ground. The rider must be seated normally during this operation, and also the pillion passenger, if one is carried regularly.

10.2 Similar procedure is applied to this type of bulb holder used on the MT50

10.1 Lift bulb holder up against spring pressure and unhook the upper clip – MB50

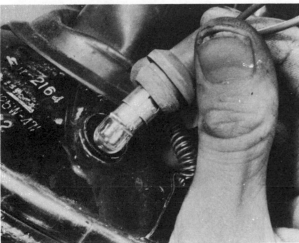

10.3 Pilot bulb holder is a push fit in reflector

10.5 Reference marks are provided to assist headlamp beam alignment

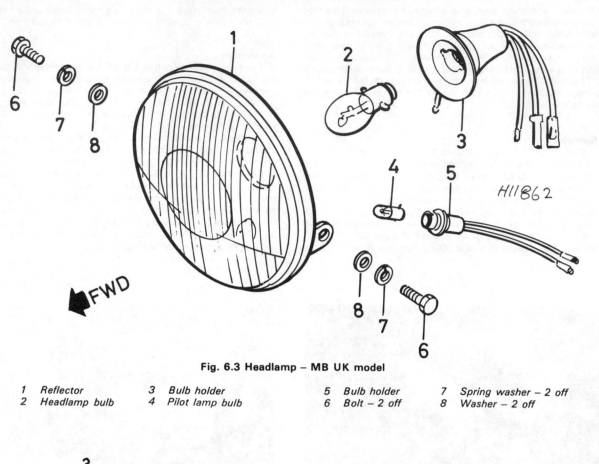

Fig. 6.3 Headlamp – MB UK model

1	Reflector	3	Bulb holder	5	Bulb holder	7	Spring washer – 2 off
2	Headlamp bulb	4	Pilot lamp bulb	6	Bolt – 2 off	8	Washer – 2 off

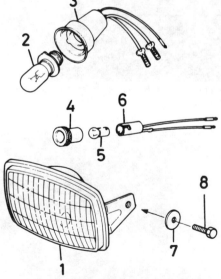

Fig. 6.4 Headlamp – MT model

1 Reflector
2 Headlamp bulb
3 Bulb holder
4 Grommet
5 Pilot lamp bulb
6 Bulb holder
7 Washer – 2 off
8 Bolt – 2 off

11 Bulb replacement: stop and tail lamp

1   The combined stop and tail lamp bulb contains two filaments, one for the stop lamp and one for the tail lamp.

2   The offset pin bayonet fixing bulb can be removed after the plastic lens cover and screws have been removed.

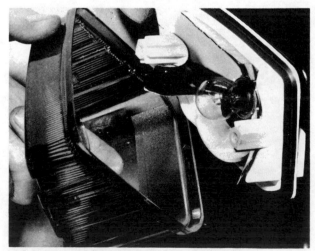

11.2 Release rear lamp lens to gain access to bulb

1 Reflector
2 Rim
3 Adjusting screw
4 Spring
5 Nut
6 Bolt – 2 off
7 Nut – 2 off
8 Cover
9 Headlamp shell
10 Collar – 2 off
11 Nut – 2 off
12 Collar – 2 off
13 Screw – 2 off
14 Screw and washer – 2 off

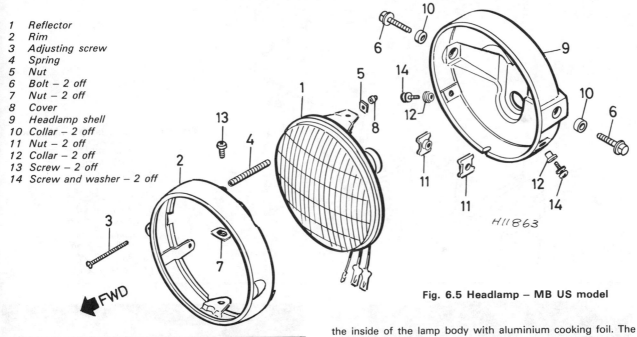

Fig. 6.5 Headlamp – MB US model

12 Bulb replacement: flashing indicator lamps

1 The indicator assemblies are plastic mouldings bolted on to metal stalks. The earth connections should be checked at convenient intervals to ensure that they are tight and free from dirt or corrosion. If a bulb or wiring connection fails, the affected lamp will cease operation, the failure being indicated by rapid flashing of the remaining bulb.

UK models
2 The lens is clipped to the body of the lamp and can be removed by using a coin or broad-bladed screwdriver in the slot provided to lever the lens off. Both the lens and the body are of plastic construction, so care must be taken to avoid damage during removal. The bulb is of the conventional bayonet type and can be removed by pushing inwards, twisting gently anti-clockwise and releasing.
3 No reflectors are fitted to the indicator lamps, and owners may wish to improve their visibility in bright sunlight by lining

the inside of the lamp body with aluminium cooking foil. The lamps are, however, adequate in most normal conditions.

US models
4 The lens is retained by a single fixing screw. Remove this and lift away the lens. Remove the bulb by pushing inwards and twisting gently anti-clockwise.

13 Bulb replacement: instrument panel and warning lamps

1 The various bulbs in the instrument panel are held in rubber holders which are a push fit in the underside of the panel. To gain access to the holders, it is best to release the panel so that it can be tilted upwards.
2 The bulbs are of the bayonet cap type and are released by depressing and twisting them anti-clockwise. When purchasing replacement bulbs ensure that they are of the specified voltage and wattage.

12.2a Indicator lens can be prised off as shown

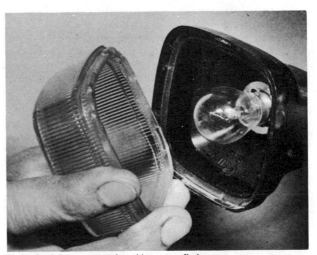

12.2b Bulb is a conventional bayonet fitting

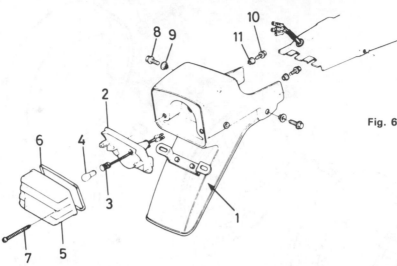

Fig. 6.6 Tail/stop lamp – MB model

1   Rear mudguard
2   Reflector
3   Bulb holder
4   Bulb
5   Lens
6   Rubber seal
7   Screw – 2 off
8   Bolt – 2 off
9   Collar – 2 off
10 Bolt – 2 off
11 Collar – 2 off

13.1a Instrument panel bulbs are a push fit in panel – MB50 ...

13.1b ... and are of bayonet fitting – MT50

14 Switches: general

1   Generally speaking, the switches fitted to the machines covered in this Manual should give little trouble, but if necessary they may be tested as described in the following Sections.
2   To test the switches, a multimeter, set to the resistance function, will be required to carry out the various continuity checks described.
3   On models fitted with a battery, always disconnect the battery before removing any of the switches, to prevent the possibility of a short circuit. Most troubles are caused by dirty contacts, but in the event of the breakage of some internal part, it will be necessary to renew the complete switch. It should, however, be noted that if a switch is tested and found to be faulty, there is nothing to be lost by attempting a repair. It may be that worn contacts can be built up with solder, or that a broken wire terminal can be repaired, again using a soldering iron. The handlebar switches can all be dismantled to a greater or lesser extent, but the ignition switch is a sealed unit. It is, however, up to the owner to decide if he has the skill to carry out this sort of work. Note also that procedures for testing the ignition and kill switches are given in Section 4 of Chapter 3.

14.1 The left-hand handlebar switch assembly (UK models)

15 Stop lamp switches: testing and adjustment

1   The front stop lamp is incorporated in the front brake lever assembly and is automatically operated by application of the front brake. No adjustment is possible.
2   The rear stop lamp switch is located by a bracket on the lower right-hand side of the frame and is connected to the rear brake pedal by a spring. It should be adjusted to operate as the brake pedal has taken up its free play and is beginning to engage the rear brake.
3   Testing is an extremely simple process for either switch. Disconnect the black and green/yellow wires and test for continuity between them with the brake lever or brake pedal firmly applied. If no continuity is found the switch must be replaced as it is not possible to effect a satisfactory repair.

16 Flashing indicator switch: testing

1   This is a horizontally mounted three-position rocker switch. To test it, the headlamp will probably have to be removed in order to gain access to the switch wires at their snap connectors (US models) or multi-pin connector (UK models).
2   Once this has been done, turn the switch to the 'R' position and check for continuity between the light blue and grey wire terminals. Turn the switch to the 'L' position and check for continuity between the orange and grey wires. If continuity is found on both sets of wires, the switch is in good order. There should be no continuity between any of the wires with the switch in the central or 'Off' position. If the tests prove the switch to be faulty in any way it must be renewed. Repairs, depending on the nature of the damage, may be possible but are not satisfactory in the long term.

17 Lighting switch: testing UK models only

1   This switch is a sliding three position unit mounted vertically on the inner side of the left-hand handlebar switch cluster. To test it remove the headlamp as previously described and disconnect the switch lead at the multi pin connector and at the snap connectors. Identify the wires as appropriate and check for continuity between them in the following order. With the switch in the 'Off' position, check the yellow and pink wires. With the switch in the 'P' position check the yellow, pink and brown together, and the black and brown/white together. With the switch in the 'H' position check the yellow and brown wires and the dipswitch.
2   If continuity is found between each group of wires when the switch is placed in the positions indicated the switch is in good order. If not, it is faulty and should be renewed, although if the owner has the necessary skill, repairs may be attempted.

18 Dipswitch: testing

1   This is a two position switch sliding vertically on the outer end of the left-hand handlebar switch cluster. To test it, remove the headlamp if this has not already been done, and disconnect the switch wires at the multi-pin connector or snap connectors as appropriate. On UK models, the main lighting switch must be in the 'H' position.
2   With the dipswitch in the 'Hi' position, check for continuity between the blue wire and the main feed from the lighting switch on UK models, and between the blue wire and the yellow wire on US models. Move the switch to the 'Lo' position and check for continuity between the white wire and the main feed or yellow wire as appropriate. Check also that with the switch in the middle of its travel, there is continuity between all three terminals.
3   If continuity exists in all cases the switch is serviceable. If not, repairs may be attempted as there is nothing to lose by doing so. It should be remembered that the only practical solution to switch failure is replacement of the part concerned. Switch failure which causes a sudden loss of lighting while riding at night can have most unpleasant consequences.

19 Horn button: testing

1   This unit is a simple spring loaded button on the lower part of the left-hand switch cluster. A simple test sequence is described in Section 8 of this Chapter.
2   If the horn button is proved faulty by this test it may prove possible, depending on the owner's ability, to strip the switch and repair the damage. If not, replacement is the only answer. It should be remembered that a horn in good working order is a legal requirement in the UK.

20 Neutral indicator switch: testing

1   Check that the transmission is in the neutral position and trace the generator lead up the lower frame tube to the multi-pin connector or snap connectors. Check for continuity between the light green/red wire and the dark green. If there is continuity the switch and wiring are serviceable. If not, the switch must be renewed.

21 Wiring: layout and examination

1   The cables of the wiring harness are colour-coded and will correspond with the accompanying wiring diagram.
2   Visual inspection will show whether any breaks or frayed outer coverings are giving rise to short circuits which cause the main fuse to blow. Another source of trouble is the snap connectors and spade terminals, which may make a poor connection if they are not pushed home fully, or if corrosion has occurred.
3   Intermittent short circuits can sometimes be traced to a chafed wire passing through, or close to, a metal component, such as a frame member. Avoid tight bends in the cables or situations where the cables can be trapped or stretched, especially in the vicinity of the handlebars or steering head.

The MBX50 S-D model

The MT50 S-F model

Chapter 7

The MBX/MTX50 and MT50 S-E/F, G, J, L models

Contents

Specifications

Note: *information is given only where it differs from that given in the Specifications Sections of Chapters 1 – 6. Except where specified information applies to MBX50 or MTX50*

Model dimensions and weights

	MBX50	MTX50
Overall length	1970 mm (77.6 in)	2045 mm (80.5 in)
Overall width	675 mm (26.6 in)	810 mm (31.9 in)
Overall height	1110 mm (43.7 in)	1130 mm (44.5 in)
Wheelbase	1250 mm (49.2 in)	1335 mm (52.6 in)
Ground clearance	170 mm (6.7 in)	230 mm (9.1 in)
Dry weight	89 kg (196 lb)	88 kg (194 lb)

Specifications relating to Chapter 1

Final drive reduction ratio – MTX50 .... 3.917 : 1 (47/12)

Specifications relating to Chapter 2

Fuel tank capacity

	MBX50	MTX50
Overall	12.0 lit (2.6 Imp gal)	9.0 lit (2.0 Imp gal)
Reserve	2.0 lit (0.4 Imp gal)	2.5 lit (0.5 Imp gal)

Carburettor

	MBX50	MTX50
ID number	PF06D-A	PF06E-A
Main jet	68	72
Pilot jet	40	42
Pilot air screw – turns out	$1\frac{1}{4}$	$1\frac{1}{4}$
Idle speed	1300 rpm	1500 rpm

Carburettor ID number
MT50 S-E/F, G PF05D-A
MT50 S-J, L PF05D-B

Engine oil tank capacity .... 1.2 lit (2.1 Imp pint)

Gearbox oil capacity – MTX50
At oil change .... 0.8 lit (1.41 Imp pint)
At engine rebuild .... 0.9 lit (1.58 Imp pint)

Torque wrench settings

Component	kgf m	lbf ft
Fuel tap filter bowl	0.3 – 0.5	2.0 – 3.5
Oil pump mounting screw and bolts	0.8 – 1.2	6.0 – 9.0

Specifications relating to Chapter 3	**MBX50**	**MTX50**

Ignition timing

	MBX50	MTX50
Retard starts at	4400 – 5600 rpm	5000 – 7000 rpm
Full retard – BTDC	10.5° ± 3.5° @ 9000 rpm	8° ± 3.5° @ 9000 rpm

Spark plug – standard

	MBX50	MTX50
NGK	BR6ES	BR9HS
ND	W20ESR-U	W27FSR

Specifications relating to Chapter 4	**MBX50**	**MTX50**

Front forks

	MBX50	MTX50
Oil capacity – per leg	143.5 – 148.5 cc (5.1 – 5.2 Imp fl oz)	119.5 – 124.5 cc (4.2 – 4.4 Imp fl oz)
Spring free length	497.3 mm (19.5787 in)	587.9 mm (23.1456 in)
Service limit	482.5 mm (18.9960 in)	569.9 mm (22.4370 in)

Rear suspension unit

	MBX50	MTX50
Spring free length	137.5 mm (5.4138 in)	160.6 mm (6.3228 in)
Service limit	135.0 mm (5.3150 in)	157.4 mm (6.1968 in)

Rear suspension linkage pivot bearings – MTX50
Bush ID .... 15.070 – 15.120 mm (0.5933 – 0.5953 in)
Service limit .... 15.135 mm (0.5959 in)
Centre sleeve OD .... 14.966 – 14.984 mm (0.5892 – 0.5899 in)
Service limit .... 14.941 mm (0.5882 in)

Torque wrench settings

Component	kgf m	lbf ft
Fork top bolt – MBX50	4.0 – 5.0	29.0 – 36.0
Fork top bolt – MTX50	1.5 – 3.0	11.0 – 22.0
Fork top plug – MBX50	1.5 – 3.0	11.0 – 22.0
Headlamp mounting bolts – MTX50	1.8 – 2.5	13.0 – 18.0
Bottom yoke pinch bolts – MBX50	2.4 – 3.0	17.0 – 22.0
Bottom yoke pinch bolts – MTX50	3.0 – 4.0	22.0 – 29.0
Damper rod Allen screw	1.5 – 2.5	11.0 – 18.0
Front wheel spindle nut	5.5 – 7.0	40.0 – 50.5
Swinging arm pivot bolt nut	5.5 – 7.0	40.0 – 50.5
Suspension linkage pivot bolt nuts	4.0 – 5.0	29.0 – 36.0
Suspension unit mountings – MBX50	2.7 – 3.3	19.5 – 24.0
Suspension unit top mounting – MTX50	4.0 – 5.0	29.0 – 36.0
Suspension unit bottom mounting eye and locknut – MTX50	3.8 – 6.0	27.5 – 43.0
Suspension unit bottom mounting – MTX50	3.8 – 4.8	27.5 – 34.5
Rear wheel spindle nut – MBX50	5.5 – 7.0	40.0 – 50.5

Specifications relating to Chapter 5

Wheels
Spindle maximum warpage .... 0.20 mm (0.0078 in)
Bearing maximum play .... 0.027 mm (0.0010 in)

Front brake – MBX50
Master cylinder ID .... 12.700 – 12.743 mm (0.4999 – 0.5017 in)
Service limit .... 12.755 mm (0.5022 in)

Piston OD	12.657 – 12.684 mm (0.4983 – 0.4994 in)
Service limit	12.640 mm (0.4976 in)
Caliper bore ID	25.400 – 25.405 mm (0.9999 – 1.0002 in)
Service limit	25.450 mm (1.0020 in)
Piston OD	25.318 – 25.368 mm (0.9968 – 0.9987 in)
Service limit	25.300 mm (0.9961 in)

Tyres

Front – MTX50	2.50 – 21 4PR
Rear – MTX50	3.00 – 18 6PR
Rear – MBX50	2.75 – 18 6PR
Manufacturer's recommended minimum tread depth – at centre of tread:	
Front	1.5 mm (0.06 in)
Rear	2.0 mm (0.08 in)

Tyre pressures

Rear type, solo – MBX50	25 psi (1.75 kg/cm^2)
Rear tyre, pillion – MTX50	36 psi (2.50 kg/cm^2)

Final drive chain

Length – MBX50	420 x 118 links
Length – MTX50	420 x 122 links
Standard length of 40 links – 41 pins	508 mm (20.0 in)
Maximum length of 40 links – 41 pins	518 mm (20.4 in)
Chain free play – MTX50	20 – 30 mm (0.8 – 1.2 in)

Torque wrench settings – MBX50 only

Component	kgf m	lbf ft
Rear sprocket mounting nuts	4.0 – 5.0	29.0 – 36.0
Master cylinder clamp bolts	1.0 – 1.4	7.0 – 10.0
Caliper bleed nipple	0.4 – 0.7	3.0 – 5.0
Caliper axle pin retaining nuts	2.0 – 2.5	14.5 – 18.0
Pad retaining pins	1.5 – 2.0	11.0 – 14.5
Drum brake arm pinch bolt	0.8 – 1.2	6.0 – 9.0

Specifications relating to Chapter 6

Electrical system	12V

Battery

	MBX50	MTX50
Type	Yuasa YB3L-A	Yuasa YB2-5L-C
Capacity	3Ah	2.5Ah
Maximum charging rate	0.3 amp	0.25 amp

Fuse	7A

Alternator output	90W @ 5000 rpm

Charging rate

Note – test conducted with regulator black wire disconnected

	MBX50	MTX50
Charge starts at – day and night	2000 rpm	1800 rpm
Day @ 4000 rpm	0.8A (minimum)/17.7V	1.2A (minimum)/17.7V
Day @ 8000 rpm	2.5A (maximum)/18.2V	3.5A (maximum)/18.2V
Night @ 4000 rpm	0.5A (minimum)/17.7V	1.0A (minimum)/17.7V
Night @ 8000 rpm	2.5A (maximum)/18.2V	3.0A (maximum)/18.2V

Resistor

	MBX50	MTX50	MT50 S-E/F, G, J
Pink to Green wires	6.7 ohm	6.7 ohm	1.4 ohm
Green/white to Green wires	4.0 ohm	3.0 ohm	N/App

Bulbs

	MBX50	MTX50
Headlamp	12V, 35/35W	12V,35/35W
Pilot lamp	12V,4W	12V,4W
Main beam warning lamp	12V,1.7W	12V,1.7W
All other instrument illuminating and warning lamps	12V,3.4W	12V,3.4W
Indicator lamps	12V,18W	12V,18W
Stop/tail lamp	12V,21/5W	12V,21/5W
Number plate lamp	12V,5W	N/App

Bulbs – MT50 S-G, J, L

Indicator lamps	6V,10W
Main beam warning lamp	6V,1.7W

1 General description

The first six Chapters of this Manual describe the Honda MB5, MB50 S-A and MT50 S-A models. This Chapter describes the later models, where working procedures differ significantly.

When working on one of the later models, refer to this Chapter first, to check whether there are any differences noted or described, then refer to the main text for full information.

2 Introduction to the later models

MBX50 S-D

1 This model replaced the earlier MB50 S-A and is easily recognised by its lack of a handlebar fairing amongst many other styling differences; the main distinguishing feature is the fitting of Honda's 'Pro-Link' rear suspension. Apart from the differences described subsequently in this Chapter, the following alterations should be noted:

2 The air filter is now behind the left-hand side panel, the battery being fitted behind the right-hand panel.

3 The square headlamp is now fitted in a nacelle unit, and a separate bulb is fitted in the tail lamp assembly to illuminate the number plate.

4 The handlebars are now secured by two clamps, each fastened by two bolts; removal and refitting is therefore as described for the MT model in Chapter 4. The flashing indicator lamp lenses are retained by a single screw, as described for the US model in Chapter 6.

5 The wheels employ a different pattern of spoke plate and the brake disc of the front wheel is now retained by three bolts passing through the hub to be fastened by nuts. A flanged cover plate is fitted to the hub.

6 The oil pump control lever reference mark is now a notch in the lever outside edge; this must be aligned with the pump body index mark as described in Routine Maintenance and/or Chapter 2.

MTX50 S-C

7 This model replaced the earlier MT50 S-A and is easily recognized by being fitted with Honda's 'Pro-Link' rear suspension. Apart from the other differences described subsequently in this Chapter, the following alterations should be noted:

8 A tachometer is now fitted; this is examined as described in the main text for the MB models and is removed and refitted as described for the MT50 S-A speedometer.

9 The headlamp is a round unit, the air filter is now behind the left-hand side panel and the battery is behind the right-hand side panel. The chain adjusters, while of a different type which use separate drawbolts, are used in a manner similar to that described in Routine Maintenance and/or Chapter 5.

10 The exhaust pipe rear mounting is repositioned and the silencer/tailpipe assembly now has only one mounting bolt.

11 When removing and refitting the front wheel, note that the spindle is no longer threaded into the left-hand fork lower leg, but is now a push fit.

12 The flashing indicator lamp lenses are each retained by a single screw, as described for the US model in Chapter 6.

MT50 S-F, S-G, S-J and S-L

13 These models replaced the MT50 S-A and the MTX50 S-C and apart from slightly re-styled cycle parts, are the same as the MT50 S-A model. Refer therefore to Chapters 1 – 6 when working on one of these machines.

14 Note that the carburettor ID number has altered (see Specifications) and that while all working procedures and specifications are identical to those given for the MT50 S-A, care will be required when ordering replacement parts as many components have been slightly modified; eg the kickstart shaft. This has been enlarged at its bearing surface in the engine right-hand outer casing (MT50 S-G, J, L only), necessitating the fitting of a modified casing and larger thrust washer and oil

seal. Also the later models are fitted with a breather tube on the petrol tank filler cap, and square black plastic-bodied indicator relays.

15 To assist the owner in identifying exactly the model being serviced, their engine and frame numbers are given below:

MT50 S-A

Engine number – AD01E-5000882 on
Frame number – AD01-5000882 to 5041188

MT50 S-F

Engine number – AD01E-5066723 on
Frame number – AD01-5109771 on
Note also that while this model is usually referred to as the MT50 S-F, the parts list refers to it as the MT50 S-E; either suffix may be encountered when ordering spare parts.

MT50 S-G

Engine number – AD01E-5071884 on
Frame number – AD01-5200034 on
In addition to the general notes above, these machines are also fitted with modified flashing indicator lamp assemblies; note that the lenses are each retained by a single screw, as described for the US model in Chapter 6.

MT50 S-J

Engine number – AD01E-5078016 on
Frame number – AD01-5400001 on
In addition to the general notes above and the modified flashing indicator lamp assemblies which are fitted to both S-G and S-J models, these machines also feature slightly modified brake wear indicator pointers and rear sprocket mountings. Note that later MT50 S-G and all MT50 S-J models are fitted with modified side stands. Refer to Section 9 for details.

MT50 S-L

Engine number – AD01E-5082581 on
Frame number – AD01-5500002 on
The S-L model is basically unchanged from the S-J, differing externally in the use of new colours and graphics. The only significant change to this model is the fitting of a combined regulator/rectifier unit, which replaces the separate rectifier and resistor units of previous models.

3 Routine Maintenance: revised schedule – MT50 S-G, J, L

1 Owners should note that while all servicing procedures for these models are as described in Chapters 1 to 6 or in the Routine Maintenance section at the front of this manual, the mileage/time intervals have been revised. Proceed as follows:

2 The pre-ride (daily) and weekly checks should be carried out as described, and the gearbox oil level should be checked at the interval prescribed. For all other work the intervals are:

Six-monthly, or every 2500 miles (4000 km)
Clean the air filter element
Clean and check the spark plug
Check the fuel feed pipe and filter
Check the oil feed pipes
Check the throttle operation and the throttle/oil pump cable adjustment
Check the engine idle speed
Check the clutch adjustment
Check the brake shoes for wear
Check the stand
Check the suspension
Check the wheels

Annually, or every 5000 miles (8000 km)
Repeat all previous service operations, then carry out the following:
Renew the spark plug
Decarbonise the engine and exhaust system

Eighteen monthly, or every 7500 miles (12 000 km)
Repeat all previous service operations, then carry out the following:
Change the transmission oil
Check the steering head bearing adjustment

4   Routine Maintenance: checking the front disc brake – MBX50

1   The front disc brake components must be checked at the same intervals as those given for the earlier model in Routine Maintenance, but noting the following procedures.

2   To check the fluid level, turn the handlebars until the reservoir is horizontal and check that the fluid level, as seen through the sight glass in the rear face of the reservoir body, is not below the lower level mark on the body. Remember that while the fluid level will fall steadily as the pad friction material is used up, if the level falls below the lower level mark there is a risk of air entering the system; it is therefore sufficient to maintain the fluid level above the lower level mark, by topping-up if necessary. Do not top up to the higher level mark (formed by a cast line on the inside of the reservoir) unless this is necessary after new pads have been fitted. If topping up is necessary, wipe any dirt off the reservoir, remove the retaining screws and lift away the reservoir cover and diaphragm. Use only good quality brake fluid of the recommended type and ensure that it comes from a freshly opened sealed container, brake fluid is hygroscopic, which means that it absorbs moisture from the air, therefore old fluid may have become contaminated to such an extent that its boiling point has been lowered to an unsafe level. Remember also that brake fluid is an excellent paint stripper and will attack plastic components; wash away any spilled fluid immediately with copious quantities of water. When the level is correct, clean and dry the diaphragm, fold it into its compressed state and fit it to the reservoir. Refit the reservoir cover (and gasket, where fitted) and tighten securely, but do not overtighten, the retaining screws.

3   To check the degree of pad wear, look closely at the pads from above or below the caliper. Wear limit marks are provided in the form of deep notches cut in the top and bottom edges of the friction material or as red painted lines cut around the outside of the material. If either pad is worn at any point so that the inside end of the mark (next to the metal backing) is in contact with the disc, or if the wear limit marks have been removed completely, both pads must be renewed as a set. If the pads are so fouled with dirt that the marks cannot be seen, or if the oil or grease is seen on them, they must be removed for cleaning and examination.

4   To remove the pads, use an Allen key of suitable size to unscrew the threaded plugs which seal the pad retaining pins, then slacken the retaining pins. Remove the two mounting bolts and withdraw the caliper, complete with its mounting bracket, from the fork leg, taking care not to twist the brake hose. Remove both pad retaining pins and withdraw the pads, noting carefully the presence and exact position of the anti-rattle spring.

5   Thoroughly clean all components, removing all traces of dirt, grease and old friction material then use carefully fine abrasive paper to polish clean any corroded items. Check carefully that the caliper body slides easily on its two axle bolts and that there is no damage to any of the caliper components, especially the rubber seals. If it is stiff, remove the mounting bracket from the caliper, clean the axle bolts and check them for wear or damage (which can be cured only by the renewal of the bolts or mounting bracket, as applicable) then smear a good quantity of silicone or PBC (Poly Butyl Cuprysil) based caliper grease over the bolts and caliper bores before refitting the mounting bracket to the caliper. It is essential that the caliper body can move smoothly and easily on the mounting bracket for the brake to be effective. **Warning:** do not use ordinary high-melting point grease; this will melt and foul the pads, rendering the brake ineffective.

6   If the pads are worn to the limit marks, fouled with oil or grease, or heavily scored or damaged by dirt and debris, they must be renewed as a set; there is no satisfactory way of degreasing friction material. If the pads can be used again, clean them carefully using a fine wire brush that is completely free of oil or grease. Remove all traces of road dirt and corrosion, then use a pointed instrument to clean out the groove(s) in the friction material and to dig out any embedded particles of foreign matter. Any areas of glazing may be removed using emery cloth.

7   On reassembly, if new pads are to be fitted, the caliper pistons must now be pushed back as far as possible into the caliper bores to provide the clearance necessary to accommodate the unworn pads. It should be possible to do this with hand pressure alone. If any undue stiffness is encountered the caliper assembly should be dismantled for examination as described in Section 21. While pushing the pistons back, maintain a careful watch on the fluid level in the handlebar reservoir. If the reservoir has been overfilled, the surplus fluid will prevent the pistons returning fully and must be removed by soaking it up with a clean cloth. Take care to prevent fluid spillage. Apply a thin smear of caliper grease to the outer edge and rear surface of the moving pad and to the pad retaining pins. Take care to apply caliper grease to the metal backing of the pad only and not to allow any grease to contaminate the friction material. Carefully fit the pad anti-rattle spring, ensuring that it is correctly located, and insert the moving pad into its aperture in the caliper mounting bracket. Check that the pad is free to slide in the mounting bracket then refit the second pad and insert the two pad retaining pins, tightening them securely to the specified torque setting. Note that the pads must be refitted so that the larger areas of friction material are downwards when the caliper is in place on the machine.

8   Replace the caliper assembly on the machine ensuring that the pads engage correctly on the disc and that the hose is not twisted, then refit the mounting bolts and tighten them securely, to the specified torque setting if possible. Check that the pad pins are securely tightened and refit the threaded plugs. Apply the brake lever gently and repeatedly to bring the pads firmly into contact with the disc until full brake pressure is restored. Be careful to watch the fluid level in the reservoir; if the pads have been re-used it will suffice to keep the level above the lower level mark, by topping-up if necessary, but if new pads have been fitted the level must be restored to the upper level line described above by topping up or removing surplus fluid as necessary. Refit the reservoir cover, gasket (where fitted) and diaphragm as described above.

9   Before taking the machine out on the road, be careful to check for fluid leaks from the system, and that the front brake is working correctly. Remember also that new pads, and to a lesser extent, cleaned pads will require a bedding-in period before they will function at peak efficiency. Where new pads are fitted use the brake gently but firmly for the first 50 – 100 miles to enable the pads to bed in fully.

5   Routine Maintenance: adjusting drum brakes – all models

1   While drum brakes are adjusted as described in Routine Maintenance and/or Chapter 5, if adjustment is no longer possible (the adjuster threads having been taken up) but the wear indicators show the brake shoe friction material to be still serviceable, the operating arms may be rotated on the camshafts.

2   Disconnect the cable or rod from the operating arm and remove its retaining pinch bolt. Carefully lever the arm off the camshaft splines, taking care not to disturb the wear indicator plate, and rotate the arm through one or two camshaft splines before tapping it back on to the camshaft. Some trial and error will be required before the arm is re-located so that the full length of the adjuster is once more available.

3   Tighten the pinch bolt to the specified torque setting, connect the cable or rod again and adjust the brake.

6   Routine Maintenance: final drive chain – all models

1   On MTX50 models, note the different chain free play

specification. On all models, adjust the chain as described in Routine Maintenance and/or Chapter 5, but note that the adjusters are fitted with locknuts on the MTX50.

2   To assess accurately the amount of wear present in the chain, it must be cleaned and dried as described above, then laid out on a flat surface. Compress the chain fully and measure its length from end to end. Anchor one end of the chain and pull on the other end, drawing the chain out to its fullest extent. Measure the stretched length. If the stretched measurement exceeds the compressed measurement by more than 2% or $\frac{1}{4}$ in per foot, the chain must be considered worn out and be renewed. Honda's own recommendation is that the maximum length of any 40 links (ie mark any one pin, count off 41 pins and measure the distance between the two) must not exceed 518 mm (20.4 in) when the chain is cleaned and stretched out.

7   Routine Maintenance: cleaning the fuel tap filter

1   This task must be performed every three months, or 1800 miles/3000 km, whichever is the sooner.

2   Switch the tap to the 'Off' position and unscrew the filter bowl from the tap base, then remove the O-ring and the filter gauze. Check the condition of the sealing O-ring and renew, if it is seriously compressed, distorted or damaged. Clean the filter gauze using a fine-bristled toothbrush or similar; remove all traces of dirt or debris and renew the gauze if it is split or damaged. Thoroughly clean the filter bowl; if excessive signs of dirt or water are found in the petrol, remove the tank as described in Section 12, empty the petrol into a clean container and remove the fuel tap by unscrewing its retaining gland nut.

3   Fit the filter gauze to the tap, ensuring that it is located correctly, then press the O-ring into place to retain it. Use only a close-fitting ring spanner to tighten the filter bowl, which should be secured by just enough to nip up the O-ring; do not overtighten it as this will only damage the filter bowl, distort the O-ring and promote fuel leaks. The recommended torque setting is only 0.3 − 0.5 kgf m (2 − 3.5 lbf ft). If any leaks are found in the tap they can be cured only by the renewal of the tap assembly or the defective seal, where applicable.

8   Routine Maintenance: checking the suspension

1   This task must be performed every six months, or 3600 miles/6000 km, whichever is the sooner.

2   On MBX50 models inspect the stanchions, looking for signs of chips or other damage, then lift the dust excluder at the top of each fork lower leg and wipe away any dirt from its sealing lips or above the fork oil seal. Pack grease above the seal and refit the dust excluder. Note that none of this would be necessary, and fork stiction would be reduced, if gaiters are fitted; they are available from any good motorcycle dealer. For obvious reasons this is not necessary on MTX50 models but it is still advisable to lift the gaiters at regular intervals to check the seals; smear grease over the stanchion to prevent corrosion.

3   To check the swinging arm support the machine so that the rear wheel is clear of the ground then pull and push horizontally at the rear end of the swinging arm; there should be no discernible play at the pivot. If the rear suspension is not to be dismantled for lubrication, pump grease into the swinging arm pivot via the grease nipple provided until fresh grease is seen at both ends of the pivot. Honda recommend the use of a molybdenum disulphide-based grease.

4   The rear suspension linkage consists of several highly-stressed bearing surfaces which are not fitted with grease nipples (except in the case of MTX50 swinging arm pivots) and which are very exposed to all the water, dirt and salt thrown up by the rear wheel. Regular cleaning and greasing is essential; owners should note that this is greatly simplified if the linkage were dismantled for all bearings to be fitted with grease nipples.

A local Honda Service Agent should be able to tell you of someone competent to undertake such work. Note that not only are the linkage components expensive to renew if allowed to wear out through lack of attention, but the machine will almost certainly fail its DOT certificate test if such wear is found.

5   To check the linkage components, two people are required; one to sit on the machine and bounce the rear suspension while the other watches closely the action of the various components. If any squeaks or other noises are heard, if the linkage appears stiff, or if any signs of dry bearings or other wear or damage are detected, the rear suspension should be removed as a complete assembly and dismantled for thorough cleaning, checking and greasing. Where grease nipples are fitted, remove the weight from the suspension by supporting the machine so that the rear wheel is clear of the ground, then inject grease into each bearing until all old grease is expelled and new grease can be seen issuing from each end of the bearing. If nipples are not fitted, the linkage must be dismantled so that the bearings can be cleaned and packed with new grease. See Sections 16 and 17 of this Chapter.

9   Routine Maintenance: checking the side stand – later MT50 S-G and all S-J, L models

1   Examine the side stand for cracks or bending, and lubricate the pivot with a multi-purpose or graphited grease. The side stand pivots about a single shouldered bolt; check that its retaining nut is securely fastened. Check the return spring and renew it, if weak or strained; if the pivot is correctly lubricated and the spring sufficiently strong, a pull of 2 − 3 kg (4.4 − 6.6 lb) as measured with a spring balance hooked on to the stand foot, should be required to retract the stand when it is in the 'down' position (machine supported upright).

2   Inspect the rubber pad on the side stand for wear. If it is worn down to or past the wear mark, it should be renewed. Renew with a pad marked 'Below 259 lb only'.

10 Engine/gearbox unit: removal and refitting

1   Since the MBX50 and MTX50 models are both fitted with full cradle type frames, a slightly modified procedure is required to remove and refit the engine.

MBX50

2   Remove the seat, both side panels and the fuel tank as described in Section 12 of this Chapter. Remove the carburettor as described in Chapter 2.

3   Remove or disconnect all other components as described in paragraphs 1 − 9 of Chapter 1, Section 4.

4   Remove their retaining nuts and tap out the three engine mounting bolts noting the spacer on the upper rear bolt. Withdraw the engine unit.

5   Refitting is the reverse of the removal procedure.

MTX50

6   Remove the seat, both side panels and the fuel tank as described in Section 12 of this Chapter. Remove the carburettor as described in Chapter 2.

7   Noting that this model is fitted with a tachometer whose drive cable must be disconnected, remove or disconnect all other components as described in Sections 4 and 5 of Chapter 1.

8   Remove their retaining nuts and tap out the three mounting bolts of the engine top mounting/cylinder head steady assembly, then withdraw the two mounting plates. Remove their retaining nuts and tap out the remaining three mounting bolts, noting the two spacers on the upper rear bolt. Withdraw the engine unit to the left.

9   Refitting is the reverse of the removal procedure.

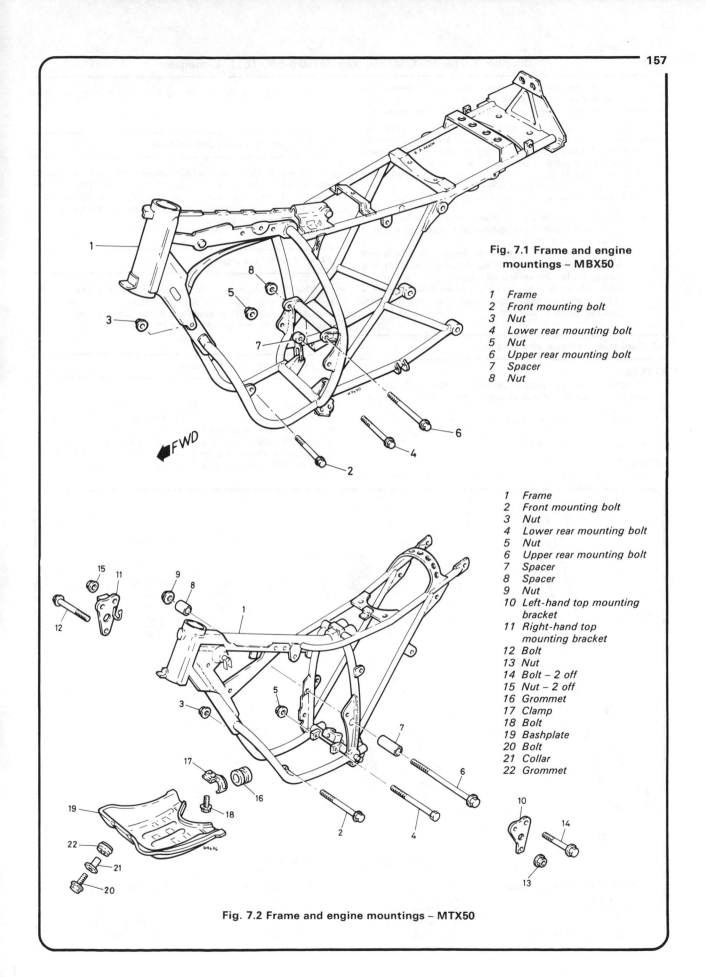

Fig. 7.1 Frame and engine mountings – MBX50

1   Frame
2   Front mounting bolt
3   Nut
4   Lower rear mounting bolt
5   Nut
6   Upper rear mounting bolt
7   Spacer
8   Nut

1   Frame
2   Front mounting bolt
3   Nut
4   Lower rear mounting bolt
5   Nut
6   Upper rear mounting bolt
7   Spacer
8   Spacer
9   Nut
10   Left-hand top mounting
      bracket
11   Right-hand top
      mounting bracket
12   Bolt
13   Nut
14   Bolt – 2 off
15   Nut – 2 off
16   Grommet
17   Clamp
18   Bolt
19   Bashplate
20   Bolt
21   Collar
22   Grommet

FWD

Fig. 7.2 Frame and engine mountings – MTX50

11 Engine/gearbox unit: modifications

1   When removing or refitting the cylinder head, note that there is no top mounting bolt to be removed on MBX50 models, but on MTX50 models the engine top mounting/cylinder head steady assembly must first be dismantled.

2   Note that the MTX50 model is fitted with a tachometer identical to that described in Chapter 1.

3   On MBX50 models, note the following modifications:

  a)   The two rear cylinder studs are fitted with tubular seals or dowels at the crankcase gasket surface; do not omit these on reassembly

  b)   The crankshaft right-hand main bearing oil seal is now outboard of the main bearing, which is therefore now lubricated by the engine oil supply

  c)   With reference to Fig. 1.10, a splined thrust washer is fitted between the output shaft 1st and 4th gear pinions (items 3 and 9)

12 Fuel tank: removal and refitting

MBX50

1   Disconnect the feed pipe as described in Chapter 2, Section 2. Unlock and remove the dual seat, then carefully pull away both side panels.

2   Unscrew the single mounting bolt, lift the tank at the rear and pull it backwards off its front mountings. Refitting is the reverse of the removal procedure.

MTX50

3   Proceed as described for the MT50 model in Chapter 2, but

note that the tank is retained by only one bolt on the later model.

13 Pilot jet – removal and refitting

On the MBX50 and MTX50 models the pilot jet can be unscrewed for cleaning purposes but requires great care on refitting. It must be screwed in carefully until resistance is encountered, then tightened by $\frac{3}{4}$ turn only. Do not overtighten the jet as it is easy to shear it off.

14 CDI Unit: testing

The CDI unit on both later models is tested as described for the US model in Chapter 3. It is mounted under the rear of the fuel tank on MBX50 models and under the seat, next to the suspension unit top mounting, on MTX50 models.

15 Front forks: modifications

MBX50

1   Note that the complete fork legs are removed and refitted as described for the MB50 S-A in Chapter 4. Dismantling and reassembly are also similar, bearing in mind the obvious differences shown in the accompanying illustration. Note that the spring retaining plug must be removed and refitted with a spanner, taking precautions to prevent it from flying out under spring pressure.

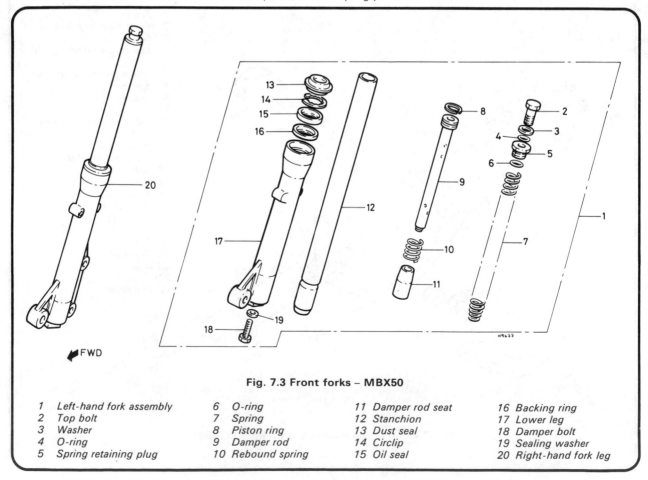

Fig. 7.3 Front forks – MBX50

1	Left-hand fork assembly	6	O-ring	11	Damper rod seat	16	Backing ring
2	Top bolt	7	Spring	12	Stanchion	17	Lower leg
3	Washer	8	Piston ring	13	Dust seal	18	Damper bolt
4	O-ring	9	Damper rod	14	Circlip	19	Sealing washer
5	Spring retaining plug	10	Rebound spring	15	Oil seal	20	Right-hand fork leg

MTX50

2   Although different in appearance, the only significant difference between the forks fitted to the MTX50 and those fitted to the MT50 S-A models is that the later model has drain plugs, gaiters, and separate damper rod seats (the latter similar to those shown for the MBX50). Proceed as described for the MT50 S-A model.

16 Rear suspension: removal and refitting

1   **Note:** while it is possible, with a little care, to remove the pivot bolts and separate the suspension unit, linkage and swinging arm so that all three can be removed individually, it is recommended that the complete suspension be removed as a single assembly, as described below. This will permit all components to be checked for wear or damage and all bearings to be lubricated at the same time.

2   First remove the rear wheel as described in Chapter 5, then remove the seat, both side panels and the chainguard. If it is necessary to gain access to the suspension unit top mounting bolt, remove also the fuel tank. On MTX50 models it may be necessary to remove the oil tank, but on MBX50 models the air filter assembly may have to be withdrawn to reach the suspension unit.

3   Remove the retaining nuts from the suspension unit top mounting, the linkage front arm/frame mounting and the swinging arm pivot bolt, then remove the bolts in the same order. If any bolt is difficult to remove because of dirt or corrosion, apply a liberal quantity of penetrating fluid and allow time for it to work before tapping out the bolt with a hammer and drift. Manoeuvring it carefully to avoid damage, lift out the swinging arm and rear suspension, disengaging it from the chain.

4   On reassembly, grease all bearings thoroughly and check that all components are in place, then manoeuvre the assembly into position, remembering to pass the swinging arm left-hand fork end through the chain. Refit the swinging arm pivot bolt, greasing it thoroughly and tighten its retaining nut to the torque setting specified. Check that it moves easily, with no traces of stiffness or free play, then align the linkage front arm with its frame mounting, grease the pivot bolt and refit it, followed by refitting the suspension unit top mounting bolt, suitably greased. Tighten their retaining nuts to the specified torque settings, but raise the swinging arm to normal working height before tightening the unit bottom mounting bolt. This is to ensure that the bonded rubber bush fitted at this point is tightened in approximately its normal working position to minimise distortion and to prevent premature wear.

5   Refit all components that were removed on dismantling and check for correct chain adjustment, suspension movement and rear brake operation before taking the machine out on the road.

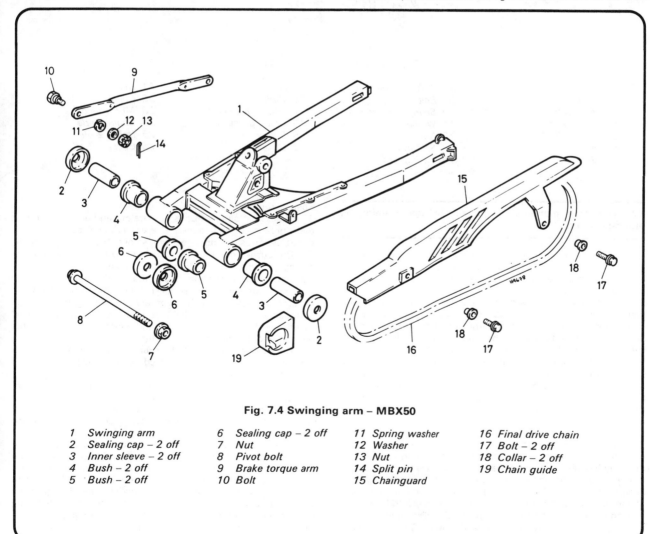

Fig. 7.4 Swinging arm – MBX50

1	Swinging arm	6	Sealing cap – 2 off	11	Spring washer	16	Final drive chain
2	Sealing cap – 2 off	7	Nut	12	Washer	17	Bolt – 2 off
3	Inner sleeve – 2 off	8	Pivot bolt	13	Nut	18	Collar – 2 off
4	Bush – 2 off	9	Brake torque arm	14	Split pin	19	Chain guide
5	Bush – 2 off	10	Bolt	15	Chainguard		

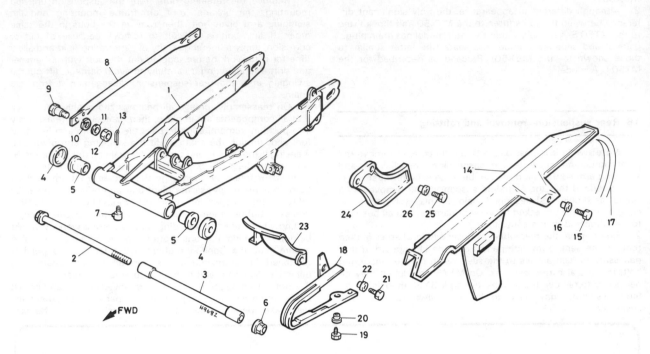

Fig. 7.5 Swinging arm – MTX50

1 Swinging arm	8 Brake torque arm	15 Bolt	21 Bolt
2 Pivot bolt	9 Bolt	16 Collar	22 Collar
3 Inner sleeve	10 Spring washer	17 Final drive chain	23 Mud shield
4 Sealing cap – 2 off	11 Washer	18 Chain guide	24 Chain guide
5 Bush – 2 off	12 Nut	19 Screw	25 Bolt – 2 off
6 Nut	13 Split pin	20 Collar	26 Collar – 2 off
7 Grease nipple	14 Chainguard		

17 Swinging arm and rear suspension linkage: examination and renovation

1   Before commencing work, check with a local Honda Service Agent exactly what is available for the machine being worked on. In some cases bushes are available only as part of a larger component.

2   Referring to the illustrations accompanying the text, dismantle the assembly into its component parts and wash carefully each one in solvent to remove all traces of dirt and old grease. Components such as the chain guides and linkage mud shields need not be removed unless necessary.

3   All pivot bearings are formed by a bush of metal or of synthetic material, or in some cases bonded rubber bushes that are pressed into the bearing housing. A steel inner sleeve is fitted in the centre of this bearing and the pivot bolt passes through the sleeve. Sealing caps are fitted at each end of each bearing.

4   Wear will only be found, therefore, between the pivot bolt and inner sleeve and between the inner sleeve and bearing. After thorough cleaning, reassemble each bearing and feel for free play between the components. If excessive free play is felt, examine each component renewing any that shows signs of deep scoring or scuffing. Also check all components for wear due to the presence of dirt or corrosion, and check the swinging arm and linkage arms for signs of cracks, distortion or other damage, renewing any worn items. On MTX50 models, wear can be assessed by direct measurement, if required (see

Specifications).

5   Check that all pivot bolts are straight and unworn and that their threads are undamaged. Use emery paper to polish off all traces of corrosion and smear grease over them on reassembly.

6   The bushes can be removed either by tapping them out or by using a variation of a drawbolt arrangement as shown in the accompanying illustration. Note that since this will almost certainly damage the bush or bearing, they should not be disturbed unless renewal is necessary. On refitting, the drawbolt arrangement shown must be used to avoid the risk of damage. Clean the housing thoroughly and smear grease over the bearing and its housing to aid refitting.

7   The sealing caps should be examined closely and renewed if worn; they must be in good condition to exclude dirt and water from the bearings.

8   On reassembly, pack molybdenum disulphide grease (containing at least 45% molybdenum disulphide) into each bearing and sealing cap, and smear it over all inner sleeves and pivot bolts. Check that all grease nipples are clear by pumping grease into the bearings.

9   Refer to the accompanying illustrations on reassembly to ensure that all components are correctly refitted. Do not forget to refit the sealing caps to each bearing, ensuring that their lips seat correctly. All linkage pivot bolts are fitted from left to right on MBX50 models; on MTX50 models the linkage front arm/frame and the swinging arm pivot bolts are refitted from right to left, all others are refitted from left to right.

10 Tighten all retaining nuts to the torque settings given in the Specifications Section of this Chapter.

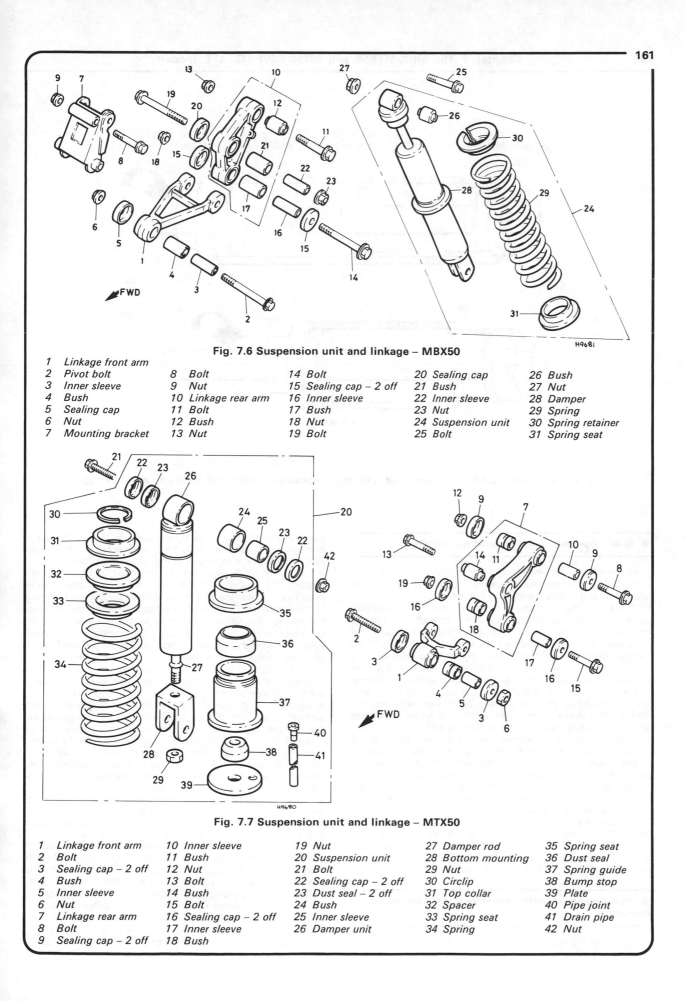

Fig. 7.6 Suspension unit and linkage – MBX50

1	Linkage front arm	8	Bolt	14	Bolt	20	Sealing cap	26	Bush
2	Pivot bolt	9	Nut	15	Sealing cap – 2 off	21	Bush	27	Nut
3	Inner sleeve	10	Linkage rear arm	16	Inner sleeve	22	Inner sleeve	28	Damper
4	Bush	11	Bolt	17	Bush	23	Nut	29	Spring
5	Sealing cap	12	Bush	18	Nut	24	Suspension unit	30	Spring retainer
6	Nut	13	Nut	19	Bolt	25	Bolt	31	Spring seat
7	Mounting bracket								

Fig. 7.7 Suspension unit and linkage – MTX50

1	Linkage front arm	10	Inner sleeve	19	Nut	27	Damper rod	35	Spring seat
2	Bolt	11	Bush	20	Suspension unit	28	Bottom mounting	36	Dust seal
3	Sealing cap – 2 off	12	Nut	21	Bolt	29	Nut	37	Spring guide
4	Bush	13	Bolt	22	Sealing cap – 2 off	30	Circlip	38	Bump stop
5	Inner sleeve	14	Bush	23	Dust seal – 2 off	31	Top collar	39	Plate
6	Nut	15	Bolt	24	Bush	32	Spacer	40	Pipe joint
7	Linkage rear arm	16	Sealing cap – 2 off	25	Inner sleeve	33	Spring seat	41	Drain pipe
8	Bolt	17	Inner sleeve	26	Damper unit	34	Spring	42	Nut
9	Sealing cap – 2 off	18	Bush						

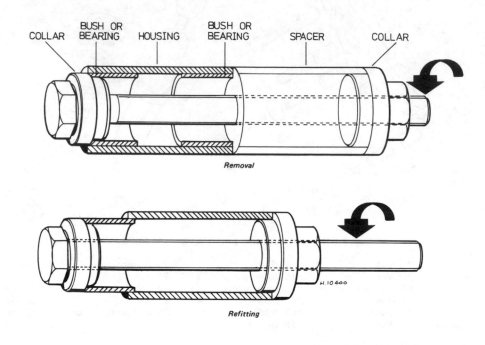

Fig. 7.8 Drawbolt tool for removing and refitting suspension linkage and swinging arm bearings

18 Rear suspension unit: removal and refitting

1   As mentioned in Section 16, the suspension unit is best removed as part of the rear suspension, but if it is necessary to detach the unit alone, proceed as follows.

2   Place the machine on a stand so that it is supported securely with the rear wheel clear of the ground, then remove the seat, the side panels and if necessary to reach the suspension unit top mounting bolt, the fuel tank. On MTX50 models remove the oil tank mounting bolts to gain working space; it may be necessary to remove the tank but if a little ingenuity is exercised it should be possible to manoeuvre the tank from position without disturbing it unduly. On all models, take the weight off the rear suspension by wedging a wooden block under the rear wheel, then remove its retaining nut and tap out the suspension unit top mounting bolt.

3   Exposing the unit bottom mounting may prove to be awkward; remove if necessary the mud shields and chain guides to gain extra working space, then either lift the wheel and support it on blocks as soon as the mounting bolt is accessible, or remove the linkage pivot bolts and lower the unit to the ground; it may be necessary to remove the linkage front arm to permit this. Be careful not to damage the unit.

4   Reassembly is a reversal of the dismantling procedure chosen. If the mounting bolts are to be renewed, use only genuine Honda parts to be sure of mountings of sufficient strength. Smear grease over the bolts and refit them from left to right. Tighten all bolts to the torque settings specified.

19 Rear suspension unit: dismantling, examination and reassembly

1   Note that the suspension unit is sealed for life and can only be renewed to rectify any faults such as if it is dented or damaged, if the damper rod is bent, or if any signs of oil leakage can be seen. To remove the spring, proceed as follows.

2   On MBX50 models some means must be found of compressing the spring safely so that the spring retainer can be pulled out. While this is usually achieved by placing the unit bottom mounting in a vice and having an assistant pull down on the spring, the safest method is to apply a pair of spring compressors to the spring coils. Compressors are readily available in auto accessory shops for use on the MacPherson strut front suspension of many cars, particularly Fords.

3   On MTX50 models, clamp the unit top mounting eye in a vice and compress the spring as described above, then use a pointed instrument to displace the spring top seat retaining circlip from its groove in the unit body; note carefully which groove is used of the two provided. With the spring still compressed, note how many threads of the damper rod are exposed, hold the unit bottom mounting and slacken its locknut, then unscrew the bottom mounting and the locknut. Withdraw the metal plate with the drain tube attached, followed by the spring bottom seat, the spring guide, the dust seal and the spring itself with its top collar and seat.

4   When it has been removed, measure the spring free length and renew it if it is settled to less than the service limit specified. Renew the damper assembly if any of the faults listed above are found, or if the damping action is weak.

5   The unit top mounting is a bonded rubber bush on MBX50 models and a metal bush with a steel inner sleeve on MTX50 models, check it for wear or damage and renew it if faulty. The bush is removed and refitted using a modified version of the drawbolt assembly described in Section 17 of this Chapter.

6   On MBX50 models reassembly is a straightforward reversal of the dismantling sequence. On MTX50 models the same applies but the following points should be noted. When refitting the top seat retaining circlip, note that while it should be refitted

in the groove from which it was removed, a measure of preload adjustment can be achieved, if desired, by fitting the circlip in a different groove; the groove nearest the unit bottom mounting will give the hardest spring setting, this gradually softening as the circlip is moved up towards the unit top mounting.

7   Also on MTX50 models, when refitting the spring it must be compressed safely while the bottom mounting components are refitted in their correct positions. Apply thread locking compound to the damper rod threads, screw the bottom mounting fully on to the damper rod followed by the locknut, screwing both into the previously noted position and tightening them securely. Note that a torque setting of 3.8 – 6.0 kgf m (27.5 – 43 lbf ft) is specified and should be used if a means can be found of applying it. Slowly release spring pressure and rotate the metal plate until the pin projecting from it aligns with the cutout in the bottom mounting so that the drain tube will be in the correct position when the unit is refitted to the machine. Pack the unit top mounting with molybdenum disulphide grease before refitting the inner sleeve and check that the seals and sealing caps are correctly fitted.

20 Front brake master cylinder – modifications – MBX50

Although now a cast one-piece unit with an inspection window to check the brake fluid level (see Section 4), the master cylinder is serviced in the same way as that described in Chapter 5. The only difference is that the washer (item 5, Figure 5.3) is no longer fitted. Note that if the necessary measuring equipment is available, the dimensions of the cylinder bore and piston can be checked against those specified and any worn components can be renewed.

21 Brake caliper: examination and renovation – MBX50

1   If the regular checks described in Section 4 reveal the presence of any fluid leaks or of any wear, damage, or corrosion which will impair the caliper's efficiency, the unit must be removed and dismantled for checking. Start by removing the brake pads as described in Section 4 of this Chapter.

2   Pull the mounting bracket out of the caliper body. If they are damaged or worn, the two axle bolts can be unscrewed from the bracket and renewed individually. Detach the rubber dust seal from the upper axle bolt and pull out of the caliper body the rubber dust seal/bush which fits around the lower axle bolt; these should be renewed if cracked, split or worn in any way.

3   The simplest way of ejecting the pistons from the caliper bores is to place the caliper in a plastic bag, tying the neck tightly around the brake hose to catch the inevitable shower of brake fluid. Apply the brake lever repeatedly, using normal hydraulic pressure to force out the piston. Ensure that the pistons leave the bores at the same time; if one sticks at any point the other piston must be restrained by firm hand pressure so that the full hydraulic pressure can overcome the resistance. It would be very difficult to extract one piston alone from this type of caliper without risking damage. When the pistons have been ejected, apply the brake lever until all remaining fluid is pumped into the bag, then unscrew the union bolt to disconnect the brake hose and remove the caliper from the machine, taking care to prevent the spillage of any brake fluid.

4   An alternative to the above method will require a source of compressed air. Attach a length of clear plastic tubing to the bleed nipple, placing the tube lower end in a suitable container. Open the bleed nipple by one full turn and pump gently on the front brake lever to drain as much fluid as possible from the hydraulic system. When no more fluid can be seen issuing from the bleed nipple, tighten it down again, withdraw the plastic tube and disconnect the hydraulic hose at the caliper union. Wrap a large piece of cloth loosely around the caliper and apply a jet of compressed air to the union orifice. Be careful not to use too high an air pressure or the pistons may be damaged.

5   If either of the above methods fails to dislodge the pistons, no further time should be wasted and the complete caliper assembly should be renewed. If the pistons and caliper bores are so badly damaged or so corroded that hydraulic or air pressure cannot move the pistons, the caliper will not be safe for further use even if a method can be devised of removing the pistons and cleaning the bearing surfaces.

6   When each piston has been removed, it should be placed in a clean container to ensure that it cannot be damaged and the seals should be picked out of the caliper bores, pressing each inwards to release it, and discarded. Wrap the exposed end of the hydraulic hose in clean rag or polythene to prevent the entry of dirt. Carefully wash off all spilt brake fluid from the machine using fresh water, brake fluid is an excellent paint stripper and will attack any painted metal or plastic component.

7   Clean the caliper components thoroughly in hydraulic fluid. **Never** use petrol or cleaning solvent for cleaning hydraulic brake parts otherwise the rubber components will be damaged. Discard all the rubber components as a matter of course. The replacement cost is relatively small and does not warrant re-use of components vital to safety. Check the pistons and caliper cylinder bores for scoring, rusting or pitting. If any of these defects are evident it is unlikely that a good fluid seal can be maintained and for this reason the components should be renewed. If measuring equipment is available, compare the dimensions of the caliper bores and the pistons with those given in the Specifications Section of this Chapter, renewing any component that is worn to beyond the set wear limit.

8   Inspect the shank of each axle bolt for any signs of damage or corrosion and clean or renew each one as necessary; if the matching bores in the caliper body are worn or damaged, the body must be renewed. It is essential that the body can move smoothly and easily on the axle bolts. Check also that the bleed nipple is clear and its threads undamaged, and that the dust cap is in good condition; renew either component if faulty.

9   On reassembly, the components must be absolutely clean and dry; cleanliness is essential to prevent the entry of dirt into the system. Soak the new seals in hydraulic fluid before refitting them to the caliper bores; check that each seal is securely located in its groove without being twisted or distorted. Smear a liberal quantity of clean brake fluid over the pistons and caliper bores then very carefully insert the pistons (with their recessed faces outwards) with a twisting motion, as if screwing them in, to avoid damaging or dislodging the seals. When the piston outer ends project 3 – 5 mm above the caliper they are fully refitted; do not press them fully into the caliper bores. Wipe off any surplus brake fluid.

10   Fit the rubber bush and seal to the caliper body and mounting bracket, check that the axle bolts are tightened securely on the bracket and smear silicone- or PBC-based brake caliper grease over the bolt bearing surfaces. Pack a small amount of grease into the matching caliper passages and refit the mounting bracket, ensuring that the seals are correctly engaged on their locating shoulders. Renew the sealing washers if worn or distorted and connect the brake hose to the caliper. Check that the hose is correctly aligned and tighten the union bolt to the specified torque setting. Refit the pads to the caliper and the caliper assembly to the machine, as described in Section 4.

11   Refill the master cylinder reservoir with new hydraulic fluid and bleed the system by following the procedure given in Chapter 5. On completion of bleeding, carry out a check for leakage of fluid whilst applying the brake lever. Push the machine forward and bring it to a halt by applying the brake. Do this several times to ensure that the brake is operating correctly before taking the machine out on the road.

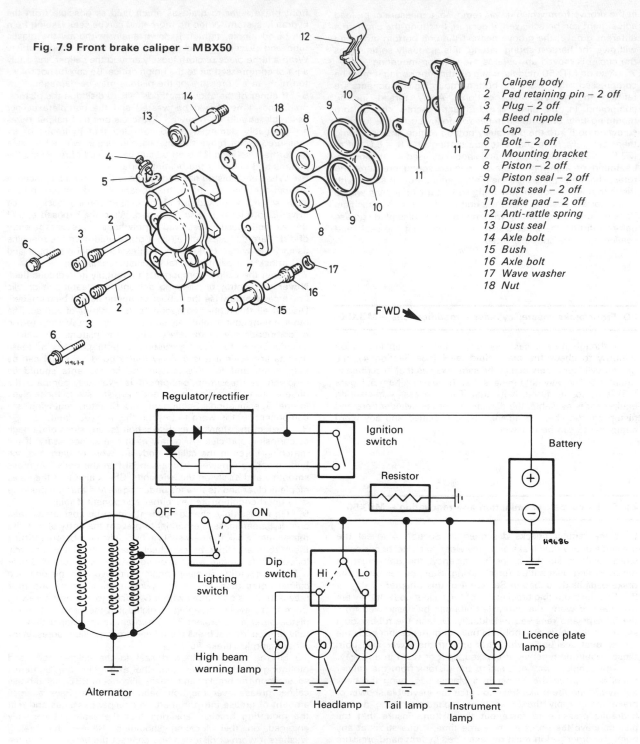

Fig. 7.9 Front brake caliper – MBX50

1 Caliper body
2 Pad retaining pin – 2 off
3 Plug – 2 off
4 Bleed nipple
5 Cap
6 Bolt – 2 off
7 Mounting bracket
8 Piston – 2 off
9 Piston seal – 2 off
10 Dust seal – 2 off
11 Brake pad – 2 off
12 Anti-rattle spring
13 Dust seal
14 Axle bolt
15 Bush
16 Axle bolt
17 Wave washer
18 Nut

FWD

Fig. 7.10 Charging system circuit diagram – MBX50

22 Charging system: checking

Alternator

1 The alternator is tested as described in Chapter 6, Section 3, comparing the results obtained with those given in the Specifications Section of this Chapter. The resistance values of the coils themselves are the same as those given in Chapter 6.

Regulator/rectifier unit

2 On MBX50 models, the regulator/rectifier unit is a sealed, finned, metal unit, mounted on the left-hand side of the frame top tubes, immediately to the rear of the steering head. Remove the seat, both side panels and the fuel tank to gain access to it. On MTX50 models the unit is mounted under the seat, next to the suspension unit top mounting.

3   To test the unit, disconnect it at the multi-pin block connector joining it to the main wiring loom; the test must be carried out using either a Sanwa SP-10D (Honda part number 07308-0020000) electrical tester set to the kilo ohms scale, or a Kowa TH-5H electrical tester set to the x100 ohm scale. Measure the resistance between the pairs of wires as shown in the accompaning test table, comparing the readings obtained with those specified. If the specified equipment is not available, some idea of the unit's condition may be gained by using an ordinary multimeter or ohmmeter, determining by trial and error the correct resistance range; the results of any such test should be confirmed by a Honda Service Agent using the correct equipment before any firm conclusions are reached.

4   If the results obtained differ from those specified at any point, the unit is faulty and must be renewed; repairs are not possible.

Resistor

5   On MBX50 models the resistor is mounted on the right-hand side of the frame top tube, under the fuel tank; on MTX50 models it is on the left-hand side of the frame front downtube.

6   The unit is tested as described in Chapter 6, but the test connections and the results to be expected are given in the Specifications Section of this Chapter. Since the resistor is now a double unit, two separate tests are necessary to check each side; note that the wire colours may refer to the wires themselves or to coloured identifying sleeves fitted over black wires, whichever is fitted.

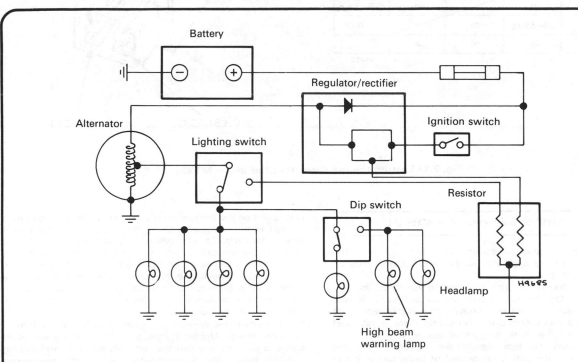

Fig. 7.11 Charging system circuit diagram – MTX50

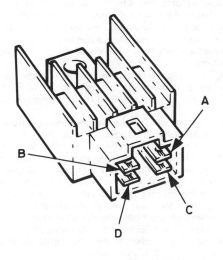

+PROBE −PROBE	A	B	C	D
A		1~5 kΩ	∞	∞
B	1~5 kΩ		∞	∞
C	∞	∞		∞
D	∞	∞	0.5~1.0 kΩ	

Fig. 7.12 Testing the regulator/rectifier unit – MBX50

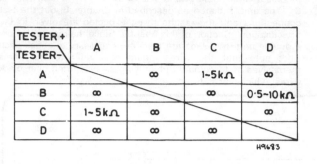

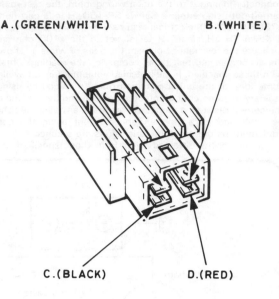

A.(GREEN/WHITE)   B.(WHITE)

C.(BLACK)   D.(RED)

TESTER + / TESTER –	A	B	C	D
A		∞	1~5kΩ	∞
B	∞		∞	0·5~10kΩ
C	1~5kΩ	∞		∞
D	∞	∞	∞	

H9683

Fig. 7.13 Testing the regulator/rectifier unit – MTX50

23 Regulator/rectifier unit: general – MT50 S-L

1 A combined regulator/rectifier unit is fitted to the MT50 S-L, in place of the separate rectifier and resistor units on previous models.
2 The regulator/rectifier unit is bolted to the right-hand side of the frame top rail, just above the carburettor. It is held by a single bolt and can be removed after disconnecting its wiring at the block connector. Note that there is no need to remove the fuel tank to gain access to the unit.
3 Unfortunately no test details are available from the manufacturer; if the unit is suspected of being faulty, it can only be tested by the substitution of a new unit.

24 Low oil level warning lamp circuit: testing

1 The circuit consists of a float-type switch mounted in the top of the oil tank and the bulb itself, which is mounted in the instrument panel (MBX50) or in the tachometer (MTX50).
2 When the ignition is switched on the lamp should light for approximately 5 seconds as a check that the system is working, then it will go out. If it does not go out there is insufficient (200 cc/0.35 pint or less) oil in the tank; top up the tank as described in Routine Maintenance and check again that the lamp goes out. If the lamp does not light at all the system is faulty and must be checked.
3 The most likely cause of failure will be a blown bulb, but it is worth checking first that the battery is fully charged; check that all other systems are working normally as a quick test of this. The bulb is removed and refitted as described in Section 24 of this Chapter and/or Section 13 of Chapter 6.
4 If the bulb is in good condition the fault must lie in the switch or in the wiring. Remove the seat and side panels to gain access to the oil tank top surface and disconnect the switch at the multi-pin block connector joining it to the main loom. Test the wiring in the main loom as follows.
5 First check that full battery voltage is available, connecting a DC voltmeter between the black wire terminal and a suitable

earth point on the frame and switching on the ignition. If battery voltage is not measured check the black wire back to the ignition switch and the switch itself. Next use a multimeter set to one of the resistance scales to check that there is continuity between the green wire terminal and a good earth point on the frame, and between the green/red wire terminal and the warning lamp bulb holder; if resistance is measured in either case the wire is damaged or broken and must be checked carefully until the fault is found.
6 If the bulb and wiring are in good condition the fault must lie in the switch. Unplug it from the oil tank and wash off all traces of oil, checking that the terminals are clean and making good contact. Use a multimeter set to the appropriate resistance scale to test the switch. With the float at the bottom of the switch column, measure the resistance between the switch green/red and black wire terminals; a reading of 5 – 15 ohms should be obtained. Check that there is no continuity (ie infinite resistance) between the green and black wire terminals when the float is fully lowered. Finally lift the float fully to the top of the column and measure again the resistance between the green/red and black wire terminals, the reading should now be 340 ohms.
7 If any of the above tests reveals a fault in the switch, or if obvious signs of damage can be seen on removing the switch from the oil tank, the switch must be renewed; repairs are not possible.
8 To test the accuracy of the switch, remove it from the tank and clean it, as described above, then connect it again to the main loom, switch on the ignition, raise the float to the top of the column and wait for the lamp to go out. When the lamp goes out move the float to the bottom of the column, whereupon the lamp should light again, and slowly move the float back up the column until the lamp goes out. Measure the distance between the float stop at the bottom of the column and the bottom of the float; the distance should be 4.5 mm (0.18 in) although a tolerance of 1.0 mm (0.04 in) above or below this figure is allowed. If the lamp lights above or below these limits the switch is inaccurate.
9 The only solution to an inaccurate switch is to renew it, although it must be up to the owner to decide whether this is justified; it is a simple matter to drain the oil tank and to pour

in oil until the lamp goes out, measuring carefully and recording for future reference the amount of oil necessary to do this.

25 Instruments, bulbs and headlamp – removal and refitting

MBX50

1 Remove the four mounting bolts and withdraw the headlamp nacelle, then remove its two mounting bolts and withdraw the headlamp assembly. The bulb connectors can be unplugged so that the unit can be removed completely, if required. The bulbs are removed and refitted as described in Chapter 6.

2 The instrument illuminating and warning lamp bulbs can be unplugged from the base of the instrument panel once the nacelle and headlamp have been removed.

3 To remove the instruments, withdraw the headlamp, disconnect the wiring connectors joining the panel to the main wiring loom, disconnect the instrument drive cables and remove the two panel mounting nuts.

4 To separate the panel assembly unscrew the two retaining screws in its top surface, followed by the four screws (one at each corner) in its bottom surface. Withdraw the panel top cover; each instrument can be removed after its two retaining screws have been unscrewed.

5 Reassembly is the reverse of the removal procedure. Note the headlamp alignment marks (see Chapter 4).

MTX50

6 Remove its two retaining bolts and pull forwards the headlamp casing, disconnect the bulb wires and withdraw the headlamp assembly. The bolts can be removed and refitted as described in Chapter 6.

7 To unplug the instrument illuminating and warning lamp bulb holders from the instrument bases it is merely necessary to remove the headlamp casing.

8 To remove the instruments first withdraw the headlamp casing and headlamp then remove the single securing screw and open the connector box mounted on the fork bottom yoke. Disconnect all wires joining the instruments to the main wiring loom, then disconnect the instrument drive cables. The instruments can then be removed individually, each being retained by two nuts, or as a complete unit by removing the bolts securing the mounting bracket to the fork top yoke.

9 Reassembly is the reverse of the removal procedure.

MT50 S-G, S-J and S-L

10 The main beam warning lamp bulbholder is a press fit in the headlamp casing. Access to the bulb can be gained by releasing the headlamp casing bolts and easing the assembly forwards until the bulbholder can be reached.

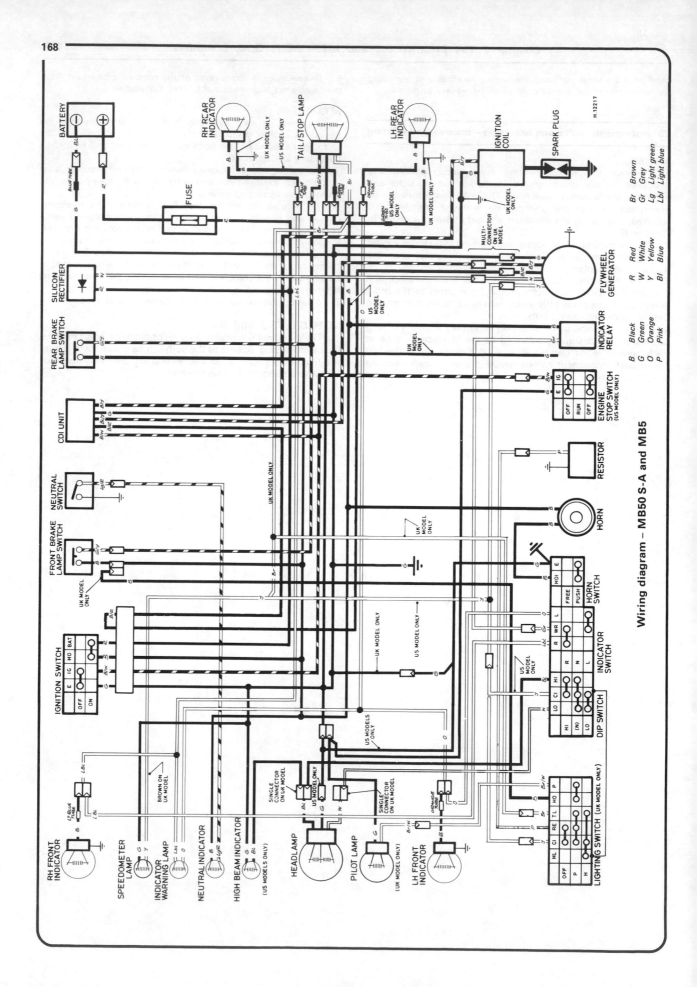

Wiring diagram – MB50 S-A and MB5

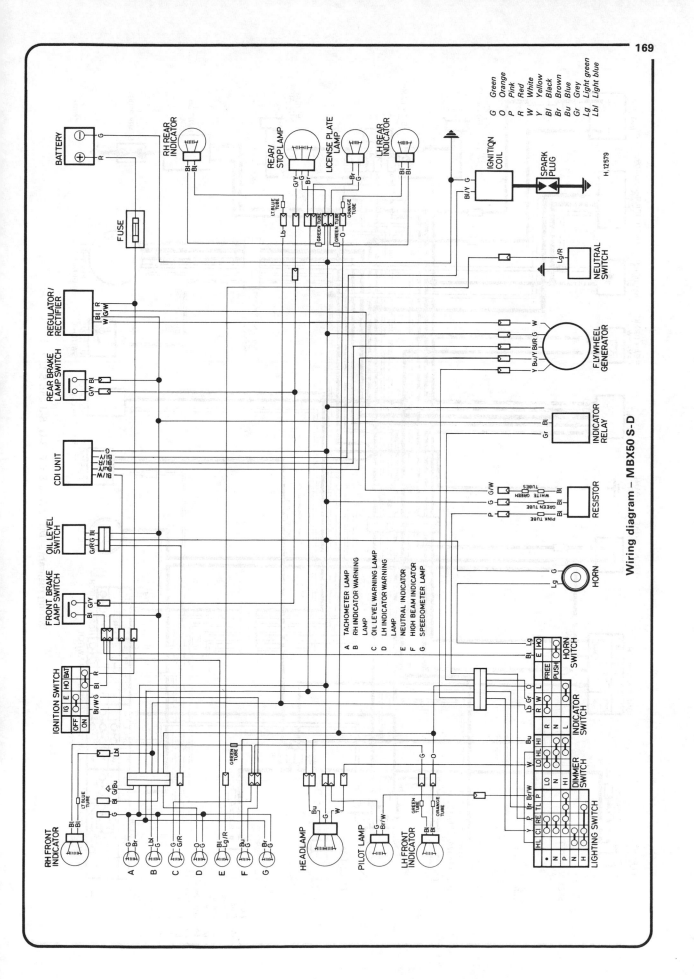

Wiring diagram – MBX50 S-D

H.12579

G	Green	
O	Orange	
P	Pink	
R	Red	
W	White	
Y	Yellow	
Bl	Black	
Br	Brown	
Bu	Blue	
Gr	Grey	
Lg	Light green	
Lbl	Light blue	

A TACHOMETER LAMP
B RH INDICATOR WARNING LAMP
C OIL LEVEL WARNING LAMP
D LH INDICATOR WARNING LAMP
E NEUTRAL INDICATOR
F HIGH BEAM INDICATOR
G SPEEDOMETER LAMP

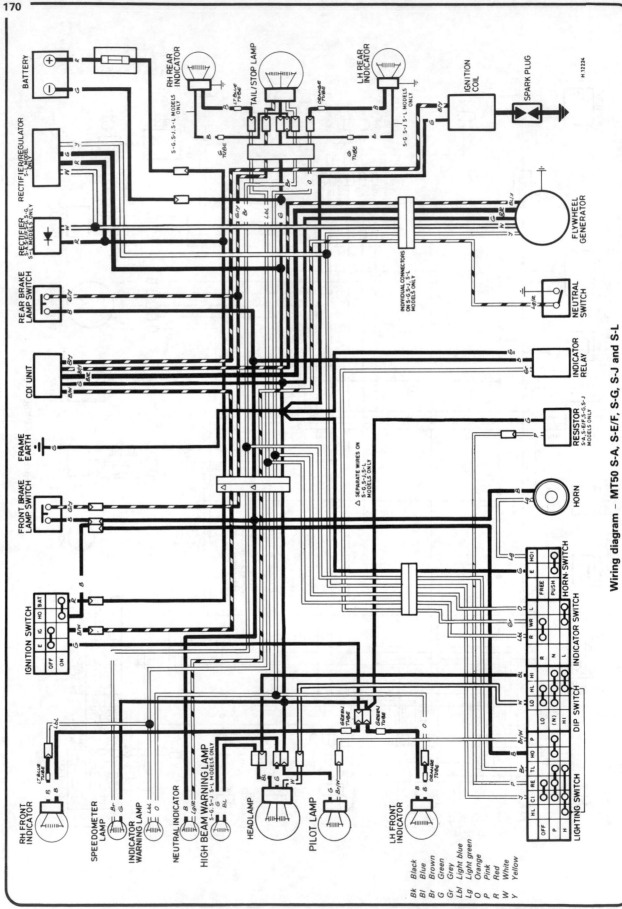

Wiring diagram – MT50 S-A, S-E/F, S-G, S-J and S-L

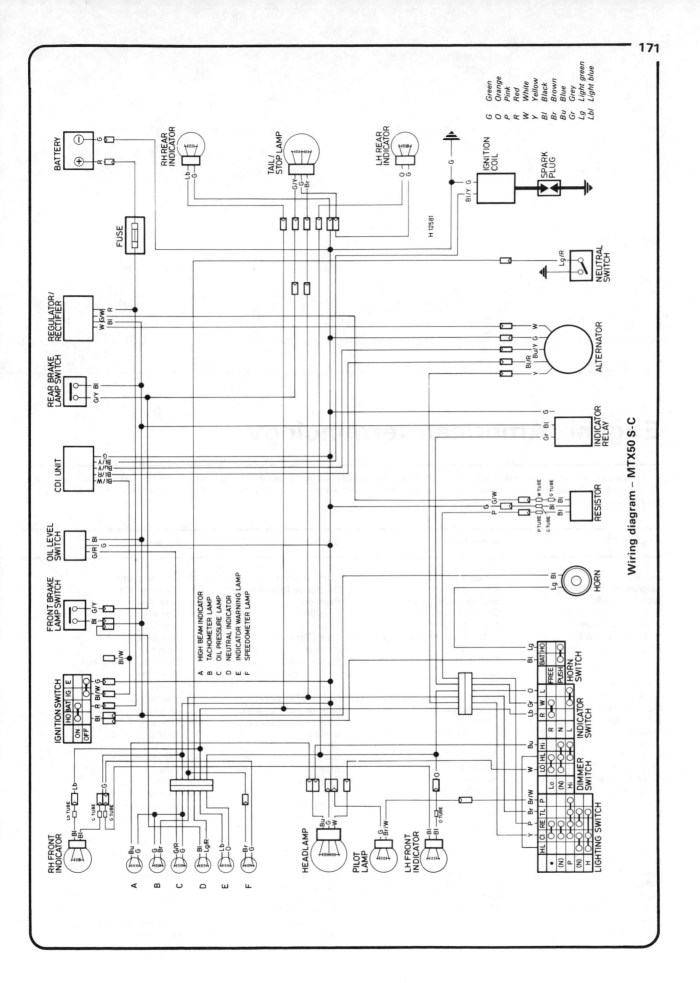

Wiring diagram – MTX50 S-C

English/American terminology

Because this book has been written in England, British English component names, phrases and spellings have been used throughout. American English usage is quite often different and whereas normally no confusion should occur, a list of equivalent terminology is given below.

English	American	English	American
Air filter	Air cleaner	Number plate	License plate
Alignment (headlamp)	Aim	Output or layshaft	Countershaft
Allen screw/key	Socket screw/wrench	Panniers	Side cases
Anticlockwise	Counterclockwise	Paraffin	Kerosene
Bottom/top gear	Low/high gear	Petrol	Gasoline
Bottom/top yoke	Bottom/top triple clamp	Petrol/fuel tank	Gas tank
Bush	Bushing	Pinking	Pinging
Carburettor	Carburetor	Rear suspension unit	Rear shock absorber
Catch	Latch	Rocker cover	Valve cover
Circlip	Snap ring	Selector	Shifter
Clutch drum	Clutch housing	Self-locking pliers	Vise-grips
Dip switch	Dimmer switch	Side or parking lamp	Parking or auxiliary light
Disulphide	Disulfide	Side or prop stand	Kick stand
Dynamo	DC generator	Silencer	Muffler
Earth	Ground	Spanner	Wrench
End float	End play	Split pin	Cotter pin
Engineer's blue	Machinist's dye	Stanchion	Tube
Exhaust pipe	Header	Sulphuric	Sulfuric
Fault diagnosis	Trouble shooting	Sump	Oil pan
Float chamber	Float bowl	Swinging arm	Swingarm
Footrest	Footpeg	Tab washer	Lock washer
Fuel/petrol tap	Petcock	Top box	Trunk
Gaiter	Boot	Torch	Flashlight
Gearbox	Transmission	Two/four stroke	Two/four cycle
Gearchange	Shift	Tyre	Tire
Gudgeon pin	Wrist/piston pin	Valve collar	Valve retainer
Indicator	Turn signal	Valve collets	Valve cotters
Inlet	Intake	Vice	Vise
Input shaft or mainshaft	Mainshaft	Wheel spindle	Axle
Kickstart	Kickstarter	White spirit	Stoddard solvent
Lower leg	Slider	Windscreen	Windshield
Mudguard	Fender		

Index

Printed by

J H Haynes & Co Ltd

Sparkford Nr Yeovil

Somerset BA22 7JJ England